Debating Zimbabwe's Land Reform

IAN SCOONES

Correct citation: Scoones, I. (2014). *Debating Zimbabwe's Land Reform*. Brighton: Institute of Development Studies

Photo credits: Photography is by B.Z. Mavedzenge. Front cover: Ruchanyu garden. Back cover: Rwafa maize crop

ISBN: 978-1-4936-8062-7

TABLE OF CONTENTS

FOREWORD

This is a book of a blog. This may seem odd, given that all 60 of the chapters have appeared on the Zimbabweland blog[1], and remain free to view in the archives. But I thought that it would be good to put a selection together in one place to save all that clicking. There are also eight new essays summarising the different sections. The book is published in low cost format with no royalties accruing, allowing a small cover price for print-on-demand copies, as well as an electronic version. The book has been distributed widely in Zimbabwe, including in all our study sites in Masvingo.

The blog has gathered quite a following: both those who appreciate it, and those who hate it. There are several thousand page views each month from all over the world, but particularly from Zimbabwe, South Africa, the UK and the US. It was set up soon after our 2010 book, *Zimbabwe's Land Reform: Myths and Realities*, was published by James Currey, Weaver Press and Jacana Media. The book's publication resulted in a massive amount of commentary that has persisted in various forms, some of which you can see in the media and review sections of our website at www.zimbabweland.net. The website also offers further resources, including photos, booklets, videos and more.

The blog has served a number of purposes. It allows a weekly opportunity to comment, to let off steam and express frustrations, irritations, sometimes anger, at the wider commentary on Zimbabwe, and the land question in particular. More positively, it also offers a chance to share with readers things I have found interesting, challenging and inspirational. Because, amongst the dross that is written about Zimbabwe, there are plenty of excellent contributions, most of which do not get any air time. The blog also allows us to keep the debate provoked by our book alive, to respond to the critiques, and to share new material in advance of formal publication.

The Masvingo research project was established in 2000 in response to the land invasions, and subsequent Fast Track Land Reform Programme. As researchers who had worked in the province for many years, finding out what happened after

---

1 www.zimbabweland.wordpress.com; see also www.zimbabweland.net

land reform occurred was important. The research has been funded by grants from the UK's Economic and Social Research Council and Department for International Development, and has been linked to work at PLAAS (the Institute for Poverty, Land and Agrarian Studies at the University of the Western Cape, South Africa), the University of Zimbabwe and others over the years. The research in Masvingo has been led by B.Z. Mavedzenge, and has involved Felix Murimbarimba and Jacob Mahenehene in recent years (and also Nelson Marongwe and Chrispen Sukume previously). Thanks are especially due to the many people in the land reform settlements and beyond who have been involved in the research, as well as Agritex and others for engaging with the work. For the production of this book, thanks are due to to Jake Cornwall Scoones for his expert design and production skills, to Mar Maestre Morales for putting the blogs into the book format and to Ollie Burch for his continued administrative support.

Now over 13 years, our research has documented what happened in Masvingo province across 16 sites, including A1 (small-scale), A2 (medium-scale commercial farms) and informal (not registered) sites, across a transect from the relatively higher potential areas to the north to the dryland areas in the lowveld, and including sites in the irrigated areas around Chiredzi. 400 households were included in our original sample and we have documented in detail what has happened using both quantitative and qualitative methods. In the light of extensive misperceptions and inaccuracies in media and academic commentary alike, our aim has been to shed light on the controversial issues, and find out what was actually happening on the ground.

The empirical data published in our book challenged five oft-repeated myths, and provided an empirical base for subsequent explorations. We have continued work in Masvingo since the book's publication, allowing us to explore the dynamics after 2009, and the stabilisation of the economy. Others have taken up the challenge to explore similar questions in different areas, providing an increasingly comprehensive overview of the land reform aftermath.

This sort of empirical data is essential if solid, informed debate about future directions is to take place. That our results have been used by some for political purposes is inevitable in the highly charged debate around Zimbabwe's land, but in the blog and other writings we have tried to stay above the fray, and focus on the results on the ground. A particular effort has been invested in encouraging others to do more work – to challenge, question and deepen our findings. The small grants competition the Institue of Development Studies at Sussex (IDS), the African Institute for Agrarian Studies, Harare (AIAS), Ruzivo Trust, Harare and PLAAS developed for young Zimbabwean researchers was one example. In the blog, and in this book, some of the work of this next round of research is profiled.

I hope you enjoy the chapters in this book. Remember that they were written to a weekly deadline and usually respond to events and policy moments that now have been superseded. However, bearing this in mind, the contributions do show how the debate has moved on. Sometimes this has been painfully slow, held back by a lack of understanding, poor engagement with the empirical realities and a set of ideological biases that blinkers, closes down and constrains debate. But today there is much more empirical data, from a range of sources and places, and this has substantially enhanced our ability to debate the evidence and the policy implications more thoroughly.

With Zimbabwe entering (yet another) phase following the 2013 elections, land will inevitably remain high on the agenda. For any post-settler economy redistributing economic assets, including land, is an essential precondition for justice, but also longer term economic growth and social and political stability. How it is done, and how the negative impacts are addressed, is an essential debate, but the imperative to do something is clear, whether in Zimbabwe, South Africa, Namibia or elsewhere.

For this reason, I hope this collection will be read widely, both inside and outside Zimbabwe. For the lessons from Zimbabwe are important in the wider southern African region; and crucially important for donors, investors and supporters of Zimbabwe in the wider world to understand. I hope this book – and the blog that for now continues online – offers some small contribution to this. And if you object to anything written here – or indeed find it useful and have something else to add – rather than throwing this book at the wall, or shouting at your computer screen, do write a comment on the blog.

The book is organised in eight sections plus an Endpiece. The blogs (identified as 'chapters' here, with some minor edits from the originals) are not presented chronologically, but in thematic sections, each of which is introduced with a short overview essay, aiming to put the different contributions in context. The sections cover agricultural and livestock production, the economy, political dimensions, land, livelihoods and rural development, aid and development, comparative lessons and researching land and agrarian change. In the e-book version you can click through to the sources; in the paper version sources are referenced in footnotes.

For more updates, make sure you subscribe to future blogs at http://zimbabweland.wordpress.com.

Ian Scoones, Brighton, November 2013

ABOUT THE AUTHOR

Ian Scoones is a Professorial Fellow at the Institute of Development Studies at the University of Sussex, is co-director of the STEPS Centre and has been the joint convenor of the Future Agricultures Consortium. He has worked in Zimbabwe on livelihoods, land and rural development since the mid 1980s. Since 2000, he has been leading research on what happened to people's livelihoods in Masvingo province following the land reform. He is the co-author of *Zimbabwe's Land Reform: Myths and Realities* (James Currey, Weaver, Jacana Media, 2010). For more information, see www.ianscoones.net

ACRONYMS

A1 – small-scale resettlement farm

A2 – medium-scale commercial resettlement farm

ACP – Africa, Carribean and Pacific agreement

Agritex – the agricultural extension agency

AIAS – African Institute for Agrarian Studies

ANC – African National Congress

ANU – Australian National University

ARDA – Agriculture and Rural Development Authority

AU – African Union

BBC – British Broadcasting Corporation

BIPPA – Bilateral Investment Promotion and Protection Agreement

BRICS – Brazil, Russia, India, China and South Africa

CA – Conservation agriculture

CAMPFIRE – Communal Area Management Programme for Indigenous Resources

CFU – Commercial Farmers Union

CGIAR – Consultative Group on International Agricultural Research

COMESA – Common Market for Eastern and Southern Africa

COPAC – Zimbabwe Constitution Select Committee

CSC – Cold Storage Company

CSO – Central Statistics Office, now ZIMSTAT

DFID – Department for International Development (UK)

ESRC – Economic and Social Research Council (UK)

EU – European Union

FAC – Future Agricultures Consortium

FAO – Food and Agriculture Organisation of the UN

FCO – Foreign and Commonwealth Office (UK)

FMD – Foot and Mouth Disease

FSRU – Farming Systems Research Unit

FT – Financial Times

G20 – Group of 20 leading nations

GAPWUZ – General and Agricultural Plantation Workers Union of Zimbabwe

GDP – Gross Domestic Product

GNU – Government of National Unity

GoZ – Government of Zimbabwe

GPA – Global Political Agreement

Ha – Hectare

HIPC – Heavily Indebted Poor Country

IDS – Institute of Development Studies, Sussex

ICFZ – Indigenous Commercial Farmers Union of Zimbabwe

IMF – International Monetary Fund

JAG – Justice for Agriculture Group

JPS – Journal of Peasant Studies

LRAD – Land Redistribution for Agricultural Development programme, South Africa

M and G – Mail and Guardian (South Africa)

MDC-T – Movement for Democratic Change, Tsvangirai

MIT – Massachusetts Institute of Technology

MOD – Ministry of Defence (UK)

NYT – New York Times

PLAAS – Institute for Poverty, Land and Agrarian Studies

SADC – Southern Africa Development Community

UEA – University of East Anglia (UK)

UN – United Nations

USAID – United States Aid

USDA – United States Department of Agriculture

UZ – University of Zimbabwe

ZANU-PF – Zimbabwe African National Union – Patriotic Front

ZFU – Zimbabwe Farmers Union

ZIMSTAT – Zimbabwe Statistical Services

SECTION A
AGRICULTURAL AND LIVESTOCK PRODUCTION

Zimbabwe's agricultural and livestock production has been transformed by land reform since 2000. While earlier attempts at land reform had met with some success, as documented by Bill Kinsey and colleagues over the years, they had not fundamentally changed the agrarian structure. This meant that a classic settler economy 'dualism' had persisted, with a small-scale (black) farming in the communal areas, and a few resettlement areas, contrasting with a highly capitalised large-scale (largely white) commercial agriculture. Despite a boom in the 1980s thanks to substantial new government investment and support following Independence, the small-scale sector struggled. The large-scale sector, made up of around 6000 farms, had profited from agricultural liberalisation on the back of long-term state subsidy. Some believed that this pattern was the most efficient and effective response to both domestic food needs and international agricultural markets, with small-scale farmers eventually moving off the land into urban jobs as the economy transformed. Yet the inherited dualism was highly unjust, and actually not as efficient as some wanted to believe. Crucially, while having significant successes, the 1980s and 90s resettlement programmes did not resolve the outstanding question of land in distribution and access in Zimbabwe, perhaps the key rallying call for the liberation struggle, and so the pent up demand for land was evident.

Today, following the major land reform from 2000, precipitated by a combination of spontaneous land invasions and state orchestrated appropriation, there is a very different agrarian structure. A 'tri-modal' pattern is evident. It is dominated by a large small-scale sector, critically added to by around 175,000 new A1 farms.

These land holdings are larger than in the communal areas, and so offer more potential for production of crops and livestock. This is complemented by a medium-scale commercial sector (largely A2 farms) that have the potential, as yet largely unrealised, of providing a more distributed alternative to large-scale commercial production. And then there is still a large-scale commercial and estates sector. Some large-scale farms were left intact – some with former farmers, others grabbed by political-security elites – and most of the former estates continue to function, although often with new outgrower arrangements with A2 farms.

While production initially collapsed, in part due to the challenges of getting established in the new farms and in part due to the parlous state of the economy, the agricultural sector since 2009 in particular, when the Zimbabwe dollar was abandoned and the economy stabilised under the unity coalition government, has grown significantly, with some crops – notably tobacco and cotton – booming. The following chapters offer some profiles of this change for some key commodities, including tobacco [chapter 2], sugar [chapter 3], beef [chapter 5] and poultry [chapter 6], where very different patterns of change are evident.

At the core of the debate over agrarian structure is the long-running question of the relative efficiency of small and large farms. The opening chapter addresses this for the Zimbabwe context, but argues that actually the debate should not be about either large or small, but about what combinations of farm sizes in what spatial configurations.

All new farms, big and small, are 'commercial' in some sense, as all new farmers are vigorously engaging with the market. But these markets are new, with value chains associated with them radically restructured. Much of the debate about Zimbabwe's agricultural sector forgets this. Old data, based on old structures are used, and the new configurations remain poorly understood. Certainly in the period of hyperinflation there was a necessary growth in the informal economy, often involving illegal, cross-border and barter exchanges. Since 2009, the economy has stabilised, and more formal channels have opened up again. However, the informal economy still exists – and it is very large, and often completely uncounted. Also there are new players in the market, including traders, contractors and transporters. They exist in large numbers. These are often new entrants into the agrarian economy, generating surpluses, employing labour, although sometimes circumventing the formal economy. In chapter 4, for example, I look at the growth of contract farming, and its implications.

The new agrarian structure requires a radical rethink of all aspects of production, including technology. Chapter 8 looks at conservation agriculture and tractors, both promoted currently but both, in different ways, inappropriate to the new context. There has been much disappointment that the infrastructure and equipment formerly deployed on large-scale farms is not being used, and lies derelict or destroyed. Sometimes this is due to neglect and lack of finance, but very often it is due to the fact that such equipment is no longer appropriate. Few new farmers have farms big enough to use centre pivot irrigation systems, combine harvesters or even tractors, for example. But equally they are not keen, for very good reasons, on highly labour intensive gardening techniques like conservation agriculture. There is an urgent need for a rethink in research and extension, as well as in private sector provision and aid programmes, to come up with technologies appropriate to the scale and capacities of the new farmers.

In our 2010 book, we showed how farm production had been increasing progressively through the 2000s. This pattern has continued, but not always consistently. Some crops on some farms have fared better than others. Overall, it remains the case that the smaller-scale A1 farmers have done better, and the commodities with a clear market chain (tobacco, cotton) or with a growing domestic market (beef, poultry) have done better, while others have not. Maize production in particular, without irrigation and in a period with occasional droughts and low prices, has done less well, resulting in a greater frequency of food imports.

The sector is in transition; and a decade or so is a short time for such a major transformation in production, labour regimes, infrastructure, markets, value chains and so on. With limited support, the transition has been longer than hoped for, but any future efforts must take account of what has happened, and what is happening, rather than rely on old models and assumptions from the past. These definitely no longer apply. Our work, with others, is mapping out the new realities on the ground, encouraging a radical rethink of approaches to agriculture and livestock production and marketing suited to the new agrarian structure.

CHAPTER 1
SMALL FARMS, BIG FARMS

There is a classic debate in agricultural economics and development policy about the relative efficiencies of small and big farms. It is centred on what is known as the 'inverse relationship' which posits that as farms become smaller they become more productive per unit area, as costs – such as the supervision of labour – get reduced (or at least passed on to cheaper family labour arrangements). The argument is that small farms[2] are the ideal, efficient solution to agricultural production.

Of course there are qualifications – and these are important, perhaps increasingly so in a globalised world[3]. Very small farms, fragmented in different ways, are clearly not ideal, and suffer from many inefficiencies. Yet, what is 'small' and 'very small' is often not clear in the literature. Equally, there may be economies of scale in certain production-marketing systems, making larger farms more efficient. For example, getting high value products into international markets may mean complying with quality standards which small farmers would find difficult to adhere to.

This discussion remains at the centre of the debate about agricultural development in Africa. The African Union's Comprehensive Agriculture Development Programme (CAADP)[4] makes a strong case for smallholders being at the centre of agricultural growth, as does the Gates-funded Alliance for a

---

[2] Hazell, P.B.R., Poulton, C., Wiggins, S. and Dorward, A. (2007) *The future of small farms for poverty reduction and growth, 2020 Discussion Paper*, No. 42, Washington, D.C.: International Food Policy Research Institute

[3] Lipton, M. (2005) The family farm in a globalizing world: The role of crop science in alleviating poverty, *2020 Discussion Paper,* No. 40, Washington, D.C.: International Food Policy Research Institute

[4] http://www.nepad-caadp.net/

Green Revolution in Africa (AGRA).[5] In a new book, Gordon Conway[6], of Imperial College in the UK, argues that smallholders must be at the centre of strategies to feed 9 billion people.

For decades, then, smallholder agricultural production has barely been questioned as the central pillar for agricultural development in Africa. But now there are some dissenting voices; and influential ones too. In a provocative paper for an FAO meeting [7] on African agriculture in 50 years, Paul Collier [8] - author of the best-seller, 'The Bottom Billion', and professor at Oxford University – and Stefan Dercon[9] – now Chief Economist at the UK's Department for International Development, and a well-respected research economist who has worked extensively in Africa – make the case that the advocacy of smallholder farming was sometimes wildly overblown, often inappropriately romanticised. They argue that the inverse relationship debate was misleading, and did not provide the definitive evidence sometimes supposed for smallholder farming, and that large farms are increasingly the way forward, for some commodities and in some places.

The arguments presented certainly have merit and deserve scrutiny, but they are also potentially flawed in important ways. The arguments for large farms are that economies of scale in today's globalised world are such that smallholder farming can never really be expected to generate sufficient growth to facilitate the necessary transition out of agriculture into industrial-led growth trajectories. In Africa in particular access to global markets, and so positioning of agriculture near road infrastructure and ports, is seen as crucial, if comparative advantages in a highly competitive market setting are to be realised.

---

[5] http://www.agra.org/

[6] Conway, G. (2012) *One Billion Hungry: Can We Feed the World?* Ithaca and London: Comstock Publishing Associates

[7] Collier, P. and Dercon, S. (2009) *African Agriculture in 50 years: Smallholders in a Rapidly Changing World?* Proceedings of an experts' meeting on "How to feed the world in 2050", 24-26 June 2009. Rome: Food and Agriculture Organization of the United Nations (FAO)

[8] http://users.ox.ac.uk/~econpco/

[9] http://www.economics.ox.ac.uk/index.php/academic/stefan-dercon

Yet the argument ignores some key facts. First, smallholders have been very successful at producing a range of key commodities. In a review for a World Bank study[10] on competitive commercial agriculture in Africa, Colin Poulton and colleagues[11] found that "Large-scale agriculture has proven more competitive in export horticulture, sugar and flue-cured tobacco, whilst smallholders dominate in cotton, cashew and food staples. For tea and burley tobacco there are mixed stories. Second, markets are not all global, governed by highly stringent standards. Niche selling into such markets may offer good returns, but the costs of entry are high. Perhaps better is to produce for growing domestic and regional markets[12], and here the flexible strategies of smallholders in feeding urban Africa have long been seen to be effective. Third, the negative effects of large scale farming on local economies, food security patterns, environmental conditions and labour and employment conditions are not factored into these arguments. Large scale commercial farming does not have a universally good track-record, frequently resulting in enclave economic operations, with poor labour conditions and high externalities, focusing on single export-oriented crops, leading to negative impacts on the local food economy[13].

What are the implications of this debate for Zimbabwe? Following land reform, Zimbabwe has a radically reconfigured agrarian structure. Gone is the dualism of the past – with tracts of very large scale farming, separated off from the small-scale farming areas in the communal lands and resettlement. The limited 'Purchase Area' land was anomalous, fitting neither model, but not integrated

---

[10] http://go.worldbank.org/XSRUM2ZXM0

[11] Poulton, C., Tyler, G., Hazell, P., Dorward, A., Kydd, J., and Stockbridge, M. (2008) *All-Africa Review of Experiences with Commercial Agriculture: Lesson from Success and Failure* Background paper for the Competitive Commercial Agriculture in Sub-Saharan Africa (CCAA) Study. Washington, DC: World Bank.

[12] Diao, X and Hazel, P. (2004) Exploring market opportunities for African smallholders, *2020 Africa Conference Brief*, No. 6. Washington D.C.: International Food Policy Research Institute

[13] Scoones, I. (2013) *What role for large-scale commercial agriculture in post-land reform Zimbabwe? Africa's experience of alternative models*, blog, zimbabweland.wordpress.com

either. Today, we have a huge mix of farm sizes, as Sam Moyo[14] has described. Large-scale farms and estates remain, but the majority is now a mix of small and medium scale farms.

Crucially these are much more integrated, both spatially in terms of their proximity and economically in terms of their connections, of labour, marketing, skill and knowledge transfer and so on. The economic apartheid of the past, divided by racialised social and economic barriers, has given way to a more complex, integrated patchwork. While smallholder farming dominates, it is not the only farm type. It is the mix that is important, which is different in different parts of the country, depending on agroecology, market access, infrastructure and, of course, politics.

Getting to grips with this new farm size configuration, and the implications for economic development is an important challenge. Yet it is one that policymakers have yet to get their heads around. So fixated are people on the small versus large dichotomy, often with an implicit assumption that small is backward and big is better, that the potentials of the new agrarian structure are not being grasped. The small farm populists argue for peasant efficiencies, while the big farm advocates claim business and growth opportunities.

In my view neither is correct. But where the gains are to be had is in the mix: in the economic multiplier linkages [15] between farm sizes, in the capturing of the comparative advantages of different farm configurations, in the growth of district level economies, in the sharing between groups of equipment, skills and knowledge, and in the flexible movement of labour in a certain area. None of these opportunities could be realised in the old dualistic agrarian structure, but today there are many potentials.

---

[14] Moyo, S. (2011) Three decades of agrarian reform in Zimbabwe, *Journal of Peasant Studies*, 38(3):493-531

[15] Scoones, I. (2012) *Beyond the farm: getting local economies moving*, blog, http:// zimbabweland.wordpress.com

But it requires a different mindset: rather than thinking about the 'ideal type' farm (small or large), and fixed and outdated notions of what is 'viable'[16], we should shift to thinking about processes of economic development based on agriculture in an area. A territorial approach to local economic development, as we argued in our book, *Zimbabwe's Land Reform*, is the way forward, and will help us shed the often unproductive and diversionary obsession with farm size.

---

[16] Cousins, B. and Scoones, I. (2010) Contested paradigms of 'viability' in redistributive land reform: perspectives from southern Africa, *Journal of Peasant Studies*, 37(1): 31-66

CHAPTER 2

THE GOLDEN LEAF: BOOM TIME IN ZIMBABWE

Zimbabwe's tobacco industry is booming once again. From the low point in 2008, at the peak of hyperinflation, when only 48m kg was sold, optimistic estimates for 2012 suggest that around around 150m kg will be sold[17], with prices early in the selling season around 30% higher than 2011[18]. Production levels are not back to the peak level in 2,000 of 236m kg, but the trend is ever upwards, with sales rising from 65m to 123m to 132m kg between 2009 and 2011. In 2011, the sales generated around US$360m, helping to fuel the dramatic 34% growth in the agricultural sector in the past year. With the season not yet concluded over US$440m has been sold in 2012.

Once the almost exclusive preserve of around 3,000 large-scale white farmers, tobacco is now being produced and sold by around 60,000 black farmers from the new A1 and A2 resettlement areas. With average sales of around 10 bales per farmer, this will result in an income of around US$5,000 – no mean sum in Zimbabwean terms. And of course tobacco creates employment along the value chain, as well as tax revenues[19].

This is one of the really unexpected success stories of the land reform. While many accepted that small-scale A1 farmers with larger areas of land could engage in successful staple production and 'accumulate from below', as we described across our sample areas in Masvingo, for new farmers to participate so successfully in the high value export industry of tobacco farming was seen as unlikely. Most had written off the industry, expecting it to atrophy and die.

But contrary to expectations, the tobacco industry has been transformed, from the farms to the auction floors. A whole new set of people are involved. It is not

---

17 Meldrum, A. (2012) 'Zimbabwe's tobacco making a comeback', *GlobalPost,* 10 May

18 Sherekete, R. (2012) 'Zimbabwe: tobacco sales increase 25 percent', *All Africa,* 20 April

19 Dube, G. (2013) 'Zimbabwe Revenue Authority surpasses first quarter tax collection targets', *Voice of America. Zimbabwe,* 2 June

only the farmers who have changed, but also the labourers, the buyers and the financiers. Women are increasingly involved, particularly in the processing, sorting and auction-floor activities. White farmers are still involved too in the high quality/high cost end of the industry, in a few farms remaining under their control, but also in lease arrangements with A2 farmers, who needed the skills and expertise for the production of top quality flue cured Virginia.

New contracting arrangements have emerged to support smaller scale farmers grow tobacco. Contracting reputedly resulted in the production of 34m kg in 2011, out of the total of 132m. Some major new entrants have emerged in the market, notably those with Chinese connections. Tianze, for example, has around 250 growers linked to it[20]. Overall there are around 13 contract companies operating, as well as multiple smaller scale leasing and other arrangements.

It is this financing aspect that has been critical for the dramatic growth of the small-scale sector. This has allowed farmers to invest in inputs, and the rate of refusal has declined, and overall quality has increased. Chinese contract companies, loan facilities and other forms of finance have transformed the system. More traditional players, from the western based companies and other commercial lenders, are now re-engaging knowing that there is money to be made.

There are downsides of the tobacco economy, of course. Curing is largely carried out using local fuelwood sources, and the impact on forests and woodland resources is significant[21]. A more sustainable source of fuel will clearly be necessary. Equally, the high labour demands have resulted in accusations of child labour[22] on the farms, flouting labour laws and undermining child rights. These of course were core issues when white farms took on tobacco as a core crop some decades ago, and will hopefully only be transitional challenges.

---

[20] Xinhua (2012) 'Zimbabwe tobacco farmers hail support from Chinese firm', *Capital News*, 25 April

[21] Masau, P. (2012) 'Zimbabwe: Indigenous trees under siege from farmers', *Africa News*, 25 April

[22] 'Zimbabwe NGO tackles rising child labour in farming communities', *Voice of America. Zimbabwe*, 2 June

For the longer term, the tobacco story in the last five years has some important lessons for the wider agrarian transition. While tobacco is not a crop appropriate everywhere (and is not significant in our study areas in Masvingo, for instance), there are some more generic insights worth noting. First, A2 farmers, who have really struggled elsewhere, including in Masvingo, with poor production due to low capitalisation and investment, can make it under the right circumstances. Second, markets are key, but so is support to engage in markets. It is not just price levels, demand and supply, but up-front investment, skill development and knowledge building about quality control and market niches. Third, finance is vital; and that's where Chinese finance and contracting count [chapter 48]. Fourth, there are definitely roles for white farmers with skills and capacities in a particular commodity area, but probably involving engagement in different ways, at the high end of the market [chapter 15].

Hopefully the lessons from the tobacco transition can be applied to other aspects of the agricultural economy, leveraging finance [chapter 14], expertise and market access for the benefits of a larger group of people than the previously narrow, privileged large-farm sector.

CHAPTER 3

THE SWEET SMELL OF SUCCESS: THE REVIVAL OF ZIMBABWE'S SUGAR INDUSTRY

A report by the USDA's Global Agricultural Information Network[23] has shown that Zimbabwe's sugar industry is rebounding fast on the back of a 6% increase in area cultivated mostly by private outgrowers who are part of the A2 land reform allocations. Sugar output in 2012/13 is expected to increase by almost 16% to 430,000 tonnes from the 372,000 tonnes in 2011/12 season, with 160,000 tonnes expected to be exported, earning important revenue for the country.

Much of this is happening in the lowveld of Masvingo province, and in the large estates, including Hippo Valley and Mkwasine where we have been studying sugar production on A2 outgrower plots since 2000 (see our video[24]). The Hippo Valley story reflects the wider picture.

Towards the end of last year the Zimbabwe newspapers carried a double page spread reporting the annual results of Hippo Valley Estates Ltd[25], which are majority owned by the South African conglomerate Tongaat Hulett[26]. The highlights were: revenue up by 30% at US$90m, with an operating profit of over US$17m. The commentary was upbeat: "The relatively stable operating environment continues to provide a platform for the recovery, growth and development of the sugar industry ... The Company remains focused on its goal to achieve full milling capacity utilization of more than 300,000 tons annual sugar production over the next three years".

---

[23] Esterhuizen, D. (2012) *Zimbabwe. Sugar Annual*. USDA Foreign Agricultural Service, GAIN Report.

[24] http://www.zimbabweland.net/Part_7.html

[25] http://www.huletts.co.za/ops/zimbabwe.asp

[26] Karombo, T. (2013) 'Research shows surge in Zimbabwe's sugar output', *Business Day BDLive*, 10 January

Although a way off the target in 2012 at just over 160,000 tons, total deliveries of cane were up 40% on 2011, with 1.349m tons of cane produced by private growers and the company. Private growers' deliveries were up 55% on the previous year, and an additional 178k tons was delivered by Green Fuel Ltd, the biofuel company linked to the infamous Billy Rautenbach [chapter 23]. With the integration of the once separately controlled estates at Triangle and Hippo Valley, the company envisages a total combined capacity of 4.8m tons of cane production, resulting in 600,000 tons of sugar.

With both company funds and external support, channelled through the EU, there has been considerable investment in cane production on 'uncontested' private land (mostly in the Chipwa and Mpapa areas). Private cane growing has expanded dramatically from the relatively small outgrower arrangements that existed in the past. The company report notes that "in the current season, 611 indigenous private cane growers, farming 11,138 ha and employing 5,569 people will supply 772,000 tons of cane generating for them US$50 million in revenue".

The company estimates that private growing could increase substantially on the basis of existing mill capacity. They estimate an additional 661 growers farming 12,742 ha could supply 1.4 million tons of cane each year to the Hippo Valley mill, creating employment for 12,000 and additional revenue of US$150m. This would amount to a total employment in the sugar industry of 30,000, and revenue of around US$250m. This would surely be the sweet smell of sugar success.

The rebounding of the Zimbabwe sugar industry is attracting attention in the business press in South Africa clearly seeing the investment value for South African companies. Interestingly and typically, the Business Day report failed completely to mention that the growth of production is being driven by a revived partnership between South African capital and new land reform beneficiaries.

But to achieve such ambitious targets, and to continue the impressive growth, will require much new investment, not least in rehabilitating and replanting cane fields, and supplying new water resources for newly cleared land. Sugar has long been a central part of Zimbabwe's agricultural economy, providing stable revenues for the treasury, and earlier when part of ACP (Africa, Carribean and Pacific) agreements, benefiting from a guaranteed and profitable market. Rather overshadowed by the success of the tobacco sector, sugar has not been much in the spotlight, but deserves to be. Just as in tobacco, but in a more organised, estate linked production system, an increasing proportion of production is now coming from outgrower areas allocated as A2 plots as part of the land reform.

As we showed in our book[27], production in these sites in Hippo Valley in the remote lowveld area of Chiredzi district (and also in Triangle and Mkwasine estates) increased over time from the establishment of A2 plots in 2002. In parallel these farmers accumulated equipment, transport and invested in their land. They also employed considerable amounts of labour. As we documented, they had at that time an uneasy relationship with the core estate. The estate management did not know how to deal with the new outgrowers. They had been used to dealing with a relatively few white and Mauritian outgrowers, but now there were hundreds (registered in Chiredzi district as A2 farms across Hippo Valley and Mkwasine). Many new farmers felt they were being squeezed, with low prices offered, quality controls dubiously applied and transport being supplied late. They thought, perhaps correctly, that the estate management was waiting for them to give up, so the old regime, which was easier to manage and control, could be reinstated.

From around 2007, when the economy was in freefall, sugar production collapsed. Payments being offered in Zimbabwe dollars were meaningless and credit arrangements and cheque payments were wiped out by hyperinflation. Many did indeed give up, ripping out their cane and planting other crops, including maize and tomatoes. But with the stabilisation of the economy through dollarization in 2009, the situation changed. The incentives to reinvest in sugar production returned, and the estate management changed its tune. Now they needed cane desperately so they could break even running the huge mills and vast estates. They belatedly realised that they had to accept private outgrowers, and encouraged them to reengage. And in the period from 2009 they have done on a massive scale as the company figures show.

Now the company is more upbeat about the new outgrower model. It is not as if this is alien to them, as in other operations in the region, this sort of relative

---

[27] Scoones, I., Marongwe, N., Mavedzenge, B., Mahenehene, J., Murimbarimba, F., and Sukume, C. (2010) *Zimbabwe's Land Reform: Myths and Realities.* Oxford: James Currey

smallholder model is dominant. Indeed compared to operations in Zambia and South Africa the new A2 plots are large, averaging 20-30ha, enough to produce a substantial amount of cane, and some other crops besides. Cane farmers in our study sample in Hippo Valley are much more optimistic now.

However there are constraints. The company report alludes to these obliquely mentioning the performance has been "despite the prevailing liquidity and socio-economic challenges". These are many of course; not least the on-going uncertainty over tenure arrangements in the outgrower areas. Leases have been promised, but only offer letters exist. More significantly there has been a rumbling of discontent among the Shangaan political elite from the area, complaining that 'outsiders' got the prime sugar areas. Some influential people have barged others out of their plots, asserting their 'indigenous' rights. Most A2 sugar farmers are indeed from outside the area; many are (or were) civil servants, many from the ministry of agriculture. In the scramble for A2 plots through a chaotic and patronage-influenced allocation system, sugar plots were seen as prime targets for those in the know, and they carefully filled their forms and 'business plans' to ensure they were successful. By the mid-late 2000s many regretted this move, but now they are much more happy, which is why the land is become contested again.

Questions of finance (or 'liquidity') are also significant, as the company notes. It is not cheap to farm sugar: you need equipment, significant amounts of inputs, a lot of labour, irrigation and expensive transport. And you need to replant on a sustainable rotation: crops planted one year may not yield significantly for several years hence. At the farm level cash flow is the perennial challenge, and without effective credit and banking systems in rural Zimbabwe, this is tough without company support. Yet reliance on a single company, just as any contract farming arrangement, puts the grower at a disadvantage in terms of negotiating a good deal. But there are also other pressing financing issues in the sugar sector. The infrastructure was originally built in the 1950s and 60s, and much of it is decrepit and in need of repair. Irrigation canals need constant attention, as do rail lines and mill machinery. Extending farmed areas requires clearing, levelling and laying of canals. None of this is cheap. With profits being scarce in recent years, the company has not invested. External strategic investments financed by the EU[28] under the post ACP regime Adaptation Fund are constrained. Euro 45m have been allocated, but only 10m euro have been released to date via the Canelands Trust[29], a body controlled by the company. Due to sanctions, only areas which were not part of the 'fast-track' land reform programme are eligible, meaning that most new private outgrowers – some of the largest producers today of Zimbabwean sugar – cannot benefit from the industry rehabilitation programme (at least officially) – there is of course considerable leakage and wider investments benefit everyone. These anomalies created by the political stand-off between the EU, and other western donors, and the Zimbabwean government, despite much evidence that sanctions do more harm than good, continue, and are likely to at least until after the next elections.

Meanwhile, and despite these constraints, the sugar industry continues to grow, providing livelihoods, income and employment for many, and much needed revenue for the government exchequer too.

---

[28] European Commission (2012) *The EU supports the recovery of the sugar sector in Zimbabwe*, Press Release, 22 November

[29] European Commission (2009) *Zimbabwe Annual Action Programme 2009 Accompanying Measures for Sugar*, Annex, Program Document, Sugar Facility, CRIS Decision 021446, http://ec.europa.eu/europeaid/documents/aap/2009/af_aap_2009_sugar_zwe.pdf

CHAPTER 4
FARMING UNDER CONTRACT

Contract farming is all the rage in Zimbabwe at the moment. Indeed, more generally across Africa[30], there is growing interest in linking up smallholder farmers with larger business operations to produce and market certain agricultural commodities. Advocated by the World Bank and others, it seems like a perfect 'win-win' scenario. Smallholders get access to inputs and markets, and agribusiness gets guaranteed products at good prices and at scale, without having to take over large areas of land and produce everything themselves. Thus, in the great 'land grab' debate, some offer contract farming, with smallholders linked into global value chains, as an alternative[31].

Of course contract farming arrangements[32] are not new in the Zimbabwean agricultural sector. The great cotton boom from the 1990s when smallholders entered cotton production in a big way was driven by contract arrangements, initially with the parastatal Cottco, and then with a variety of companies following liberalisation. This has been hailed as a massive success. Production increased and quality was maintained, and the Zimbabwe cotton industry thrived. The same is now happening in tobacco [chapter 2], as contract producers, on new resettlement farms, both A1 and A2, are hooking up with contractor, including some major contracts with the Chinese company Tianze. Other commodities have seen positive contracting experiences, including specialised crops like paprika. Where there are high demands for expensive inputs (fertilisers, sprays, seeds) and a need for specialist marketing support, then contracting makes much sense.

---

[30] NEPAD (2006) Contract farming offers fresh hope for Africa's declining agriculture, *East Africa Policy Brief*, No 2. Pretoria: NEPAD

[31] Cotula, L. and Leonard, R. (eds) (2010) *Alternatives to Land Acquisitions: Agricultural Investment and Collaborative Business Models,* London/Bern/Rome/Maputo: IIED/SDC/IFAD/CTV

[32] Dawes, M., Murota, R., Jera, R., Masara, C. and Sola, P. (2009) *Inventory of Smallholder Contract Farming Practices in Zimbabwe*, Revised Final Report, Support Capacity for Enhanced Market Access and Knowledge Management (SCAPEMA), Netherlands: SNV

Now though contracting arrangements are expanding to other crops, including food staples like maize. This is in response to a different set of drivers, created in particular by the land reform programme. The land reform distributed over eight million hectares to some 170,000 households. Many, especially in the A1 smallholder schemes, have got going on production, based on relatively low capital inputs and investments. But there are also quite a number of particularly A2 farmers and some A1 farmers with larger plots who have found it difficult to get production moving on their new farms. This is for a variety of reasons, including lack of credit, poor access to machinery, limited skills and knowledge of larger scale farming, tenure insecurity and so on. There are quite a few A2 farms that remain underutilised. Of course this was also the case in the former large-scale sector, where over 1,400 farms were deemed underutilised in the late 1990s, but under the land reform where new land is supposed to be put under production to meet national food security needs and enhance agricultural incomes, this situation needs to be reversed.

Contract farming provides a way of overcoming some of the obstacles facing the new farmers, and is being embraced by many, particularly it seems in the higher potential areas of the Highveld. With contractors offering credit, inputs and transport and marketing facilities, and the new farmers offering land and labour, there is a matching up of capacities not being provided either by government or the banking/credit system.

Who then are the new contractors and contractees, and what problems are being faced? There has been little in-depth research on this evolving phenomenon, and it will be important to dig deeper. But a number of patterns are clear. The new contractors are not the classic large-scale agribusiness operations who run the tobacco, cotton or paprika contracting arrangements, they are often new entrepreneurs with some capital and out to make a buck (or many in fact). For the maize trade, purchasing a three-tonne truck is a key investment, as well as having contact with multiple land owners in an area. Supplying some inputs, and supporting a network of contract farmers, requires good social relations and some keen business acumen. The new contractors are often urban based, with jobs in town, but perhaps no land, or not enough of it. They are well connected and highly entrepreneurial. Their operations are small, but sometimes allowing considerable quantities of produce to be traded in a season. They play the price differentials well, selling into informal markets at key moments to maximise profit. A number of such players are former white farmers, often in consortia with others, who know the production system, and the economics and technical requirements of production and trade.

On the other side, the A2 farmers with spare land have a range of arrangements, from classic contracting where they produce the crop to land leasing, where the contractor takes on the production on their land. Maize and livestock production seem to dominate, as these both have high demand local markets into which products can be sold. For the new farmers demonstrating that the land is being used is also important, as the threat of a land audit is always around the corner. There are downsides of 'living under contract'[33], as the classic literature shows. There may be little competition and it is often a buyers' market, with produce being sold off at knock-down rates. Contracting tends to benefit men more than women, and the cash that comes may come late or not at all. Inputs supplied may be sub-standard or inappropriate, and becoming reliant on one product and one market may increase risks for producing households.

There are also particular risks to these new contracting arrangements in the post-land reform context in Zimbabwe. These revolve around land ownership and tenure security. In many of the Highveld areas, particularly where high value land with infrastructure is at stake, there continues to be insecurity in land holdings, especially on the A2 farms. An avaricious politician or military officer may eye up land that looks productive, and try and take it over. This process of politically-driven land grabbing continues today, despite attempts to stop it. Leases have not been issued, as uncertainty about the legal status of 'contested land' persists, and so land holders have little recourse to law, and must rely on local political connections to hold on to land – a risky and volatile strategy. In the same way contractors must balance the risks of this highly uncertain land ownership situation. They usually spread their risks, preferring to invest in multiple, smaller land areas than contract at scale in one place. This increases transaction costs substantially, but offsets the risks of default, take-over and disruption. Indeed, many prefer the more stable and settled A1 schemes to the more politicised, turbulent A2 areas, where well connected big chefs can intervene at any time.

---

[33] Little, P. and Watts, M. (eds.) (1994) *Living Under Contract: Contract Farming and Agrarian Transformation in Sub-Saharan Africa*, Wisconsin: University of Wisconsin Press

There are pros, cons, risks and opportunities of the new contract farming boom in Zimbabwe. Past experiences show the need to be cautious, as outlined in the excellent review by Carlos Oya[34]. But it's certainly a trend worth tracking, and especially the new, private entrepreneur led strategies. As new farmers, particularly on larger plots, fail to get production moving due to lack of credit and other input support from government or the private sector, a contracting arrangement may be a positive solution, especially as it draws new entrepreneurs with new finance and skills, as well as former white farmers who lost their land, into the sector, reshaping economic and political relationships and spreading the gains of land reform in new ways.

---

[34] Oya, C. (2012) Contract farming in sub-Saharan Africa: a survey of approaches, debates and issues, *Journal of Agrarian Change*, 12(1):1-33

CHAPTER 5
ZIMBABWE'S BEEF INDUSTRY

The beef industry was once the pride and joy of the commercial farming sector. As we show in a paper on the history of the Zimbabwe livestock industry and veterinary control[35], white ranchers enjoyed extraordinary levels of support from colonial and post-colonial governments. The industry also profited from generous import agreements to the EU supported by the aid budget. The result was that beef exports became an important foreign exchange earner for the country through the 1980s and 1990s.

But this export trade was reliant on compliance with stringent EU disease control regulations, particularly around foot-and-mouth disease (FMD). Huge amounts of money were invested by the EU, creating a series of disease control zones to facilitate export. The beef export industry migrated northwards, away from the traditional cattle ranching country of the lowveld towards the Highveld, and so far from the FMD infected zones. FMD is a natural disease in Africa and is found in wildlife, and particularly buffalo. A beef export strategy and wildlife do not mix, and even with FMD-free buffalo herds maintaining disease freedom. Compliance with EU regulations became an expensive challenge.

And then everything changed. With the land invasions of 2000, there was a massive movement of livestock and a breakdown in veterinary controls. FMD outbreaks occurred and the export trade was lost. The beef industry as it had been known collapsed. The massive infrastructure built up around the CSC (Cold Storage Commission, later Company)[36] became a white elephant, and the investment in disease control by the EU became largely an irrelevance.

Today, the livestock industry is based on multiple small herds owned mostly by small scale farmers. FMD is under control again, and movement controls are in

---

[35] Scoones, I. and Wolmer, W. (2007) Land, landscapes and disease: the case of Foot and Mouth Disease in southern Zimbabwe, *South African Historical Journal*, 58:42–64

[36] Cross, E. (1971) An economic appraisal of the production and marketing of Rhodesian beef, *Rhodesian Journal of Economics*, 5(19).

place. But the prospects of regaining the export market look remote. This is seen by some as another example of the tragedy of Zimbabwe's land reform. But has this transition in the structure and focus of the livestock industry been all bad?

The subsidised investments in the old white ranching sector, which continued for 20 years after Independence, through the beneficence of government and the donors, meant that beef ranching was rarely economic. The subsidised parastatals like the CSC were a massive drain on public resources. The meat supplied was not geared for domestic demand ('*nyama*') but to export (fillet steaks for Europeans). The ranches that were required for this industry were vast, amounting to thousands of hectares, and increasingly in the higher potential areas of the country. Was this really the optimal use of this land? And the fences, market bans, slaughter and quarantine controls that were imposed on everyone for the benefit of a few exporters, resulted in cost and inconvenience for many.

Today, Masvingo's 'real markets'[37] for meat are based on a diverse group of producers, and linked to a distributed network of traders, sellers, brokers and suppliers, spreading the economic gains further (see our report on livestock in Masvingo[38]). The unit value is lower, but the overall benefits for economy and development may be greater. In another paper on options for disease control in the southern African beef industry[39], we made the case that the 'disease freedom' approach adopted before 2000 and required by the EU and OIE (the World Animal Health Organisation), does not make sense in areas where FMD is endemic. Other more appropriate ways to control and manage make more sense, although enclaves of high-value production could still exist through 'compartmentalisation' but would have to be factored into private business

---

[37] Mavedzenge, B., Mahenehene, J., Murimbarimba, F., Scoones, I. and Wolmer, W. (2008) The dynamics of real markets: cattle in southern Zimbabwe following land reform, *Development and Change*, 39(4): 613-639

[38] Mavedzenge, B., Mahenehene, J., Murimbarimba, F., Scoones, I. and Wolmer, W. (2006) *Changes in the Livestock Sector in Zimbabwe Following Land Reform: The case of Masvingo province*, Research Report, Brighton: IDS

[39] Scoones, I. , A. Bishi, N. Mapitse, R. Moerane, M.-L. Penrith, R. Sibanda, G. Thomson and W. Wolmer (2010) Foot-and-Mouth Disease and market access: challenges for the beef industry in southern Africa, *Pastoralism*, 1 (2): 135-164.

plans. For others, a commodity-based trade system would make more sense, with a focus on different domestic and regional markets.

As Zimbabwe's herds are rebuilt, but under very different ownership patterns, important policy decisions will be required. Will there be a vain attempt to recreate the past glories of the commercial beef export system, or will a more sensible focus be on different markets, productions systems and disease control measures?

CHAPTER 6

ZIMBABWE'S POULTRY INDUSTRY: RAPID RECOVERY, BUT MAJOR CHALLENGES

Zimbabwe's poultry industry has shown massive growth since 2009. A range of sizes of units have sprung up everywhere – from the medium size units of 1000 birds to massive industrial scale operations. Chickens are big business.

Meat consumption has changed significantly in Zimbabwe over the last 20 years. Beef used to be the most consumed, with Zimbabweans eating on average 13kg per annum in the 1980s. According to a 2012 USAID report[40], today this has dropped to only 3.3kg, the lowest in the region. Chicken and pork in particular have replaced this; chicken consumption is now half of all meat consumed. Beef has dropped to only 35%. Meat consumption has rebounded since 2009 as the economy has improved, now estimated to be 11,000 MT per month, up by 20%. But the pattern of consumption has changed. This has been driven in part by taste, but also austerity as people looked to cheaper sources of protein. According to the USAID report, the retail price of economy beef which has the highest demand is between US$4.60 – US$5.00 per kg compared to the average chicken retail price of about US$3.30 per kg.

After the stabilization of the economy, many invested in poultry as a sure-fire way of making money. Ministry of Agriculture data show the rapid increase in both broilers and layer production of day old chicks from 2009, with over 50m day old chick production of broilers by 2011, for example.

But there are significant challenges to these new producers. These centre in particular on competition from cheap imports, including illegal dumping. ZIMSTAT shows that in 2011 chicken imports were 25,500 MT at a value of US $13.644 million or an average of only US$0.53/kg. The low price suggests much

---

[40] Sukume, C. and Maleni, D. (2012) '*Beef CIBER Study. Constraints to Competitiveness*', unpublished report to the Zimbabwe Agricultural Competitiveness Program, Harare: DAI/ USAID

of this is offal (including 'waste' pieces), which is illegal to import. Additionally the volume exceeds the official quota by over 100%, representing 20% of the total demand for chicken nationally, according to the USAID report.

In addition, the costs of feed have escalated. Soya production has been slow to rebound in Zimbabwe, and imports are costly as only Zambia produces GM-free soya in the region. These imports are expensive as Zambia tries to protect its own growing poultry industry. This really took off when Zimbabwe was suffering outbreaks of avian influenza in the early 2000s, and then subsequently when the Zimbabwe economy collapsed, and along with it its poultry industry.

The 2013 budget statement laid out the challenges for the Zimbabwean industry clearly:

- Stiff competition from cheap imports for both table eggs and meat, threatening viability of producers.

- Rising input costs, particularly maize and soya meal, following poor harvests.

- High volumes of illegal imports which are being sold in the domestic market at sub-economic prices.

The USAID study highlighted the challenge of cheap and illegal poultry imports for the meat industry as a whole. Much of the imported poultry meat comes from Brazil which has a massive poultry industry. Products that cannot be sold in the Brazilian markets are often transported elsewhere in the world. Feet, skin, necks and other 'offal' are frozen and packaged and sold at rock bottom prices. Chicken pieces too are packaged and sold, again at highly competitive rates. Go to any Zimbabwean supermarket and you will find 1kg of chicken pieces being sold at US$3, sometimes considerably less.

How these prices can be so low is beyond me. Maintaining a cold chain from Brazil to Zimbabwe must cost a fortune, let alone the cost of the product and its processing and packaging. While there are import quotas, many believe these are being exceeded through illegal imports. The import of offal is also illegal due to health and safety concerns. The USAID study recommended tighter import controls and the banning of offal imports, arguing that cheap imports were not only damaging the poultry industry, but also the beef industry as cheap meat alternatives were suppressing demand.

This is not just a Zimbabwean problem. In 2012, the South African government slapped on surcharges, provoking a row with the Brazil[41]. Brazil responded by taking the dispute to the WTO[42], claiming that the South African's protectionist actions were threatening the new friendship developed between the nations as a result of the BRICS partnership. It seems the diplomatic heat, and the threat of a WTO case that the South Africans have backed down[43], at least for now.

Undeterred by this dispute from across the border, Zimbabwe has now responded to the same problem. The 2013 budget statement noted:

> "*Due to unfair competition from imports of chicken, local breeders are increasingly cancelling orders for day old chicks... Investigations indicate that chicken imports are either smuggled or are grossly undervalued for duty purposes. In instances of smuggling, the necessary veterinary and health hazard permit controls are undermined...*"

The government introduced a higher customs duty "in order to level the playing field between imported and locally produced chicken". This is an important and welcome move. Let's see if it has the effect it needs to. Hopefully the Brazilians will be less heavy-handed with Zimbabwe where the market is much smaller, and a trade dispute can be avoided.

Unfortunately, the issue is not just about formal trade. As already noted, it is perhaps the illegal trade which is most significant, and damaging. This is well embedded in local Zimbabwean business networks, sometimes with high-level connections, and veterinary control and customs enforcement capacity remains weak. While chicken smuggling is perhaps less dramatic than drugs or diamonds, it has just as devastating an effect on the economy, lives and livelihoods.

---

[41] Fihlani, P. (2012) 'Could chicken row threaten Brazil-South Africa friendship?', *BBC News Africa*, 3 October

[42] 'Brazil contests South African chicken dumping surcharge', *World Poultry*, 25 October 2012

[43] 'No SA action on 'dumped' chickens', *The Poultry Site*, 24 December 2012

CHAPTER 7
MECHANISING ZIMBABWEAN AGRICULTURE

What is it about the allure of tractors? They seem to be the archetypal symbol of development and progress. Everyone needs one. But are they worth it? Tractors can plough fields, pull equipment and even be used to drive around town. But they are expensive, difficult to maintain and not much use on small plots where they often do substantial damage through compacting soil.

Tractors of course are also a symbol of power. They show status, prestige and access to the places that matter. In the mad-cap mechanisation scheme of the mid-2000s organised by the Reserve Bank of Zimbabwe, they were handed out to all and sundry. With hyperinflation raging, the 'loans' could be paid off for as little as US$20. Every chef worth their salt got a shiny new red Chinese tractor. Hundreds of tractors were distributed, representing a considerable amount of generous Chinese loan money. Were these funds really helping to keep the country afloat during a time of austerity due to sanctions?

In the 1980s tractors were all the rage too. A symbol of modernity they could not be missed from the standard development package. A new, modern Zimbabwe had to have agriculture which was mechanised; the ox plough was from the old era when Africans did not have access to resources and the opportunity to practise modern agriculture like whites did.

Joseph Rusike did an important piece of research[44] back then showing how in most circumstances in the communal areas tractor use through individual ownership was far from economic. The tractor hire schemes run through the District Development Fund served some with the cash, and were especially useful in times of drought when cattle were too weak to pull ploughs. And as cattle numbers were hit by drought mortalities in the early 1990s, tractors again became useful as herd numbers were not sufficient to form spans. At a similar

---

[44] Rusike, J. (1988) *Prospects for agricultural mechanisation in communal farming systems: a case study of Chiweshe tractor mechanisation project,* Thesis, Harare: University of Zimbabwe

time, Rusike's work was backed up by a major historical survey by then World Bank economist Hans Binswanger[45].

And now again there is more talk of tractors. This time from the Brazilians, who are offering nearly US$100m worth of farm machinery as part of a solidarity deal with the Zimbabwean government[46], channelled through the 'family farming' and agrarian reform ministry, the MDA. This is supposed to assist in particular the land reform programme, increasing efficiency and reducing the underutilisation of land through the expansion of cropped areas.

The Chinese too are showing off their tractors, and in particular the industrial machines produced by Menoble, the company that runs the new Chinese Agricultural Demonstration Centre at Gwebi College near Harare. There is also apparently a John Deare representative based at the Centre, apparently posted to Zimbabwe from China. Even the Iranians are offering tractor aid too[47]. A large plant, jointly run and built by the Iranian government was being mooted recently.

The Brazilian tractors have not arrived yet, and the Chinese ones remain in the courtyard at Gwebi. Representatives from both countries' agencies genuinely believe that tractors will make a difference to Zimbabwe's agriculture. Will Zimbabwe be flooded with tractors, of different makes with different spare parts and repair needs? Will this really help Zimbabwe's agricultural revitalisation? Or will it be another source of patronage, with tractors blessing people's homesteads as shining, then decaying, examples of misspent development money?

Of course agricultural mechanisation helped transform the large-scale farms of northeast China, and Brazil has pushed agricultural mechanisation to a new peak in the mega farms of the Brazilian *Cerrado*. But these are very different contexts to Zimbabwean agriculture.

---

[45] Binswanger, H. (1986) Agricultural mechanization. A comparative historical perspective, *World Bank Research Observer*, 1(1):27-56

[46] Kadzere, M. (2011) 'Zimbabwe to acquire farming equipment from Brazil', *The Herald Online*, 23 August

[47] Nasseri, L. (2012) 'Iran invests in Zimbabwe tractor-assembly plant, press TV says', *Business Week*, 26 February

Arable area sizes today range from an average of 2-5ha in the communal areas to 10-15ha in the A1 schemes to 70ha and above in the A2 farms (although in many instances only a small fraction is cultivated). Shared tractor arrangements may make sense for A2 schemes, allowing farmers to increase cultivated areas. However it is probably not tillage that is constraining this expansion, but more credit and finance for increasing production.

The Reserve Bank of Zimbabwe (RBZ) programme in the 2000s was a disaster and was simply an exercise in profligate patronage. But other schemes have failed too. But rather than shun the generosity of the Brazilians, Iranians and Chinese — and no doubt in the future many other donors wanting their farm machinery manufacturers to benefit from aid and investment programmes — it will be important to assess mechanisation needs and the institutional design of such programmes, taking account of the very particular political economy of tractors in Africa. A good starting point for those in the Ministry — currently called the Ministry of Agriculture, Mechanisation and Irrigation Development — would be to re-read Joe Rusike's and Hans Binswanger's papers from the 1980s.

CHAPTER 8
APPROPRIATE TECHNOLOGIES?

In December 2012 I had the opportunity to discuss technology options for Zimbabwean farming with two different groups. They had very different ideas about what was appropriate. And neither seem to have asked farmers themselves. Nor had they taken account of the particular technological challenges of Zimbabwe's agrarian structure. Both, for different reasons, seemed, to me at least, inappropriate technologies for the vast mass of Zimbabwean settings.

The first was a discussion around 'Conservation Agriculture' (CA)[48] in Wondedzo Extension, a villagised A1 scheme in Masvingo district where CA is being promoted by an NGO, Hope Tariro. This low-till approach, involving digging planting pits by hoe in small areas to concentrate moisture and fertility inputs, is being pushed by donors in Zimbabwe in a big way. It is central to programmes led by the FAO, as well as across numerous NGOs. It is supported by the EU and DFID among other donors, and is backstopped by a range of technical support agencies. These include the River of Life Church and the Foundations for Farming[49], where CA is inspired by 'callings from God' and the Sustainable Agriculture Trust, led by a group of former white farmers and supported by substantial EU-FAO funds, as well as CGIAR Centres like CIMMYT and ICRISAT.

I talked to the local extension agent in the area who was preparing for the planting season with his demonstration farmers. He estimated he spent around 60% of his time during the farming season on supporting CA activities in the area. He was politely equivocal about the approach, but he was clear it was diverting his time from other activities. It is an extremely intensive gardening approach, which requires an area to be fenced off and all crop residues returned to the land. Farmers refer to it as 'dig and die' due the back breaking work

---

[48] Scoones, I. (2012) *Conservation agriculture: the problem of donor fads*, blog, zimbabweland.wordpress.com

[49] http://www.foundationsforfarming.org/

involved, but they are glad of the free seeds (and in some cases fertiliser too). But is this an appropriate technology for the new resettlements?

On very small areas, with substantial labour inputs, yield increases are clearly possible, but this is not an approach that will deliver sustained growth in farm production in the larger arable plots of the new resettlements. Designed for micro garden plots, it may be appropriate for some areas, but not many. In a discussion at the nearby irrigation scheme, we raised the idea of testing out CA there. A woman immediately jumped up and exclaimed: "No! We will not do this! This is *our* cooperative irrigation. If we have the NGO here, they will make us irrigate with buckets!" There was general agreement: the NGO imposed ideas were fine to get hold of seed and could be done on small areas near the villages, but they should not disrupt their core economic activities on the irrigation scheme. The discussion moved to the problems of CA, and the usual list spilled out. Too much labour, small areas, burning of crops with concentration of fertiliser and so on.

The next opportunity to discuss farm technology came a few days later at the China Agricultural Technology Demonstration Centre [chapter 48], built by the Chinese Government on the campus of Gwebi College just outside Harare. This is being run by the agricultural machinery company, Menoble, an offshoot of the Chinese Academy of Agricultural Mechanisation Sciences[50]. The facility is impressive as is the shiny machinery in the courtyard. The Centre hosts regular training programmes for Zimbabwean farmers and extension officials. But with some exceptions, the machines are only useful for massive farms – of the order of 1000 hectares or so. The model, it was explained, is the large-scale commercial farms of north-east China, where the company has its major market. What about the famous small-scale farms of China?, I asked. No, this is backward farming, not the future, it was argued by one official.

Neither group had, it seems, thought about the demands of the new agrarian structure. Today, 90% of Zimbabwe's farmers are smallholders, representing 80% of the farmed land. This is a dramatic change from the past. The argument of the donors and NGOs pushing CA is that many of these farms in the communal areas are very small – perhaps only one or two hectares. Here an intensive

---

[50] http://menoble.en.alibaba.com/company_profile.html

gardening approach may be appropriate, if the labour is available. But what about the new resettlements? The average holding per household in the A1 schemes is 30-40ha, with cultivated areas in our study sites in Masvingo increasing, now averaging 5-10ha. CA does not make sense in these areas. But nor does most of the Chinese machinery on offer at Gwebi. The Chinese company officials argue that production should occur on large, modern, efficient farms, equipped with the latest machinery (huge cultivators, combine harvesters and planters pulled by 15HP tractors). A familiar tale about the supposed superiority of large-scale farming, and the need to transform a backward smallholder sector [chapter 1], forgetting of course how Chinese economic growth was supported by millions of smallholder farms following the reforms.

Neither the western donors and NGOs nor the Chinese seem to have thought hard enough about the contexts into which their technologies are supposed to fit. Nor have they discussed properly with their clients and customers. Of course Zimbabwean farmers are very polite, and will not turn away an NGO, in case its work can be redirected towards something useful. They are happy to take free inputs (worth around US$40 per household), but, as with the outburst at the irrigation scheme and the derogatory nick-name for CA, they are reluctant to see this as a solution. Equally, extension workers and farmers alike will attend the Chinese training courses and marvel at the big machines, but will they take up the suggested technical options? Even if they could afford them, this is extremely unlikely. Only a small proportion of farmland is now over 1000ha, representing only a few farmers. Is this the target market for Chinese machinery, and could be basis for a long term business plan for Menoble? I doubt it.

So here we have two sets of inappropriate technology being pushed by two very different sets of donors, driven by particular perceptions and assumptions. Technology transfer has come back into fashion in the aid world, but all the critiques that Robert Chambers and others made way back on the problems with this paradigm still apply. In a new agrarian setting, there are some real technological challenges, but these will have to be met together with inputs from farmers and a much better sense of scale requirements and farmer needs and priorities. Perhaps the Chinese, the Brazilians (also offering tractors) [chapter 48] and the 'traditional' donors could support this – focusing on rehabilitating Zimbabwe's agricultural research and development capacity.

SECTION B
THE ECONOMY

In the period to 2009, the economy was in freefall. Inflation rose to a peak of 231 million percent, and the currency was worthless. Parallel markets existed for everything, and normal market exchange had to cease, or go underground. Since 2009, inflation has been low, the US dollar and South African rand have been adopted as currencies, and growth has been impressive, peaking at 9%. Much credit must go to the MDC Finance Minister of the Government of National Unity that operated from 2009-13, Tendai Biti.

Before 2009, the economy was in turmoil. There was a massive flight of capital, as investors withdrew, and the economy became captured by those with the political clout and economic resources. The security services and their business partners were involved in a complex and corrupt web of economic and political relations across all sectors. In parallel the informal economy exploded – partly out of necessity as the formal system collapsed, but also out of the opportunities for entrepreneurship that opened up. The land reform is part of this story, but not as some suggest the sole 'cause' of the collapse: there were a number of factors: sanctions, capital flight, lack of international credit, as well as the impact of restructuring a major sector in the economy. Chinese support and the commodities boom in the minerals sector offset some of the worst, and have helped spur recovery. Indeed, land reform-based production has been an important part of economic growth in recent years [section A].

In this section, various chapters explore these issues, starting in chapter 9 with a discussion of the dangers of the 'resource curse' and the reliance on a narrow and politically-controlled, minerals sector. This is followed in chapters 10 and 11 by an overview of the macro economic picture as seen at the time of the 2013 budget, and a further discussion of how a successful, stable and sustainable economic recovery needs to see agricultural growth as an important part of it, and reliance on the minerals boom is unwise. For in 2013 growth prospects are looking less rosy than a few years back. Growth projections are downwards, and the 2013 election outcome will only make matters worse, bringing more uncertainty and questions about investor confidence. This is why attention to agriculture is essential, as this provides the basis for sustained, broad-based, inclusive growth.

Other chapters in this section look at different aspects of the agricultural economy. A key issue is the question of farm labour. Farm workers were displaced in large numbers due to the land reform. But not on the scale as some suggest, and chapter 12 tries to get behind the facts and figures. They have also been replaced by a new labour force, as employment is being generated on the new farms. This new rural labour economy is poorly understood, and highly variable across the country, but it is an important. Generating employment in agriculture will be essential for any long-term recovery, and the improvement of lives and livelihoods more broadly.

One of the key claims of redistributive land reform, especially to a mix of smallholdings and larger farms, is that this spatial reconfiguration, with different niches and specialisations, but also with far more people on the land, will result in a major local economic regeneration, with positive linkage effects and spin offs for businesses, employment and growth more generally. This has been slow to happen, although there were already emerging signs even in 2010, as reported in our book. Chapter 13 looks at this issue, and makes the case that a territorial approach to local economic development should be a central component of economic policy.

A key constraint to agricultural growth has been the lack of capital and finance. This has been less of a problem for smallholders who have used their own resources and labour, but more for A2 farmers who are trying to establish larger operations under very difficult economic conditions. Credit and finance arrangements are essential, and chapter 14 argues that some major rethinking is required in rural finance arrangements to allow funding to flow on a secure basis. This will mean overhauling inappropriate collateral arrangements, as well as innovative approaches to co-financing, including contracting arrangements [chapter 4].

It is of course not only land ownership that has changed through land reform, but also wider value chains and markets (see also section A). There are many new entrants – as market agents, transporters, contractors, input suppliers, equipment dealers, financiers and more – and this has been generating important income earning and employment opportunities, as the new farms establish themselves. Former farmers who had been displaced from their land through land reform have also found new roles. With skills, market knowledge, capital and connections, they have been able to capitalise on new business opportunities in a number of ways [chapter 15]. Whites may no longer be the dominant presence at the production end, but they remain important in the wider agricultural economy, and crucial to its longer-term recovery.

The land reform requires a radical rethinking of economic policy – from the macro level to the specific detailed policies on finance, regulation and so on. The 'real markets' of the new economy are not the same as what went before. There is little data, poor understanding, and so inadequate policy responses. Getting to grips with the transformation of the agricultural economy is an important precursor to a sustained recovery, and will avoid any quick-fix reliance on mineral revenues to drive growth.

CHAPTER 9

'RESOURCE NATIONALISM': A RISK TO ECONOMIC RECOVERY?

In a presentation during 2012 Professor Tony Hawkins from the University of Zimbabwe, offered some notes of caution about Zimbabwe's economic recovery, despite the high growth rates being recorded. He argued that Zimbabwe is becoming "increasingly resource-reliant with the share of GDP of agriculture and mining together now virtually double that of manufacturing".

This structural change is illustrated in a table, contrasting the share of GDP and percentage of exports in 1990 and 2010/11.

SHARE IN GDP	1990	2010
Mining	4%	9.1%
Agriculture	15%	13%
Manufacturing	22%	11.5%
EXPORT SHARES	**1990**	**2011**
Primary	82%	94.5%
Manufactures	18%	5.5%
Exports: GDP	28%	50%

Exports he explained "now contribute half of GDP – up from 28% – while the share of primary exports is up 95% from 82%. This reflects the de-industrialization of the economy". He continues: "...if Zimbabwe is to re-industrialize, firms will need to have very different business models from those of the past". But, he says policymakers are fixated "on capacity utilization, strategic industries, import substitution, self-sufficiency and local ownership". This, he says, is "more likely to accelerate de-industrialization than reverse it".

This is overlain with what he calls a "toxic cocktail of resource nationalism and the resource curse". He explains: "The two interact as politicians, desperate for revenue and votes, prioritize wealth exploitation over wealth creation. The resource curse is evident where policymakers use diamond revenues to finance current – not capital – spending". Policymakers, he says, "argue that Zimbabwe is not a poor country – its diamond, gold and platinum wealth could – and should – be used to repay our foreign debt, rather than seeking debt relief. This is a political – sovereignty – argument, not an economic one. Those who tout this argument believe not just that Zimbabwe can – and should – go it alone, but also that this is a means of escaping the governance and structural reforms implicit in HIPC debt relief." [chapter 46].

He argues: "Resource nationalism takes many forms ranging from higher mining taxes to indigenization and local ownership laws. Regardless of what form it takes resource nationalism fails unless its long-run focus is on wealth generation, not asset ownership and short-termist wealth exploitation". Reflecting on the statistics, he comments: "Today the Zimbabwe economy is recovering – not growing – by consuming its wealth. The country has increased its reliance on resource-depletion growth, while failing to diversify production and exports and invest in the future".

He concludes that policy needs to shift the focus

- "from consumption to investment

- from asset ownership and wealth consumption to wealth creation

- from needs-based remuneration to productivity-based earnings

- from reviving uncompetitive firms that have passed their sell-by date to start-ups and new entrants.

- from near-term income growth, reliant on wealth depletion and consumption, to long-term growth sustainability based on investment and competitiveness".

These are all certainly good aims, and the note of caution about how mineral and agricultural riches can be fragile, if not reinvested is important. But the commodity boom driving economic growth across Africa is not going to go away. Africa is resource rich, and the demand for these riches is growing, particular in Asia. The new geopolitics reflects this as China [chapter 48], India, the Middle East, Brazil and others seek out alliances in Africa in order to secure access to resources to fuel their own economic growth.

This new world order is what Hawkins calls the 'new normal'. Rethinking the political economy of growth in the era of the commodity boom will require accommodating these new realities, but also guarding against the risks, making sure the new riches are broadly shared and appropriately invested, and keeping the new investors accountable and avoid dependency in a new periphery. This will be a major challenge for future economic policy, in Zimbabwe and beyond; one that will require some major rethinking.

CHAPTER 10

GROWTH IN JEOPARDY? REFLECTIONS ON ZIMBABWE'S 2013 BUDGET STATEMENT

The 2013 budget[51] was, in the words of Minister of Finance Tendai Biti, his most difficult yet. He revised growth projections downwards to only 4.4%, because of continued depression in the global economy and uncertainty about Zimbabwe's economic and political prospects.

But there were some bright spots. The minister has presided over a remarkable period of recovery. Zimbabwe has grown faster than any other country in the region, and mining and agriculture have been the greatest contributors to growth. By 2010 mining contributed a massive 18% to overall economic output as measured by formal GDP indicators, and nearly 50% of export revenue. Growth in agriculture was stronger than expected in 2012, as both tobacco and cotton performed better than projections. Maize was however heavily affected by drought. The treasury expects a continued pattern of growth in the sector, around 5-6%.

But the success of agriculture has been overshadowed by the growth of mining, with annual growth rates of around 30%. Exports increased by a massive 230% in the period from 2009-2011. By the end of 2011, mineral exports accounted for 47% of total exports, made up of platinum (43%), gold (28%), and diamonds (20%) in particular. Furthermore, the average share of mining to GDP has grown from an average of 10.2% in the 1990s to an average of 16.9% from 2009–2011 overtaking agriculture. Diamond output is expected to increase to 16.9 million carats in 2013, largely driven by enhanced production from the major diamond mining houses at Marange diamond fields. Platinum output is expected to rebound to 11.5 tons in 2013.

However, while growth has occurred at impressive levels since dollarization in 2009, it has not continued at such rates. Zimbabwe's seemingly miraculous

---

[51] http://www.zimtreasury.gov.zw

recovery from the dire doldrums of the late 2000s may have stalled, a concern raised in the budget. With continued investment uncertainty, question marks are raised about the robustness of the economy. While minerals and agriculture can continue to underpin some growth, the levels required for recovery to earlier levels are still not being achieved.

How can the economy be revived for the longer term? This will require investment, including by the state. The 2013 budget offered US$3.8bn in government expenditure. But this is a pathetically small amount in relation to needs, and much of it already accounted for in terms of salary obligations. Government taxation and revenue collection is improving, but the economic base remains small. Any Zimbabwean finance minister is in a bind.

In the next chapter, I look at some future scenarios, making the case for a greater focus on agriculture, and avoiding an overly strong reliance on minerals, despite their allure.

CHAPTER 11
AN UNBALANCED ECONOMY

In the previous chapter I reviewed some of the facts and figures in the 2013 budget statement. There are some definite bright spots, and the rebound since 2009 is impressive. But can Zimbabwe's economy continue to grow sustainably and inclusively on the back of mineral revenues without a more balanced economy?

In his budget statement, Finance Minister Tendai Biti argues for moving beyond an 'enclave economy' towards what he calls a 'cheetah economy'. Where is the investment for this transition going to come from? And what would such an economy look like?

Unfortunately, there is not much room for manoeuvre. The total budget committed for 2013 was only US$3.8bn, much of which was taken up by already committed salaries. Commitments to agriculture were only US$160m, 'regrettably' 6% below the Maputo Declaration target. Donor and multilateral support remains small in relation to overall need, and focused on welfare, humanitarian emergency and social services. As one commentator cruelly pointed out Zimbabwe's total budget is much smaller than the turnover of Pick n' Pay[52], a large South African retailer. So where is the strategic investment in a 'cheetah economy' going to come from?

One scenario is to rely on mineral revenues. But, as Cambridge professor Ha-Joon Chang[53] points out, this is risky. The current buoyancy of African economies is very contingent on high commodity prices and continued demand from the developed world, and perhaps especially China. A downturn elsewhere will see a sharp downturn in Africa. Even leaving aside the risks associated with the capture of mineral revenues by elites (the 'resource curse'), reliance on even an array of minerals to finance the rebuilding of an economy may be foolhardy.

---

[52] 'Biti presents paltry US$3.8bn budget', *Zimbabwe Independent*, 16 November 2012

[53] Ha-Joon Chang: growth in developing world shouldn't overexcite people – video, *The Guardian, Global Development*, 21 December

Another scenario would see agriculture more in the limelight. Rather than offering the paltry sums seen in the 2013 budget a much braver, more substantial agricultural rehabilitation initiative is required. This will inevitably require external support – including donors, multilateral banks, finance houses and the private sector – but it must be led by government, and backed by the state. Agriculture has a different demand profile to minerals, and so different economic elasticities. It employs people in potentially larger numbers per unit of output, and the growth potentials are significant, given Zimbabwe's comparative advantages. There remain outstanding issues of issuing leases and offering compensation [Chapter 47], but planning for such a mission-style effort should start now.

The alternative will indeed be the take-over by Pick n' Pay, and other elements of South African, Chinese, and Euro-American capital. You only have to go over the border to Zambia to see what a mineral led economy can offer. Growth, yes, but not more broad-based development. This is not the sort of 'middle income' country that Zimbabwe wants to become. Instead it needs a firm national economic base, owned and controlled by Zimbabweans. Perhaps surprisingly for many, the land reform has provided just this platform for growth and recovery, if only the imagination, vision and of course finance are in place.

However it seems clear the [now former] Minister of Finance is currently backing the first, risky mineral-led scenario. The budget statement is replete with statements about the dramatic potentials of the mining sector. We have heard this since Cecil Rhodes, who ultimately was disappointed. And indeed in Minister Biti's own words: "The mining sector is a tiny enclave with little connectivity with the rest of the economy and, therefore, despite its high rentals, it has not been able to sustain growth or socio-economic development".

He argues for a "major rethink" to allow forward, backward, spatial and other linkages with the rest of the economy, but does not reflect on the political economy of such a rethink. Mining capital is in Zimbabwe for a reason – minerals can be extracted and exported at a cheap price for profit. An enclave economy suits them just fine.

While Zimbabwe should not ignore its considerable mineral wealth, and it should tap it for maximum benefit, through appropriately balanced indigenisation policies, effective taxation and maximising local processing and value addition, it should also focus on its other sources of wealth: land and people, and give agriculture the boost it needs. The turn-around in tobacco, sugar and cotton, has shown the potential [chapters 2 and 3]. In my view, agriculture following land reform can not only deliver growth, but pro-poor, inclusive growth if supported in the right way.

CHAPTER 12
THE NEW FARM WORKERS: CHANGING AGRARIAN LABOUR DYNAMICS

Farm labour has been highlighted by many as one of the big losers from land reform. Certainly, the post-2000 land reform in Zimbabwe has resulted in a significant displacement of farm workers from former large-scale commercial farms. However, the scale and implications of this are much disputed, and poorly understood. In assessing the implications for employment, livelihoods and agrarian relations, it is critical to have a proper assessment of what has happened since 2000. Unfortunately, as with so much in the Zimbabwe land debate, this discussion is coloured by inaccurate figures and ideological positions, unsupported by empirical data.

Fortunately, a new paper by Walter Chambati[54], one of Zimbabwe's leading researchers on agrarian labour, has just been published the Future Agricultures Consortium in association with the African Institute for Agrarian Studies (AIAS). This helps move the debate forward by providing a detailed examination of changing agrarian labour relations based on detailed research from Goromonzi district, one of the high potential farming areas of Zimbabwe influenced by land reform.

One of the big problems with the debate about farm labour since 2000 has been (once again) the lack of data on what happened to farm workers following land reform. The figures regularly trotted out in the media, and by many others too are usually wildly inaccurate. For example the MDC, in their 2013 policy paper[55], claimed (p. 44) that "some 400,000 farm workers have been displaced with their families plunging nearly 2 million people into destitution and homelessness" due to what they term the 'chaotic' land reform. This is way off the mark, and inevitably colours the analysis and the policy conclusions reached.

---

[54] Chambati, W. (2013) *Agrarian Labour Relations in Zimbabwe after Over a Decade of Land and Agrarian Reform*, Working Paper 056, Future Agricultures Consortium: Nairobi

[55] Movement for Democratic Change (MDC) (2013) *Policy Proposals*, presented in the MDC's 8th policy conference 'Towards Real Transformation'

When we were putting together our book in 2010, we searched across the available data and tried to triangulate between sources. Our best estimates (based on CFU, GAPWUZ, CSO/ZIMSTAT and other sources) were that before land reform in the late 1990s, there were between 300,000 and 350,000 permanent and temporary farm workers working on large-scale farms and estates. Of these 150,000-175,000 (169,000 in 1999 according to the CSO) were permanent workers, making up a total population of around one million, including any dependents. In the new settlements established after 2000, around 10,000 households were established by those who were formerly permanent farm workers, along with others who were temporary farm workers and joined the land invasions. A further 70,000 permanent worker households remained in work on estates, state farms and other large-scale farms. There were also substantial numbers of *in situ* displaced people still on farms living in compounds, seeking work on the new farms and perhaps with access to a small plot – perhaps around 25,000 households. These were predominantly in the Highveld areas where significant farm worker populations resided on the farms, many without connections elsewhere and originally migrants from elsewhere in the region. Thus nationally this all means 45,000-70,000 permanent farm worker households were displaced and had to move elsewhere – to other rural areas or towns – while others who were temporary workers had to seek new sources of income but remained based at their original homes, some continuing as labourers on the new farms.

These figures suggest a very different pattern to that suggested in many media commentaries, donor reports and policy documents. It is disappointing that some more thorough cross-checking does not take place before these are published. Of course such patterns of displacement and resettlement vary dramatically across the country. In the Highveld areas where highly capitalised farms required large amounts of labour – for instance for tobacco or horticulture operations – displacements were significant. Outside these areas, the pattern was different. This was the case in Masvingo province, where land reform displaced largely ranch operations which offered limited employment. However, while there has undoubtedly been displacement and associated hardship, the scale and implications are very different to what is often suggested.

And what has replaced the former pattern of farm employment? Again this varies significantly, depending on the intensity of the farm operations, type of crops and the type of labour required. Across the farms in our study sample in Masvingo[56], we found that in the late 2000s on average 0.5 and 5.1 permanent workers were employed in A1 and A2 farms respectively, while 1.9 and 7.3 temporary workers were employed. This is shown in Chambati's studies of labour in Goromonzi, and his earlier studies in Chikomba and Zvimba, and is confirmed by the AIAS six district study[57] that showed how the average number of permanent workers increased from 1.28 on the smallest farms (up to 5 ha arable area – largely A1) and increased to 4.87 labourers for farms with arable areas of above 40 hectares (largely A2). The number of casual workers increased from 5.43 to 10.69 labourers across these ranges (p.118). Aggregating such figures up across new resettlement farms nationally, this represents a considerable amount of employment generated, including for many women.

When the new farms replaced low employment operations such as ranching as in many of our Masvingo sites, the amount of employment available now far exceeds what was there before. However for farms that employed greater amounts of labour before, the opposite may well be true. And in addition to the numbers of jobs, there is of course the question of pay, conditions, and the type of skills required. This again is highly variable.

Chambati explains how the labour regime has continued to evolve, especially following the dollarization of the economy:

> *"Non-wage labour such as sharecropping and labour tenancies are emerging in response to shortages of finance to hire labour. The integration of farm labour and land beneficiary communities through familial relations and other social networks provides prospects for the improved social reproduction of*

---

[56] Scoones, I., Marongwe, N., Mavedzenge, B., Mahenehene, J., Murimbarimba, F., and Sukume, C. (2011) *Zimbabwe's Land Reform: A Summary of Findings*. Brighton: IDS

[57] Chambati, W. (2013) Agrarian labour relations in Zimbabwe after over a decade of land and agrarian reform, *FAC Working Paper* 056, Nairobi: Future Agricultures Consortium; Chambati, W. and Moyo, S. (2007) Land reform and the political economy of agricultural labour in Zimbabwe, *Occasional Research Paper* 4, Harare: AIAS; Chambati, W. (2007) *Impact of FTLRP on Farm Workers and Labour Processes in Zimbabwe*, Harare: African Institute for Agrarian Studies; Chambati, W., Dangwa, C., Moyo, S., Mujeyi, K., Murisa, T., Nyoni, N. and Siziba, D. (2009) *Fast Track Land Reform Baseline Survey in Zimbabwe: Trends and Tendencies, 2005/06*, Harare: African Institute for Agrarian Studies

labour. The new form of social patronage based on kinship ties is being extended as more relatives are brought in for farm work to minimise cash outlays on the dollarized farm wages."

It is important to keep up with these changes, and understand the transformations in labour regimes that are occurring, with their implications for wages, rights, gender access, skill requirements and overall employment levels. With small-scale, medium scale and large-scale farms competing for labour in a particular area, there is a range of new dynamics of play. In the Highveld, the farm compound, although transformed from the past, remains a site of contestation, as Chambati explains for Goromonzi.

The social relations of labour on the new farms are of course a far cry from the exploitative residential tenancy system of the old large-scale commercial farms, with a diversity of new arrangements seen. But this does not mean that exploitation has disappeared. The new farm workers, dispersed over many more farms and often embedded in kinship networks, are poorly organised and unable to articulate demands effectively, and there has been downward pressure on wages. The organisations that once assisted farm workers on large-scale farms have yet to re-orientate their activities towards these new vulnerable groups.

With the debate still focused on the discussion of displacement, and informed by a poor understanding of what happened, a thorough reappraisal of rural labour regimes and their implications following land reform has yet to happen. Sadly the policies of Zimbabwe's farm worker labour unions and all the political parties remain largely silent on this issue, stuck in old debates informed by poor data. The same is true of much of the policy and media commentary.

Farm labour on the new resettlement farms generates a considerable number of livelihoods. As a source of employment, this sector is underestimated and poorly understood, yet is highly significant in the rural economy. As a group with poor labour rights and in need of organisation and support, the new farm workers are also an important constituency for unions, support groups and others.

CHAPTER 13

TRANSFORMING ZIMBABWE'S AGRARIAN ECONOMY

In a 2013 article in the Cape Times[58], prompted by Max du Preez's review[59] of Joe Hanlon and colleagues' book, *Zimbabwe Takes Back Its Land*, Tony Hawkins and Sholto Cross make the case that Zimbabwe's land reform has been a disaster, and that a smallholder, 'peasant' farming is not a route to economic growth.

The full-page article starts with a slightly bizarre critique of what has become to be known as 'peasant studies', a strand of academic work that has built over the years that examines the dynamics of change in agrarian societies. But it is a very odd caricature. There are very few who argue for a permanent condition of subsistence peasantry, somehow preserved in aspic. The point is that as a labour intensive, efficient form of production, small-scale agriculture, given the right support, can be an important driver of economic growth and poverty reduction (inclusive, pro-poor growth to use the current jargon). Diversification out of agriculture is an important dynamic too, as Frank Ellis' work[60] has shown from across Africa. As Michael Lipton argues in his magisterial book[61], based on a mass evidence and experience, land reform can be an important spur to such a transformation. This is the foundation for the so-called East Asian economic miracles – in Korea, Taiwan, Japan and elsewhere.

This process of change is always dynamic, and takes time. Resettlement success, just as wider economic change resulting from large-scale redistribution, is never

---

[58] Cross, S. and Hawkins, T. (2013) 'Zimbabwe's inconvenient truths', *Cape Times,* 24 May

[59] Scoones, I. (2012) *Difficult lessons from Zimbabwe that some South Africans just don't want to hear*, blog, zimbabweland.wordpress.com

[60] http://www.uea.ac.uk/international-development/People/staffresearch/ladder

[61] Lipton, M. (2009) *Land Reform in Developing Countries. Property Rights and Property Wrongs*, London: Routledge

immediate, as Bill Kinsey and Hans Binswanger[62] have shown. Restructuring of agricultural production has to be combined with the reconfiguration of supply industries and wider value chains. And following any redistributive land reform, there are inevitable processes of differentiation among agrarian classes. Some end up with larger plots, some smaller, others as labourers. It is the well-known multiplier effects[63] of small-scale agriculture that can create economic opportunities elsewhere, and provide other non-farm livelihood opportunities, and so broader based growth. Migration to urban areas is also important, but maintaining a rural base as part of a wider social security mechanism is also crucial. And, yes, as the economy grows, there is a greater pull towards higher paid, industrial jobs and people leave the countryside over time. In their article, Hawkins and Cross forget this historical experience, and misinterpret the experience of China. Ha-Joon Chang has written a brilliant piece in the *Journal of Peasant Studies*[64] that is well worth a read if you want to get to grips with the comparative historical lessons – from Europe, Asia, Latin America and beyond.

Such transformations are therefore long-term processes, and always highly context specific. In the developmental states of East Asia (and elsewhere, and earlier in Europe), the state has an important role to play: protecting people and new businesses, and so guiding and nurturing the transition through targeted incentives and subsidies. You cannot expect the existing arrangement to be appropriate to a new scenario, so it's important to facilitate the change of the wider agro-industrial base. What we are seeing in Zimbabwe is not so much "deindustrialisation" but a fundamental restructuring. Supporting such a transformation is essential, and this requires investment – something starkly absent in Zimbabwe due to a bankrupt government, a lack of private finance and donors refusing engagement due to sanctions.

Hawkins and Cross appear to reject such an agrarian vision for Zimbabwe. A welter of statistics are presented that fail to engage with the now substantial

[62] Binswanger-Mkhize, B. and Kinsey, H. (1993) Characteristics and performance of resettlement programs: a review, *World Development*, 21(9): 1477-1494

[63] Delgado, C., Hopkins, J. and Kelly, V. (1998) *Agricultural Growth Linkages in sub-Saharan Africa,* Vol. 107, Washington DC: International Food Policy Research Institute

[64] Chang, H. J. (2009) Rethinking public policy in agriculture: lessons from history, distant and recent, *Journal of Peasant Studies*, 36(3): 477-515

evidence base on Zimbabwe's rural economy, presenting once again dubious production[65], employment [chapter 12], displacement [chapter 40] and GDP [chapter 59] figures to support their argument. Without reviewing the data (in Hanlon *et al's*[66] book, as well as ours[67], Matondi's[68], Moyo and Chambati's[69] and many others), they proclaim that Zimbabwe's land reform has been a failure, and that only option for economic growth in Zimbabwe is the old model of a large-scale commercial agricultural sector, combined with industrial manufacturing, reclaiming the assumed halcyon days of the 1990s (which of course they were not).

This view is deeply problematic. A focus on the large-scale agricultural sector may produce some growth, although in the globally competitive markets of today it is unlikely to produce much, but will it produce jobs and livelihoods? Jobless growth creates social divisions, inequality and pressure on the state to provide social protection to the economically disenfranchised. Look at the 'third world' in Europe and you can see the challenges. Zimbabwe's own history, from the liberation war to the events of 2000, should show anyone that a return to an economic structure dominated by a few, but excluding the majority is not a politically viable option, even if it made any economic sense (which is very doubtful).

Hawkins and Cross seem blind to the opportunities of the new agrarian structure, rejecting these out of hand. Research from diverse sources [chapter 59] has shown how across the new resettlements there are large numbers of new farmers 'accumulating from below' – generating surpluses, investing and accumulating. Not everyone, but enough to generate an economic dynamic that creates investment and employment. This has been done with vanishingly little

[65] Scoones, I. (2012) *Fact check*, blog, zimbabweland.wordpress.com

[66] Hanlon, J., Manjengwa, J. M., and Smart, T. (2012) *Zimbabwe Takes Back Its Land,* Boulder: Kumarian Press

[67] Scoones, I., Marongwe, N., Mavedzenge, B., Mahenehene, J., Murimbarimba, F., and Sukume, C. (2010) *Zimbabwe's Land Reform: Myths and Realities.* Oxford: James Currey

[68] Matondi, P. (2012) *Zimbabwe's Fast Track Land Reform*, London: Zed Books

[69] Chambati, W. and Moyo, S. (2013) *Land and Agrarian Reform in Zimbabwe : Beyond White-Settler Capitalism*, Dakar: CODESRIA

external support. What more could be done if such support was larger and more effectively directed?

Hawkins and Cross begrudgingly acknowledge the successes of some communal farmers in the 1980s, but this time the impact could be much wider, as there are more people involved, and they are geographically spread. In our book we argue for a form of local economic development that capitalises on this new agrarian dynamic, rooted in smallholder farming, but spinning out to new businesses and value chains. The new farmers are creating new local economies – currently small-scale, but with clear opportunities for generating further economic linkages [chapter 60].

Take the tomato farmers in Wondedzo resettlement areas near Masvingo – one of the case studies being documented by the PLAAS project[70] on non-farm economies[71]. Recognising the importance of the local market, they have invested in small-scale irrigation pumps, cleared land near the river areas, and have started to produce vegetables on a large scale. As their businesses have grown, they have employed more people, mostly women from nearby areas, and have worked with suppliers to get their crops to market. This has generated more employment along the value chain, with traders, transporters, retailers, supermarket chains and others becoming involved. Several have bought new one tonne trucks in the last year, to ensure prompt delivery to market. Again, this has brought new economic activity, with drivers, mechanics and others finding work. Input suppliers are attracted to the area, offering seeds, fertilisers, pesticides, piping, pump spare parts and more. And all of this is happening in the new land reform areas without external support; yes on a small scale, but with significant cumulative impacts.

By area this sort of economic activity generates far more jobs and livelihoods than the large-scale commercial farms ever did. Being economically and socially integrated within rural settings, not set apart as was the case before, the multiplier effects are greater. Sales occur to supermarkets but also to small-scale

---

[70] http://www.plaas.org.za/smead

[71] Scoones, I. (2012) *Beyond the farm: getting local economies moving*, blog, zimbabweland.wordpress.com

traders – women who travel by bus to other towns and business centres to sell vegetables, sometimes processing them too to add value and to avoid losses.

But of course an agricultural economy cannot be just small-scale. The new agrarian structure of Zimbabwe is 'tri-modal', with a majority being small-scale (in the communal, A1 and old resettlement areas), but there are also medium scale commercial farms (A2) and the large-scale estates. Each can seek out their comparative advantages, and specialise production and marketing appropriately. But the important point is that there are now much greater opportunities for interaction – through contract farming, sharecropping, labour and market exchanges, and so on. This sort of integrated approach across farm scales to agricultural and rural development can have many spin-offs, and appropriately banishes the old dualism – a separation between 'peasant' agriculture and 'modern' commercial agriculture with its stark racial and economic divides – firmly to the past.

Hawkins and Cross seem to wish that this returns. They argue – on quite what basis it is not clear – that this is the only route to economic recovery for Zimbabwe. Yet they seem to reject the potentials of the dynamic entrepreneurialism and economic multipliers of the new agrarian system. With the potential of substantial state revenues from mining (as yet not fully captured of course), this is a moment when Zimbabwe could and should become southern Africa's new developmental state, rebalancing the economy [chapter 11], and directing and supporting development in ways that allows for long-term, inclusive, poverty-reducing growth, initially rooted in smallholder production, but always transforming, as the economy rebuilds and restructures. Looking east, may well be the right thing to do, and the lessons from East Asia, as well as now SE Asia [chapter 52], may well provide important lessons.

Political parties, media commentators, and academics alike need to engage with the realities on the ground, and avoid the posturing, the ideological grandstanding and the bitter, personal attacks and get to grips with the new realities. Harking on about the past, and failing to accept that there have been important successes of Zimbabwe's land reform means that new thinking does not emerge. Hawkins and Cross need to engage with the facts of the present, not some idealised notion of the past.

CHAPTER 14
CREDIT AND FINANCE

The abandonment of the Zimbabwe dollar and the creation of a dollarized economy in 2009 had a massive impact. Many outside Zimbabwe still have the vision of empty supermarkets, barter trade and people lugging around suitcases of old Zimbabwe dollars. No one seems to know how fast the Zimbabwean economy is growing, but Tendai Biti estimated it to be around 9% in 2011, driven in particular by the growth of the mining and agricultural sectors.

The Economist's[72] article on the growth potential of African economies highlighted Ethiopia, Angola, Nigeria, Zambia among others. Zimbabwe, intriguingly, was left off the map of growth statistics, as it would probably have registered the highest level of all. Too awkward perhaps for the Economist's map makers. Of course Zimbabwe's economy is growing from a very low base, but nevertheless things are happening [chapter 10].

In 2009 we did an enterprise survey across our Masvingo sites, and the story while positive was not startling. Businesses established soon after land reform had closed down during the hyperinflation period, and were only just being opened up. Today they are fully open for business, and others are getting set up. There are new entrants into rural markets, and those with cash and capital are returning bit by bit. These include black business elites as well as former white farmers and businessmen who are all active in establishing new operations – abattoirs, transport businesses, small shops and so on. Small-scale Chinese and Asian business is much evident too, although only in the towns.

The rural businesses are the usual staples of grocery shops, bars and butcheries, but they are complemented with other businesses, such as mobile phone repairs, tailoring, farm equipment repair and manufacture, veterinary medicine sales and many others. There appears a new confidence, and business people are sure there is money to be made. The restrictive regulations and political interference that characterised the period from around 2006, peaking around 2008, have gone, and gung-ho entrepreneurialism is evident.

---

[72] 'Africa's hopeful economies. The sun shines bright', *The Economist*, 3 December 2011

What is driving this? There is certainly more money in the economy. The flash cars in Harare are witness to this. Small-scale mining has taken off in a big way, and many are making a mint. And of course there are diamonds. Not only in the famous Marange mines, but also elsewhere [chapter 11]. The well-connected elite is making a fortune, and many are concerned about the diversion of resources away from the finance ministry towards private individuals and the party machinery of ZANU-PF. But even corrupt money has an influence on the local economy, improving flows of resources, creating demand, generating investment and so on, and this is having a tangible effect.

Yet the repeated complaint from small-scale rural business people is that, while the 'chefs' may have access to cash through whatever means, they don't – and the banking and credit system is not helping. This is hampering them from getting going. This is the complaint of A2 farmers, as well as shop owners and business people across our study areas [chapter 14]. While the absurdities of the era when the Reserve Bank, working with the army, tried to direct the agricultural economy, has thankfully gone, credit and banking institutions are not functioning well. This is limiting the opportunities of new farmers to scale up operations, to invest in irrigation, mechanisation and inputs, and to re-connect with higher value chains, which requires attention to standards, marketing and so on. This lack of rural finance is holding the sector back, and particularly the more entrepreneurial A2 farmers (and larger A1 farmers too) and the array of rural businesses linked to agriculture in the rural areas that can generate the spin-off benefits and multipliers that land reform can bring.

This needs urgent policy attention, bringing the public and private sectors together. But who is working on this? Not the donors, not the government, not the banks. Some claim that the lack of collateral through leasehold title is limiting loan-making and credit offers, but this is only part of the story [chapter 27]. The lack of policy thinking is a gaping hole. Some more effective rural economic policy, with new or rebuilt finance institutions is a top priority right now, if the new commodity boom and the post dollarization financial environment is to be capitalised upon.

CHAPTER 15

THE WHITES WHO STAYED IN AGRICULTURE

Following land reform some white farmers stayed on the land. The CFU says nationally this is only 200, but I suspect there are more. Often they do not have their full former farm (or multiple farms), but they do have a core operation. In Masvingo it has been impossible to date to get total numbers. There are not many within our study areas, but a few were 'allowed' to stay. How have they fared, and what are they doing?

There are at least four different categories of such farmers – those who have maintained strong political connections; those who have had good relationships with local communities; those who were producing strategically important things; and those who have just kept under the radar.

Those who fared best are clearly those in the first category. But given the whims of political factionalism in Masvingo especially, this is a tough job, and requires substantial transactions costs. Keeping friends with everyone in such a volatile situation can be costly.

Many former white farmers had good relations with local communities. Sometimes this was in an anachronistic, paternalistic way, but nevertheless with apparent genuine good will. Some such farmers have continued very actively to contribute to the neighbouring communities' production and welfare, sometimes on parts of their former farms. But being friends with the locals does not necessarily mean being friends with the big wigs who have designs on your farms. Although local people have tried to protect such farmers from land grabs by elites, they have often not been successful.

In the bizarre world of politicised planning in Zimbabwe, committees apparently sit and decide on the fate of particular farms. At an early stage of the land reform, seed production, animal breeding, day-old chick production, high-value fruit orchards and dairy farms were highlighted by government as in need of protection. But many lost out as farm invasions and political imperatives took hold, and, as a result, important capacity – in knowledge, market connections and infrastructure – was lost. Some in this category have remained. For example, there is a thriving day-old chick business, plus a couple of dairies on 'white-owned' farms near Masvingo. Although others have been taken over, particularly around 2008 when the peak of elite grabbing took place during the election period. And it was those with infrastructure (e.g. a dairy) which made such farms visible and susceptible to elite grabbing.

Finally, there are those who have kept under the radar. There is much of this going on. And probably more than we even know about. In the period after land reform well informed vets (who were being contracted to vaccinate, dose etc.) said there were probably around 6000 cattle being herded on farms across the province by former white farmers. Some managed to get formal leases for pieces of land, others made deals with the new farmers. This has proved tough to keep going as the costs of continuous negotiation, and the terms of the deals has proved troublesome, but the stories of the mass expropriation of stock or their export to Mozambique were overblown. Many of these lease grazing arrangements continue – on municipal and state farms, as well as privately held farms – and provide an important contribution to the booming abattoirs in the province [chapter 5].

Of course there are many others who formerly had farms who are still engaged in the agricultural sector – through processing, marketing, transport, advice and other linkages, including contract farming [chapter 4]. These are immensely important part of the agricultural economy, and such former farmers have been quick to learn where the markets are, and how to tap into them. This is generating growth and employment, as well as incomes for former farmers, but on the basis of a new land ownership.

And then there is the aid business. Of course the new resettlements are not supposed to be recipients of donor funding streams, but aid has the tendency of finding its way to supporting the most unlikely of beneficiaries. For example, the European Commission funded programme to support the farmers' unions has been a significant money-earner for some former white farmers. Through some strange assumptions about 'fairness', the funds were split equally between the CFU, the ZFU and the ICFZ. The latter apparently misused funds and were cut out. Despite the disparities in membership – the CFU with supposedly 200 active members still farming and the ZFU, with many tens of thousands – equal funds were given for supporting agriculture, including especially purchasing and distributing inputs. This has allowed some former white farmers to get into trading inputs on a significant scale, as they did not have land on which to deploy them. They have also become heavily engaged in 'consultancy' support via an FAO 'conservation agriculture' scheme[73] [chapter 8]. And contract farming linked to aid investments has also blossomed [chapter 4]. For example, nearby one of our sites,   newly rehabilitated irrigation schemes have become the focus for contract farming operations organised by former white farmers, supported by EC/UN funds. Other contract farming arrangements are evolving elsewhere – although frowned upon officially, those with the cash and the knowledge who can make a go of it are often welcomed by the new farmers, as collaborators in joint ventures, whether for cropping, hunting or livestock farming.

In the new and rapidly changing context of Zimbabwe, all sorts of weird and wonderful things are possible. Everyone agrees that white business acumen and agricultural expertise must be part of the future, but it will occur in new and as yet unimagined ways. The sooner there is acceptance of this the better, and then a more honest debate can emerge which does not hark on about going back to the past (as the CFU rhetoric so often implies) but is much more pragmatic about new alliances and ventures under a new agrarian structure.

---

[73] Scoones, I. (2012) *Conservation agriculture: the problem of donor fads*, blog, zimbabweland.wordpress.com

SECTION C
POLITICAL
DIMENSIONS

Land reform is inevitably political. The redistribution of assets from one group to another, is always going to be contentious. And so it has been in Zimbabwe. While our field research has focused on the outcomes, it has not ignored the political dimensions as some suggest.

Much commentary on Zimbabwean land and politics is very shallow and one-sided (although at least some of the media coverage is improving, see chapter 25). The inevitable focus is Robert Mugabe, and all interpretations seem to be channelled through a bizarre but enduring fascination with him, illustrated perfectly by the extraordinary reaction by a whole committee of academics following Mahmood Mamdani's piece in the *London Review of Books*[74]. Chapter 16 addresses 'the Mugabe factor' through a discussion of the film, *'Robert Mugabe.. What Happened?'*, and argues that we must look beyond Mugabe to a wider pattern of politics. This must also, as the film does, look at the historical inheritance: the meanings, memories and interpretations of the past that inevitably shape the future. Chapter 24 reviews Rory Pilossof's book, *'The Unbearable Whiteness of Being'*, a portrayal of white farming and its demise. The book demonstrates clearly how isolated, violent and abusive the experience was for many, and how and why so few did not accept (and still don't) the inevitability of land reform.

In the blog, I have reviewed a number of important works that have enriched our understanding of the wider politics of Zimbabwe in the recent period. Two authors stand out, both approaching their analysis from very different standpoints, and coming, not surprisingly, to different conclusions. The first is

---

[74] Mamdani, M. (2008) Lessons of Zimbabwe, *London Review of Books*, 30(23): 17-21

Sam Moyo, Zimbabwe's leading land scholar, whose edited book, *Beyond White Settler Capitalism*[75], makes a vitally important argument about the historical context for Zimbabwe's agrarian transformation from a monopoly settler capitalist economy, and the political implications of this. The other is Brian Raftopolous whose edited books, *Becoming Zimbabwe*[76] and *The Hard Road to Reform: the Politics of Zimbabwe's Global Political Agreement*[77] are important contributions to the debate, showing in particular how the penetration of a political-business-military elite linked to ZANU-PF has dramatically altered Zimbabwe's political economy in the past decade.

Rebuilding the state, as an accountable, legitimate and effective servant of the people will be a major and long-term task in Zimbabwe. Political institutions really do matter, as pointed out in the book *'Why Nations Fail'*, reviewed in chapter 21. A view from below on issues of security and state-building is advocated in chapter 20. This emphasises the existence of 'hybrid political orders' that must be negotiated in highly charged circumstances. This is not easy, and requires an approach that goes 'with the grain' – working with what is there rather than what might be a liberal, western, democratic ideal. As we argued in our book, this means developing a better understanding of local authority structures, their power bases, the overlaps, and sources of legitimacy, and so rebuilding public authority from below.

Other chapters complement this more macro focus, and dwell on our empirical material from Masvingo, and the specific cases that our research has examined. I argue that too often in generalised commentaries, the local, context-specific and geographically-variegated dimensions are ignored. Chapter 17 is a response to Blair Rutherford's very perceptive review of our book. While accepting some of the criticisms, the following two chapters show how our work on livelihood

---

[75] Scoones, I. (2013) *'Beyond White Settler Capitalism: Zimbabwe's Agrarian Reform'*, blog http://zimbabweland.wordpress.com

[76] Raftopoulos, B. and Mlambo, A. (2009). *Becoming Zimbabwe. A History from the Pre-colonial Period to 2008*. Harare: Weaver Press

[77] Scoones, I. (2013). *The politics of Zimbabwe's Global Political Agreement*, blog, http://zimbabweland.wordpress.com

outcomes and the context specificities of particular places has implications for the interpretation of political processes at the broader level.

A study of social differentiation and class formation on the resettlements shows how an emergent group of entrepreneurial new farmers are potentially an important rural political force, especially as allied with the middle class professionals with urban links who mostly populate the A2 farms (chapter 18). This, chapter 19 argues, has important implications for electoral politics – and the results of the 2013 elections should be seen in this light[78]. Chapter 23 turns to areas outside the core 'fast-track' land reform areas, such as large parts of the lowveld. Here there are intense contests over land, and many land invasions that have remained unrecognised by the state. The capture of economic interests, as well as resistance to elite land grabbing, is seen; all embedded in a very particular, location-specific politics.

This geographic differentiation is important to understand when assessing wider political dimensions. This is particular the case when discussing violence – a terrifying feature especially of the 2008 election period. Chapter 22 looks at the data on violence in this period, and asks why patterns are different in different places. It shows how, just as with other events, such as the impact of the clearance operation, Murambatsvina, or the capture of farms by elites or party members, blanket assessments and generalisations are invalid. A much more nuanced analysis is required. This is not to reject the importance of violent conduct, corrupt practice or elite capture, but to put it into context.

The politics of land reform is complex and contested and, as the following chapters show, highly varied between different sites, even within one province. The sort of detailed understanding of livelihood change, class formation, patterns of social reproduction and accumulation that we undertook in Masvingo must be complemented by wider analyses, as offered by Moyo, Raftopolous and others that explore the historical political economy in a broader way. There is clearly no simple story, and site-specific nuance and detail must always combine with bigger-sweep analyses.

---

[78] Scoones, I. (2013) *Zimbabwe's elections 2013: more confusion, more uncertainty* http://zimbabweland.wordpress.com/

CHAPTER 16
ROBERT MUGABE... WHAT HAPPENED?

On April 20, 2012, 32 years and 2 days after Zimbabwe's independence, there was a screening of the widely acclaimed film of "Robert Mugabe... What Happened?"[79] to a packed house at the University of Sussex. The film offers an important insight into Zimbabwe's post-Independence politics.

The panel that discussed the film afterwards, included Simon Bright (the film's director), Denis Norman[80] (the first Minister of Agriculture in independent Zimbabwe in 1980 and former head of the Commercial Farmers Union), Peter Freeman (the Overseas Development Agency – now DFID – representative in Zimbabwe in the early 1980s and subsequently within DFID responsible for Africa programmes), McDonald Lewanika (Crisis in Zimbabwe Coalition[81] coordinator) and Phillan Zamchiya[82] (Oxford University and former President of the Zimbabwe National Students Union).

It was an extraordinarily powerful and effective film, and it was a great panel discussion – with participants ranging from those intimately engaged in the post-Independence transition in 1980 to those who were not even born then, but heavily involved in contemporary struggles over Zimbabwe's future.

Everyone agreed that the film offered an insightful glimpse into the complex past of Zimbabwe. It used fascinating archival footage, together with interviews with key figures in the opposition movement in Zimbabwe – intellectuals, politicians, media figures and others. It deployed music of different styles, eras and genres to keep a pace and flavour of time and location. And it told a sympathetic, if critical, story about the man himself. As Simon Bright explained, this was a very personal project. As a Zimbabwean from a white, liberal

---

[79] http://vimeo.com/24822228

[80] http://en.wikipedia.org/wiki/Denis_Norman

[81] http://www.crisiszimbabwe.org/index.php?option=com_content&view=article&id=185&Itemid=232

[82] http://nehandaradio.com/2010/01/22/philani-zamchiya-who-is-who-in-zim/

background who had been imprisoned and then fled, he felt moved to tell the bigger story. Like others who asked 'what do you do with a respected father figure who goes wayward?', Simon wanted to explore what happened to his hero, and why he felt despair and disgust at his actions today. As he explained it was not a 'balanced presentation in the way of the BBC', but a personal, political exploration. In this sense it is highly effective. And indeed far superior to the film, *'Mugabe and the White African'*[83], which portrays such a one-sided, simplistic picture, without any attention to complex and contested histories.

Of course, as the film's title suggests, the story is told around one man – Robert Gabriel Mugabe. Mahmood Mamdani pointed out in his controversial essay for the London Review of Books[84]:

> "*It is hard to think of a figure more reviled in the West than Robert Mugabe. Liberal and conservative commentators alike portray him as a brutal dictator... There is no denying Mugabe's authoritarianism, or his willingness to tolerate and even encourage the violent behaviour of his supporters... [but this] gives us little sense of how Mugabe has managed to survive. For he has ruled not only by coercion but by consent, and his land reform measures, however harsh, have won him considerable popularity, not just in Zimbabwe but throughout southern Africa. In any case, the preoccupation with his character does little to illuminate the socio-historical issues involved.*"

Mugabe has thus become such of a focus for the Zimbabwe crisis that sometimes these wider issues are not addressed. As Sabelo Ndlovu-Gatsheni points out in a review of a series of books on Zimbabwe in *African Affairs*[85], a 'big man' political analysis can undermine our understanding of the multi-layered issues at play:

> *The concept of 'struggles within the struggle' not only captures the crucial issue of continuity and change that traverses the nationalist liberation*

---

[83] http://www.mugabeandthewhiteafrican.com/; see also a review at http://zimbabweland.wordpress.com/2011/09/16/a-white-farmer-robert-mugabe-and-some-archbishops/

[84] Mamdani, M. (2008) Lessons of Zimbabwe, *London Review of Books*, 30(23): 17-21

[85] Ndlovu-Gatsheni, S. J. (2012) Beyond Mugabe-centric narratives of the Zimbabwe crisis, *African Affairs*, 111(443): 315-323

struggle and the post-colonial period. It also encapsulate issues of personal clashes, ethnic clashes, generational clashes, ideological schisms, power struggles, strategic and tactical differences informed by exigencies of the liberation struggle – all this as a broad historical and discursive terrain within which Zimbabwe was born and leadership styles were honed. It is also the terrain within which political identities of patriots, puppets, sell-outs, revolutionaries, and counter-revolutionaries were formed. Analysis of 'struggles within the struggle' and 'struggles after the struggle' reveals the failure of nationalists to nurture and build democratic traditions, and the absence of peaceful coexistence of races, ethnicities, genders, and generations that invites the rule of violence and coercion. It exposes the nationalist struggle as a school of violence, intolerance, and commandism. Mugabe is a graduate of this school.

It was these more complex issues that the panel and audience picked up in discussion. Inevitably the film has limitations: it is after all a 85 minute documentary which must sustain a strong storyline. There are gaps, omissions and an underplaying of some important complexities. The panel and audience discussion highlighted a number of these.

The role of the British, for example, was not really explored, yet the British government's complicity (for example in the silence about the massacres by the Fifth Brigade in Matabeleland in the 1980s) was significant. The failure of the British to push a more complete settlement at Lancaster House – the 'fudges' that Peter Freeman talked of in discussion – and of course the diplomatic gaffe of the infamous 'Clare Short letter' were all part of the picture. And while the film was critical of white Rhodesia, although pointing out liberal traditions in white society, it did not explore the failure of a more complete reconciliation and integration of whites in the new Zimbabwe[86] following independence. This was a question posed to Denis Norman who served in Mugabe's cabinet at that time, and came from being the head of the white commercial farmers' union. He conceded that more could have been done. But the unwritten political contract between white farmers and the new state that whites could farm and make money, but not be involved in politics (or at least oppositional politics), was not explored in the film.

---

[86] Scoones, I. (2012) *Whiteness in Zimbabwe*, blog, zimbabweland.wordpress.com

And of course the big elephant in every room when Zimbabwe is discussed is land. In the film land is of course there as part of the narrative, but the implications and consequences of land reform are not discussed fully. The 1980s land reform is identified as a success, but the reasons why land reform effectively ceased in the 1990s and the inevitable tensions around land subsequently are rather papered over. The post 2000 land reform is, as usual, painted as a universal disaster, and the standard portrayals are repeated, without sufficient nuance or qualification. The panel tackled some of these issues in discussion. Phillan Zamchiya for example highlighted the importance of understanding land in the contemporary political context, as linked to a pattern of state-led violence, while also recognising the importance of land access for those who gained it. I pointed to the findings of our research[87], showing how land reform has not been the unmitigated disaster portrayed by the film, and why a more integrated agricultural sector was necessary to break the economic, geographic social and political separation of (white) large-scale and (black) small-scale farming to create a more sustainable and productive agriculture for the long term.

A number of contributors to the discussion also pointed out the continuities in the way politics has been played out in Zimbabwe since Independence. A lack of tolerance of alternative views, violence and oppression have all been part of a consistent pattern, and stretch into a particular history of the pre-Independence period and the nationalist struggle. It is not so much a question of seeing a golden age of the 1980s to contrast with the period since 2000; while there have been important changes, there are also repeated patterns. And this, as McDonald Lewanika pointed out, is why now a democratic transition, with a strong constitutional base, is so critical, to shed once and for all this violent history.

In a documentary film, such issues are impossible to portray in full. The film still offers a rounded, historically-informed account of 'what happened'. But it does not provide any clear answers, as to 'what next?', although it does show that it is not going to be straightforward.

---

[87] http://www.zimbabweland.net/Articles.html

CHAPTER 17
MISSING POLITICS?

In a highly perceptive review of our book, Blair Rutherford [88] from Carleton University in Canada, argues that our work has been "pivotal" in the "shifting of the debate on land reform" in Zimbabwe. But in so doing, he argues, we have created a new narrative, which, while capturing the local and the specific, misses some of the bigger picture. This is an important challenge, and one that is worth exploring. It chimes, in a rather more sophisticated way than others, with the assertions that we have missed out on politics in our account, and that the wider processes of violent nationalism associated with ZANU-PF's desperate holding on to power have been ignored (see some other book reviews[89]).

Rutherford argues that our "immersion in the material details ... limits the book". At the same time, he states "this book provides an incredible wealth of detail of the diverse economic practices emerging from and intersecting with the social relations and environmental conditions shaping the agrarian dynamics in Masvingo, while attending to the uncertain and disputed authority relations seeking to govern diverse farming areas". The "exemplary strength" of the book, he says is that the book shows a "refined analysis of the particular socio-political and class positioning of individuals and households and some of the shifts over the last 10 years".

Yet, despite this, he argues that the book "occludes" and "limits" analysis. What does he have in mind? He notes that we were reluctant to draw wider generalisations on the land invasions from the specific cases – each site was different, with a different dynamic, political history. We kept instead to the "empirical particularities" However, when we looked at the outcomes – the focus of the study – we did find some emerging patterns, embedded in huge diversity

---

[88] Rutherford, B. (2012) Shifting the debate on land reform, poverty and inequality in Zimbabwe, an engagement with Zimbabwe's Land Reform: Myths and Realities, *Journal of Contemporary African Studies*, 30(1):147-157

[89] http://www.zimbabweland.net/Reviews.html

of course. And this was the focus on class-specific patterns of agrarian change that Rutherford commented on favourably.

This highlighted a group of 'middle farmers' accumulating from below on the basis of petty commodity production, employing labour, selling surpluses and investing in the land. This was not everyone in all places (and therefore highly qualified), but a broader pattern we noted, especially across the A1 schemes. We contrasted this with the patterns in the 1980s, and noted favourably the potentials of this dynamic both for production, and development more broadly. Rutherford argues that this in turn emerges as an emergent narrative – a new myth – based on a valiant picture of "yeoman effort", around which the book positions itself.

This is certainly one strand of our argument, but this is based on analysis, rooted in highly detailed empirical data, and certainly does not have the status of the 'myths' we were debunking. These were based more on ideology than fact, and although some have claimed that these were "over stated" in the book[90], any cursory look at the media, and much of the wider 'academic' commentary will show that they were not (just take a look at the sections on land in Daniel Compagnon's otherwise useful book[91], *Zimbabwe: A Predictable Tragedy*, for a typical example).

Ours is therefore an emergent, interpretive narrative – but it is not simply "a position", "a stand", but a narrative based on findings and analysis. In many respects it was unexpected and emerged from our detailed studies through rigorous empirical study, and in this sense diverse, complex, nuanced and situated 'realities' did contrast with mainstream 'myths'. Our new narrative around land and livelihoods is, we argue, of a very different status to the 'myths' being peddled elsewhere. Of course all narratives are partial, positioned and in need of unpacking. Rutherford does a good service in this regard. But, as discussed chapter 56, I don't believe our method or our team was unreasonably

---

[90] Hammar, A. (2012) Zimbabwe's Land Reform: Myths and Realities (review), *African Studies Review*, 55(1): 219-221

[91] Compagnon, D. (2010) *A Predictable Tragedy: Robert Mugabe and the Collapse of Zimbabwe*, Philadelphia: University of Pennsylvania Press

biased. Our politics were and remain incredibly diverse, and were not, I would argue, "masked" by the book.

So what then is occluded and limited by the book's focus? I think there are certainly some things which deserve further empirical investigation, analysis and scrutiny. Rutherford identifies a few.

For example, we did not include many of the experiences of those excluded from land reform post 2000 – the farm workers who were evicted [chapter 12], the white farmers [chapter 15] who lost their land or the communal area people who were excluded, for example. This is a fair point. In respect of farm workers and former white farmers we certainly tried to locate them, but they were relatively few (unlike say in the Highveld) and difficult to trace, and even if found unlikely to talk – although we did devote a full chapter to issues around labour. Those white farmers who stayed in the district we have re-engaged with, and they appear in the book, although anonymised. In terms of the impacts in nearby communal areas, we made the choice (partly through issues of logistics and resources) not to do a comparative analysis of outcomes in the resettlements and the communal areas (along the lines of Bill Kinsey's classic earlier studies). We are now filling this gap with a more focused study of what happened in nearby areas, including issues of inclusion/exclusion.

Even in retrospect, I do not regret our focus on a detailed site-by-site analysis of what happened to livelihoods after land reform, focusing on the specifics of each case within the 'fast-track' areas. When we started this work in 2000 – and even when we finished a decade later – there was a shocking absence of this sort of detailed work. It was not easy work to do, and there were many risks and challenges. But directing a forensic spotlight on these empirical particularities through a case study focus [chapter 57] was (and remains) essential. We were, as Rutherford notes, interested in outcomes (what happened to who, where), but we were also interested in the processes which account for these outcomes. We do not, I think, present an "explicit disavowal of the debates and processes of land reform". Far from it. In fact, Rutherford concurs: "this attention to the history, to the process, is another strength of the monograph, as they are able to analyse the differential consequences of land distribution on class, gender and productivity axes".

However, Rutherford argues that "this analytical positioning prevents them from addressing the wider-scale politics and power relations which have been so crucial for these micro-dynamics... This, I would suggest, leads them to make some questionable analyses and prognoses". This is an argument made by others, and one that is important to address (and in fact – partially – agree with). I definitely agree that the wider national political context is important. We addressed this as part of Chapter 1 in our book, but perhaps this was not brought back sufficiently as context for the later analysis. However, the importance of a case study approach [chapter 57] – one province, 16 sites, 400 households etc. – is that we must relate what happened in particular places to the broader setting. Sometimes wider processes impinge, sometimes not.

Rutherford, for example, critiques our treatment of Operation Murambatsvina and the 2008 election violence. In our book, we always insisted on locating our discussion in the evidence from our study areas. So, when discussing Operation Murambatsvina we did not include a long discussion of the wider politics and implications, especially in some parts of Harare (although we offered the appropriate references), but focused on the impacts in our areas, which were very different. Equally, when discussing election violence we focused on experiences in our sites (where violence was actually rather limited; see chapter 22), and located these in the wider picture.

Both these instances of high-profile, politicised events show how diverse their impacts were, and how geographically located experiences have been. This does not undermine, deny or ignore the wider political significance of such events both nationally and in other places; indeed both shaped very fundamentally the political context in this period. However, by focusing on particular localities and experiences, our aim was to contextualise them, and so provide a sense of proportion in a wider, often highly generalised discussion of the Zimbabwe situation.

Following others, and most eloquently Brian Raftopoulos who spoke at the Cape Town launch[92] of the book, Rutherford argues that the broader implications of land reform for national level politics are not brought out. How this period has reshaped the politics of the state and its relationship with people has been

---

[92] http://www.zimbabweland.net/Launch_Audio.html

fundamental. He argues that our focus on the micro-details of what happened in particular places runs the danger of ignoring these wider political processes, a point made equally forcefully by Amanda Hammar [93]. This is true, and certainly such a broader analysis should be part of a much larger project of understanding reconfigured state-society relations and the politicisation of state practices in the post-land reform period, alongside the political, economic and social consequences of a massively reshaped agrarian structure.

This is work that some scholars have now commenced, with Sam Moyo's many contributions[94] particularly important in relation to wider agrarian politics. Equally, based on our work, chapter 18 reflects on patterns of differentiation and political dynamics both in the core 'fast-track' areas and chapter 23 on and the marginal lowveld areas outside formal land reform areas of Masvingo province. This work allows us to explore alternative interpretations and future scenarios. We argue that in our case study sites we are seeing the emergence of a 'middle farmer' class who, while benefiting from the land reform, is not allied to the political-military elite and mostly reject what Hammar calls the "political project of hegemony and sovereignty of the (previous yet persistent) ZANU-PF party-state", even if they don't all vote for the opposition (although many do, if secretly). Indeed, we argue, this group may represent a progressive alternative to the elite 'land grabbers', one that opposition formations ought to mobilise and create a narrative around land, agriculture and rural development around.

By contrast, Rutherford forwards an alternative interpretation: that the successful 'accumulation from below' we observed is the direct result of the suppression of political opposition and the violence of state practice, making resettlement farmers dependent subjects of a violent, nationalist state. This is an important discussion, one again that needs contextualising in site-specific analysis. Indeed both interpretations may be appropriate, but in different places and at different times.

---

[93] Hammar, A. (2012) Zimbabwe's Land Reform: Myths and Realities (review), *African Studies Review*, 55(1): 219-221

[94] Moyo, S. (2011) Changing agrarian relations after redistributive land reform in Zimbabwe, *Journal of Peasant Studies*, 38(5): 939-966

So, in sum, I agree this is a gap and one that requires more debate, a debate that Rutherford has usefully sparked. But this does not undermine or fundamentally challenge our findings, as some seek to do. We had one main aim – investigating and telling the story of land reform from the ground. This required presenting lots of detail (which most, including Rutherford, seem to appreciate), and it already ran to 288 pages in horribly small type. What is surely needed for this wider assessment of current and future national political dynamics is a located understanding of diverse experiences in different places, as Rutherford correctly argues in his conclusion. A synthetic, analytical perspective must reflect such diversity – and the complex, contingent and specific "entanglements" that exist. As the *Journal of Peasant Studies* special issue[95] showed, Masvingo is different to Goromonzi (Marongwe's paper) and to Chipinge (Zamchiya's paper), but there are some important convergences too, as Cliffe et al.[96] note, and as highlighted by the AIAS district studies. With this accumulation of empirical evidence, it is this wider analysis that becomes so crucial.

Any wider assessment must therefore root its analysis in these diverse local contexts and contingencies or risk the kind of simplistic over-generalisation that has characterised much writing on Zimbabwe in recent years. Unfortunately, the gap between broader national-level political analysis and field-level specifics has been massive in recent debates, and has exacerbated misunderstanding and prevented productive debate. This gap urgently needs to be narrowed, and the communities of researchers engaged at these different scales, often debating in different languages and frames, need to start working together more concretely.

---

[95] Scoones, I. (2012) *JPS Special issue on land reform outcomes – just released*, blog, zimbabweland.wordpress.com

[96] Cliffe, L., Alexander, J., Cousins, B., and Gaidzanwa, R. (2011) An overview of fast track land reform in Zimbabwe: editorial introduction, *Journal of Peasant Studies*, 38(5): 907-938

CHAPTER 18

CLASS AND RURAL DIFFERENTIATION AFTER LAND REFORM

What have been the processes of rural differentiation and class formation that have occurred following land reform in 2000, and what have been their political and economic consequences? A 2012 paper in the *Journal of Agrarian Change*[97] examines the data for Masvingo.

The paper points out that "acquiring land through reform processes... and allocating it to a mix of largely land and income poor people from nearby rural areas is not the end of the story. As new livelihoods are established, investments initiated and production, business, trade and marketing commence, processes of differentiation begin – within households, between households in a particular place and between sites".

A simplistic, populist back-to-the-land narrative is therefore insufficient. Rural economies are always dynamic – some win, some lose. So what happened across the 16 sites studied over a decade in Masvingo province?

The story is interesting – and complex. The paper shows how, among 400 households, 15 different livelihood strategies are observed, classified into four broad groups (stepping up, stepping out, hanging in and dropping out, following Andrew Dorward and Josphat Mushongah). These can be broadly associated with rural classes. These include an emergent rural bourgeoisie, and a larger group of petty commodity producers doing quite well by stepping up through agricultural production and stepping out through diversified livelihoods, and often a combination of both. There are worker-peasants who farm but also sell their labour, and the semi-peasantry who are struggling.

Linking the diversity of livelihood strategies – what Karl Marx in his treatise on the method of political economy called 'the rich totality of many determinations'

---

[97] Scoones, I., Marongwe, N., Mavedzenge, B., Murimbarimba, F., Mahenehene, J., and Sukume, C. (2012) Livelihoods after land reform in Zimbabwe: understanding processes of rural differentiation, *Journal of Agrarian Change*, 12(4): 503-527

focusing on real life on the ground – and broader patterns, tendencies and class formations ('the concrete – the unity of the diverse') is not an exact science, but the paper makes an attempt.

Why is this important? First, it is vital to realise that the new resettlements are not static or homogenous. The instability of class formations, and the overall fluidity of social and economic relations are emphasised. Efforts to support the new resettlement areas must take this into account. Who to back? The new emergent middle farmers or the poor and struggling? Second, the dynamic formation of class – cross-cut by differences of gender, age and ethnicity – has implications for political dynamics in the countryside. Again, who will have the political voice in the future? Will it be the 'chefs' who are small in number but who have grabbed land, or a larger group of emerging farmers who are doing well? And will workers, poorer peasants and others ally with them in pushing for a better deal?

These political dynamics are discussed at the close of the paper. Much remains speculation, but informed by an understanding of emerging patterns of socio-economic differentiation. If political parties want to know a bit more about their constituencies [chapter 19], then the paper offers some food for thought.

CHAPTER 19

KNOW YOUR CONSTITUENCY: A CHALLENGE FOR ALL OF ZIMBABWE'S POLITICAL PARTIES

In the bad old days of one party rule, rural constituencies knew their place. They voted for the ruling party and in exchange they were offered the basics: some improvements in infrastructure, an education and health system that were an improvement on the past, and critically food in times of drought. There were exceptions of course – notably in Matabeleland in the 1980s when terrible vengeance was wrought on those deemed to be supporting 'dissidents'. But elsewhere, in exchange for compliance and consistent voting, a social and political contract was struck between the state (in essence the ruling party) and rural people. And, yes, when there was wavering, violence was meted out, as has always been the way with the party of the armed struggle, ZANU-PF.

This then was the post-independence deal which persisted until the emergence of the MDC in the late 1990s and a tangible opposition with clout (of course there were precursors, but these never changed much). Since then voting has been much more divisive. The constitutional referendum of 2000 put it all into sharp relief, and the parliamentary, presidential and senatorial elections that followed presented a similar pattern. The MDC won the urban areas and ZANU-PF won the rural. Again there were variations, especially in Matabeleland and Manicaland, but ZANU-PF's pact with the rural populace stuck. Of course in 2008 it became more frayed, and the pattern of violence [chapter 22] rose to new, more horrifying heights. But even then civil society recorded voting patterns show that largely the rural population continued to back ZANU-PF. Land reform of course helped, as did intimidation and violence, particularly in Mashonaland East, but the sense of loyalty, commitment and a recognition of strong leadership was apparent too.

As we and others have argued extensively, land reform has radically reconfigured the rural landscape. New resettlement areas now make up nearly a quarter of the land area of the country, representing a population of 170,000 households, over a million people. Perhaps even more significant than this significant demographic and geographic shift, is the pattern of class-based differentiation that has resulted.

Due to a process of 'accumulation from below' by a significant proportion of new settlers who are producing surpluses and investing profits in rural areas, a new class of 'middle farmers' is emerging [chapter 18]. Perhaps 30-40% of the A1 farmers in our Masvingo sample sites could be classified in this group. They are entrepreneurial farmers, connected to increasingly sophisticated value chains and market outlets, selling crops and livestock regularly, hiring labour and investing in their farms. This group is most prevalent in the so-called A1 self-contained farms, where a farm block was allocated to individuals, in comparison to the villagised scheme where people are resident in villages and grazing areas are communal.

Such accumulators are also evident in the A2 farms. Fewer proportionately have made it, however, due to the challenges of finance and credit constraining their abilities to invest [chapter 14]. But some have, and are doing well. Some of these include those who might be regarded as 'accumulating from above', deriving patronage from the state or political favours from the party. Even some of the 'cronies' [chapter 26], it seems, are keen to accumulate from agriculture, perhaps knowing that their sources of patronage are likely to be short-lived.

In the past when accumulation through agriculture was available to only very few in the communal or old resettlement areas, as land areas were small, capital scarce and opportunities for market engagement constrained. Even in the boom time of communal area agriculture soon after Independence only around 20% of communal area farmers in the Highveld areas regularly sold maize to the market. This smaller group of communal area accumulators persist, and remain important in terms of overall production nationally, even if they are scattered across wide areas.

As Bill Kinsey and his team have shown over the years[98], in the old resettlement areas there were processes of differentiation similar to what we have observed in the new land reform areas. Some beneficiaries did indeed do well, producing

---

98 Kinsey, B. (1999) Land reform, growth and equity: emerging evidence from Zimbabwe's resettlement programme, *Journal of Southern African Studies*, 25 (2): 173-196

surpluses and attracting others to their homesteads. But in terms of overall numbers the old resettlement areas were never going to make inroads into a broader political dynamic in the countryside. The same applied to the small-scale farming areas. These former Purchase Areas were established by the colonial regime to create a yeoman class of middle farmer; an attempt to buy off resistance to the regime, and provide a buffer to the large-scale commercial farming areas. This rural black elite had its own political trajectory, but it never really influenced national politics in any big way, beyond the impact of a few individuals.

So why is this new class dynamic unleashed by land reform potentially significant for Zimbabwean politics? An important factor is the sheer scale of numbers. A rough calculation done by Ben Cousins and myself suggests that the new accumulators in new land reform areas amount to a substantial potential adult voting population. Add to these the accumulators in the communal areas, the old resettlement areas, the small-scale farming areas, and the remnants of the commercial farming sector, we are talking of about a million rural voters seriously reliant on and committed to accumulation through agriculture. This is perhaps around 18% of the total electorate, a quarter of rural voters: a significant number in any electoral calculation (although who is on the voters' roll[99] is yet another debate).

Large numbers of people can of course be bought off or intimidated to vote, as has happened before. There are after all around three million potential voters in the communal areas, perhaps more. However, this group of accumulating middle farmers are more vocal, educated and organised than the standard image of the rural electorate, especially in the new resettlement areas. All the studies done to date show how the land invaders were generally younger and better educated than their communal area counterparts. They are also better connected: to towns and markets, to the bureaucracy and to political leaders. This makes a difference in terms of negotiating social, political and economic space for their farming activities, but also in terms of lobbying, influencing and organising. While the new settlers are not formally organised, they are certainly engaged in a range of organisational activities, whether organising cotton buying or livestock trading at a local level.

---

[99] '2008 voters roll online', *The Zimbabwean*, 18 July 2012

Geography helps too. The rural areas are not in the same configuration spatially as they were before. A1 schemes abut communal areas which are connected to old resettlements and A2 areas. And everyone meets in new rural business centres, bus routes or market places in town. Because A1 areas were largely invaded from nearby communal areas and urban centres, people are connected socially too. They are friends, relatives, sharing churches, totems, ancestors and religious sites.

Any political party should take heed. This middle farmer group is potentially an important constituency. In the past, as Jeffrey Herbst[100] and Angus Selby[101] have shown, white farmers organised effectively and managed to capture the colonial state, bending policy after policy to their advantage. They were pretty effective after Independence too, striking important deals with the new government. Can the new accumulators, centred in the new resettlement areas, and particularly the A1 schemes, form such a politically strong group? It will of course be far more difficult, as they lack the collective economic muscle and financial backing for a strong farming union, but politically they may become significant if they can bring others with them. Would any government be able to resist the demands of such a group if they allied with the rest of the communal area population demanding attention for rural and farming issues?

A strong narrative about land, agriculture and economic development is an essential precursor. No political party offers this now. ZANU-PF resorts to its tired nationalist rhetoric, while the MDC formations seem unable to create a convincing rural policy position at all. There is a political opportunity here. Whoever can respond to the new politics of the Zimbabwean countryside will win substantial backing. Rural people can no longer be fobbed off with empty promises and a commitment to provide drought relief. As up and coming entrepreneurs committed to rural businesses, they want more: finance, investment, infrastructure and strong state backing.

---

[100] Herbst, J. I. (1990) *State Politics in Zimbabwe*, Berkeley: University of California Press

[101] Selby, A. (2002) *Commercial Farmers and the State in Zimbabwe*. DPhil Thesis: Oxford University

CHAPTER 20

TRANSFORMING THE STATE: BUILDING SECURITY FROM BELOW

Zimbabwe is often held up as the typical 'fragile state' in need of wholesale 'security' and 'governance' reform. Indeed such issues are high on the agenda of those debating Zimbabwe's transition. Building a basis for effective governance and security from below is an essential part of realising the ambitions of the Zimbabwe's 2013 Constitution. Developing a framework for support, including by donors who will now hopefully reengage with Zimbabwe, is essential.

A 2013 paper from the LSE's Justice and Security Research Programme[102] by Robin Luckham from IDS and Tom Kirk from LSE offers some interesting perspectives, and challenges some of the core assumptions of a standard, donor-led reform agenda. Its findings are highly relevant to Zimbabwe. It starts from the observation that in many 'fragile state' settings, there are 'hybrid political orders' operating. Far from a situation of state failure, according to the OECD such societies:

> "[c]ontinue to function, to form institutions, to negotiate politically, and to set and meet expectations. Traditional forms of authority are not necessarily inimical to the development of rules-based political systems ... In fact, the challenge is to understand how traditional and formal systems interact in any particular context, and to look for ways of constructively combining them." (OECD 2011:103)

This is certainly the case in Zimbabwe where a lack of security is creating vulnerability and risk for many citizens. Yet as the LSE paper notes:

[102] Luckham, R, and Kirk, T. (2012) Security in hybrid political contexts: an end-user approach, *JSRP Paper* 2, The Justice and Security Research Programme, LSE: London

[103] Organisation for Economic Co-operation and Development (OECD) (2011) *Supporting State Building in Situations of Conflict and Fragility: Policy Guidance,* DAC Guidelines and Reference Series, OECD: Paris

"...much mainstream academic and policy thinking that security is an almost self-evident public good unproblematically delivered by states or by the international community in situations of state failure. For the most part, this mainstream has showed little interest in unpeeling security's multiple layers of meaning; it has not properly investigated the relationship of security to political power; it has not scrutinised security as a politically contested object; and it has not on the whole looked at it from the perspective of end-users, i.e. those who are secured. Whilst new approaches to human and citizen security have challenged the state-centric bias of previous security thinking, they still tend to overlook security's relationships to political power, including its deeply contested nature in hybrid political orders."

So what are hybrid political orders? This literature refers to such phenomena as 'legal pluralism', 'twilight institutions' and 'mediated' or 'negotiated' states. Public authority is not fixed, and is continuously produced through negotiation across a range of actors. This challenges us to rethink the nature of 'the state' in such settings, and indeed its assumed functions, including security, which may be delivered through multiple processes.

Even the World Bank, long an advocate of standard, western style governance reforms appears to accept elements of this argument. In its flagship World Development Report publication of 2011[104] it argued for "collaborative, inclusive-enough coalitions" which "restore confidence and transform institutions and help create continued momentum for positive change". This is not an image of standardised, imposed governance and security reform.

But what political processes might help form such coalitions to deliver security? This is far from straightforward. Simplistic reform measures often advocated by donors as part of 'post-conflict' reconstruction interventions will not work. The LSE paper argues that "donor policies and programmes aiming to reform the security sectors of fragile and contested states should be viewed with a heavy dose of caution". The paper notes the extreme mismatch between a policy literature which "tends to *assume* that states and their security and justice institutions are capable in principle of delivering security if reforms are pushed

---

[104] World Bank (2011) *World Development Report 2011: Conflict, Security and Development*, Washington DC: World Bank

through" and a critical research literature which "suggests that insecurity and violence may be entrenched in the heart of the state itself and 'work' to the benefit of predatory state and other elites".

The paper goes on "Thus, in countries with corrupt or abusive institutions… those responsible for delivering security and justice are often the perpetrators of insecurity…Conversely the alleged agents of insecurity… may offer alternative forms of protection or even claim to act as liberators". Thus in Zimbabwe, the state has often been a major source of insecurity, leading violence during election periods, intimidating people not towing the line, and overseeing a security apparatus that has its tentacles spread into every corner. Yet at a local level, it is sometimes war veterans – often seen as agents of disorder and disruption – who keep the peace, negotiating security through pacts with local leaders, traditional, religious and others. Allied at some moments with the central state, but highly disillusioned and resistant at others, such processes are typical of hybrid political orders, perpetually negotiated, always contingent and highly context specific. This is why generalised narratives about violence, insecurity and disorder are always inadequate, and require locating and specifying in better understandings of what happens in particular places, as we have long argued in our work on land reform.

Yet at a moment of political transition, how can the state be reformed to allow for justice, security and rights for citizens after a period of turmoil, and capture by elites? A locale-specific, negotiated arrangement is clearly not enough, and is always fragile. In terms of the literature surveyed in the LSE paper, Zimbabwe can be characterised as a 'Contested Leviathan', a setting where state power is contested, but the apparatus of control is still in place, through the armed forces and the security services in particular, allied to a narrow political elite with waning support.

As the literature shows from numerous cases, "These contested Leviathans seldom give up their claims on power willingly or peacefully. Even when they do start to cede power to democratically elected governments, as in Egypt and Burma, their security apparatus may seek to co-opt the transitions and mould them to their own security-dominated vision of the polity"… "Under hybrid governance systems, security arrangements often protect elites, including security elites, and reinforce inequalities in power and wealth. They tend all too often to be deployed to close political spaces, reduce political participation and resist accountability"... [Formal arrangements] in turn "interconnect with the parallel powers of hybrid political orders, including systems of patronage, and the manipulation of ethnic and religious identities as instruments of security policy" [Such] "regimes and their security apparatuses may sometimes even thrive upon durable disorder and insecurity". Does this sound like Zimbabwe? Certainly it does, as Brian Raftopoulos[105] and others[106] have vividly described.

As Mariz Tadros has shown in the case of Egypt[107], agents of state security act as parallel powers, intersecting with other corporate and political interests, and with influence deep into civil society. This can help perpetuate the legacies of injustice, even in supposedly democratic or 'post-conflict' states. For any country in transition, including Zimbabwe, this is an important lesson, felt acutely in Central America, and most recently in the Middle East.

The LSE paper makes the case that we need to understand what security looks like 'from below', i.e. from the perspective of 'end users' be these citizens of states, members of local communities or those who are marginalised. It is from here that a rebuilding of security must start, accepting hybrid political orders, but also addressing the political and social inequalities that come with them. A political process for rebuilding security, and with it the state itself, must start the paper argues with asking: "What are their vernacular understandings of security and how do these reflect the hybrid and contested nature of political authority at a local level? What connects their particular and local experiences and understandings to wider conceptions of citizen and of human security?"

Only with a view of security from below can a legitimate and accountable state be rebuilt. This is an important set ideas with much relevance for the immediate future of Zimbabwe.

---

[105] Raftopoulos, B. (2010) The Global Political Agreement as a 'passive revolution': notes on contemporary politics in Zimbabwe, *The Round Table: The Commonwealth Journal of International Affairs*, 99(411): 705-718

[106] Onslow, S. (2011) *Zimbabwe and Political Transition*, London: The London School of Economics and Political Science

[107] Tadros, M. (2012) Introduction: the pulse of the Arab revolt, *IDS Bulletin*, 43(1): 1-15, Brighton: IDS

CHAPTER 21

WHY NATIONS FAIL: PERSPECTIVES ON ZIMBABWE

Why Nations Fail: The Origins of Power, Prosperity and Poverty[108] is a provocative new book by MIT and Harvard economists, Daron Acemoglu and James Robinson. It is getting a lot of commentary from, among others, Thomas Friedman in the NYT, Paul Collier in the Guardian, Martin Wolf in the FT and the Economist[109]. It even is linked to a blog[110]. It seems like a big deal which is why I bought it and read it.

Why is the book of interest to those concerned about the future of Zimbabwe? Lumped together with North Korea and Sierra Leone, Zimbabwe is used as an example to illustrate the basic argument that nations fail – and poverty results – because of poor institutions. A basic contrast is made between what they term inclusive and extractive political and economic institutions. Inclusive institutions result in prosperity, and are based on secure property rights, an unbiased legal system and the provision of public services that offer a level playing field for all to be able to participate in economic activity. They result in conditions where people innovate and invest with a sense of security. By contrast, extractive institutions are dominated by elites, and create privileges and patronage, reducing incentives for entrepreneurship and development.

The nearly 500 pages of the book make the case through a series of intriguing historical examples – from the Ottoman Empire to the industrial revolution in England to post-independent Botswana. The array of cases is extraordinary, and

---

[108] Acemoglu, D. and Robinson, J. (2012) *Why Nations Fail: The Origins of Power, Prosperity and Poverty,* New York: Crown Business

[109] Friedman, T. (2012) 'Why Nations Fail', *The New York Times,* 31 March; Collier, P. (2012) 'Why Nations Fail by Daron Acemoglu and James Robinson – review', *The Guardian,* 11 March; Wolf, M. (2012) 'The wealth of nations', *Financial Times,* 3 March; 'The big why: Nations fail because their leaders are greedy, selfish and ignorant of history', *The Economist,* 10 March 2012

[110] http://whynationsfail.com/

it's a fascinating and absorbing read. Applied to so many contexts and historical periods, the definitions of inclusive and extractive institutions become at times a bit flexible. Arguments for progressive, inclusive approaches are drawn from settings where slavery exists, or where political participation is minimal, for example. And the celebration of the US and Europe is sometimes a bit rich, given growing inequalities, deep poverty within nations and the severe limits of political institutions. Also, while the authors acknowledge that extractive institutional settings can result in growth and development – and clearly China is the contemporary example used – they argue that such conditions are fragile and will not persist, although the evidence for China's decline seems currently limited.

Overall, it is a brave, big-picture argument. It emphasises history, path-dependency, contingency and uncertainty. And it makes politics and power central to the economic analysis. This is all very welcome. But it is of course not novel. Political economy analysis has long argued that politics matter, and power and class configurations, and patterns of inequality, are crucial to the assessment of economic fortunes. Karl Marx only gets two index entries, and Marxist thought no real discussion, which seems bizarre given this important heritage in economics.

So why is this particular book getting so much air time? The commendations from the great-and-the-good of development economics are certainly impressive, with a slew of Nobel Prize winners offering their endorsements. I guess it's because the book is written by some well-known and respected academic economists. Once in a while mainstream economics 'discovers' things outside its narrow disciplinary confines. Remember the hullabaloo about 'trust' or 'social capital'? Of course classical economics always addressed politics, and it is only in the relatively recent past that this was jettisoned in favour of a narrow focus. But if this is now mainstream, I am not going to complain. We spend so much time knocking at the door of the citadel of economics, that when the door is opened to debates well known outside, we should probably celebrate (even if a bit cynically).

But what does such a book imply for development? It has some harsh implications. Much of the 'policy advice' based on technocratic assumptions will, it suggests, simply not work. As William Easterly comments in his review in the

Wall Street Journal[111], the basic conditions for development are not ones amenable to aid projects or technical advice, but need political and institutional transformation. This may take long periods, requiring the capturing of particular moments – 'critical junctures' – and often almost a revolutionary overturning of existing power structures and economic relations to provide the space for inclusive institutions to emerge. Because history matters, and is so difficult to escape, some transitions – for example from colonialism to independence – may not be enough to remove the shackles of extractive institutions. A more radical change may be required.

This is fighting talk, but what does this mean for somewhere like Zimbabwe? The usual stereotypes about Zimbabwe are trotted out in the book, and the sources used for the assessment of contemporary politics seem to be solely journalistic reports, but the basic prognosis is probably sound enough. Zimbabwe inherited a highly extractive political and institutional set up at independence. This was based on a highly unequal, racialised distribution of land and economic power. This was not challenged by the new leaders, and indeed became the basis of their own power, allowing a small group to emerge as a new black elite. Extractive institutions suited their ambitions, and they made full use of them. It is, of course, a well known, depressing tale.

The book does not dwell on Zimbabwe's land reform, but comments on other reforms where elite privilege was overturned (a particularly evocative example is presented from the Roman empire). Such redistributive reforms allowed new institutions to emerge that spread the gains more widely. However, they only work if security is provided and inclusive political institutions co-evolve with new economic opportunities. The book hails 'property rights' as the solution, but this is presented in a rather uncritical and simplistic fashion, often echoing, although not referring to, the problematic analysis of Hernando de Soto. But actually it is security over property and the gains of economic activity and innovation that is critical, rather than any particular form of private property – and so is reliant on the wider political and institutional conditions prevailing [chapter 27].

So, following that other well-know political economist, Vladimir Lenin, what is to be done? In Zimbabwe a 'critical juncture' was clearly the post 2000 land reform.

---

[111] Easterly, W. (2012) 'The roots of hardship', *The Wall Street Journal*, 24 March

While there was certainly elite capture, it has opened up potential economic opportunities for many, overturning long-standing historical inequalities. But there have as yet been no moves to establish inclusive political and economic institutions to support this. The Government of National Unit (GNU) failed, and western powers and others remain at arms' length. The opportunity of this moment may have been lost, as the extractive tendencies of a powerful elite in trouble hold sway. Was land reform in Zimbabwe one of those historical moments that the book covers which did not result in the necessary institutional revolution: a tragically missed opportunity? Or is there still a chance?

This book, for all its flaws and simplifications, offers some interesting pointers to the way forward, and the urgent need in places like Zimbabwe to focus not on 'development' in the normal technocratic mould, but on some radical political and institutional transformations which will allow the land reform to realise its potential for economic change for the better. It's a long shot, and it may be too late, but progressives across the divides should take heed.

CHAPTER 22

GEOGRAPHIES OF VIOLENCE IN ZIMBABWE

Lloyd Sachikonye has written several powerful articles and books on violence in Zimbabwe. His book, *'When a State Turns Against its Citizens: 60 Years of Institutionalized Violence in Zimbabwe'*[112] is particularly important. It documents what happened particularly around the elections in 2008, and how state led terror, deeply embedded in a particular political culture, was unleashed on the population. While graphic and harrowing, the book, as many accounts, gives the impression that this is what happened everywhere. In fact, there is an important geography of violence in Zimbabwe, which requires explanation, and this explanation helps us to nuance and differentiate our accounts of Zimbabwean politics in important ways.

There is little doubt that state-led violence, largely perpetrated by agents of ZANU-PF, increased during the 2000s, and peaked in particular around the 2008 elections. But there has been less commentary on the geography of violence – where it happened, and why. The uneven distribution of violence – including 161 cases that resulted in death – is highlighted in the dramatic maps produced by civil society monitoring groups and reproduced on the Sokwanele website[113]. As these maps graphically show, violence of all sorts was massively concentrated in Mashonaland Central and East (1341 cases, around 60% of the total for the country), with ZANU-PF youth being the main perpetrators. Masvingo, bar the series of incidents associated with election intimidation by war veterans in the communal area, Zaka, was by comparison relative unscathed.

It is this geographical difference that reflects the very different perceptions of politics in the country. Our study has been accused of underplaying violent state politics [chapter 17] as a factor in land reform, but even the civil society and human rights group monitoring at the peak period in 2008 shows how limited

---

[112] Sachikonye, L. (2011) *When a State Turns Against its Citizens: 60 Years of Institutionalized Violence in Zimbabwe*. Harare: Weaver Press

[113] http://www.sokwanele.com/map/electionviolence

this actually was in the province. We just reported what we found, and it seems to reflect what other data shows. But this is not to undermine or dismiss the 33 incidents (including 8 deaths) that were recorded in Masvingo province. Nor is this to suggest that the Mashonaland violence was isolated or unusual: it wasn't – it was systematic and terrifying. However, it does push us to – yet again – nuance our analyses by place and time.

History is particularly important. Different provinces and districts have had very different political histories. The contrasts between Mashonaland and Matabeleland are obvious, usually cast in starkly defining ethnic terms. But Manicaland is different again, as is Karanga or Shangaan Masvingo. But even within these areas, there are further differences reflecting long-standing divides in political formations, histories of the liberation war and affiliations to particular leaders. This is not the place to go into these, as they are immensely complex and require the sort of detailed district histories that Terence Ranger commented on in his review of our book[114]. Only with these histories do we get a sense of the social and political history of particular places, and how this affects contemporary patterns of politics, patronage and violence.

Ranger is therefore absolutely right that the Masvingo story [chapter 57] is peculiar and particular – just as every area of Zimbabwe is in one sense. And the more fine grained you go, each village and farm is different in other ways, as we explained in our brief histories of *jambanja* farm invasion experiences in our book. So explaining the politics of land acquisition, who benefited and why requires this sort of analysis.

Arnold Chamunogwa uses different theories of politics to explore the different dynamics and outcomes in three different cases[115] all presented in the 2012 *Journal of Peasant Studies* special issue[116] – in Goromonzi near Harare (based on work by Nelson Marongwe), Chipinge in Manicaland (based on the work of

---

[114] Ranger, T. (2011) 'Zimbabwean diamonds', *Africa. The Journal of the International African Institute*, 81(4): 649-661

[115] Chamunogwa, A. (2012) *Political Economy Analysis of Fast Track Land Reform Programme in Zimbabwe*, Thesis, Brighton, UK: Institute of Development Studies

[116] Cliffe, L., Alexander, J., Cousins, B. and Gaidzanwa, R. (eds.) (2011). Special Issue on Fast Track Land Reform in Zimbabwe. *Journal of Peasant Studies*, 38(5)

Phillan Zamchiya) and Masvingo province (based on our work). He argues that theories of 'instrumentalisation of disorder' (drawing on Patrick Chabal and Jean-Pascal Deloz[117] among others) characterise some areas, while theories of 'neo-patrimonialism' (based on work by Nicholas van der Walle[118]and others) characterise others, and in other areas theories of 'informal politics' (based on arguments by David Booth, Richard Crook, Christian Lund[119] and others) are more appropriate explanations. These politics emerge from particular histories, social configurations, state relations and experiences of land reform, as well as the particular characteristics and values of the farm systems concerned. The experiences in Goromonzi, Chipinge and Masvingo were as a result very different.

That's no surprise, I hear you exclaim! Well, in a way, no. But it's important to point out, and the theorisation is helpful to differentiate between different forms of politics in practice – none conforming to the standard liberal good governance mode. So why then did 'the instrumentalisation of disorder' dominate in Mashonaland Central and East? This was the core of the Zezuru support base for ZANU-PF, and with Goromonzi so close to Harare, there were rich pickings for the elite who were able to create disorder actively and manipulate the process, grabbing land as a result. In Chipinge, with a different political configuration and a historically strong opposition from ZANU Ndonga, a political-bureaucratic network formed to allocate high value land to try and consolidate ZANU-PF support, attempting to create a support base in the midst of opposition, ousting land invaders in the process. By contrast, in Masvingo a more informal politics emerged, particularly around the invaded A1 and informal farms where a mix of people was involved, led by war veterans and traditional leaders. The factional politics of Masvingo meant that the imposition of a strong centrist party line was impossible, and locally negotiated solutions emerged. In all settings, attempts at political capture were incomplete, often failing

---

[117] Chabal, P. and Daloz, J-P (1999) *Africa Works: Disorder As Political Instrument*, London: International African Institute

[118] Van de Walle, N. (2001) *African Economies and the Politics of Permanent Crisis, 1979-1999*, Cambridge: Cambridge University Press

[119] Booth, D. (2011) Introduction: working with the grain? The Africa Power and Politics Programme, *IDS Bulletin*, 42(2):1-10, Brighton: IDS

dramatically, and war veterans and others who led invasions often turned on leading party officials attempting to grab land, accusing them of undermining the objectives of the 'Third Chimurenga'. Politics, as ever, was highly contested, yet the styles and patterns differed due to very particular, and often very long-term, socio-cultural and political histories of the different sites.

As we assess the changing nature of Zimbabwean politics, it is important to take these differences into account, and avoid the generalisations that so much commentary resorts to. Just as Zimbabwe as a whole is not explained by what has gone on in Masvingo, so too is the wider political story not explained by referring only to Mashonaland and the highly contested farms near Harare. Explaining this diversity in the geographies of violence is not to condone it, but it does help explain why the recent past has been experienced so differently in different places across the country.

CHAPTER 23
LOWVELD POLITICS

The controversy surrounding the 'indigenisation' of shareholdings in the Save Valley Conservancy involving ZANU-PF big wigs[120] was revived again in 2012. Several new developments took place, including the granting of hunting licenses to the new joint venture 'owners' and mounting pressure on aid donors to reimpose sanctions[121] ahead of the hosting of the major UN international tourism conference in Zimbabwe in 2013. Also, local chiefs, including Chief Tsovani and Sengwe, weighed in, complaining directly to the President[122] that local people have not got a good deal from the conservancy arrangements as well as the resettlements on the sugar estates. Meanwhile, in nearby Chisumbanje, Billy Rautenbach's ethanol project[123] was in trouble, as the government refused to require ethanol mixes in fuel, and local opposition around the reclaiming of ARDA land and the eviction of farmers mounted.

Lowveld politics remains hot, and the complex political wrangles that characterise Masvingo in particular are ever-present. Behind the headlines there is a more complex story. As Takura Zhangazha explains in a blog[124] for *African Arguments*, the intra-party conflicts within ZANU-PF are an important context, as the public spat[125] between former Gutu South MP Shuvai Mahofa and tourism minister Walter Muzembi clearly shows.

---

[120] Karimakwenda, T. (2012) 'Zimbabwe: More ZANU-PF Save Conservancy 'looters' named', *All Africa*, 6 September

[121] 'EU warns Zimbabwe', *Zimbabwe Independent*, 31 August 2012

[122] 'Scale of graft shocks Mugabe', *The Financial Gazette*, 6 September 2012

[123] 'Zimbabwe: Chisumbanje ethanol project exposes Zanu-PF', All Africa, 4 September 2012

[124] Zhangazha, T. (2012) *Zimbabwe's Save Valley Conservancy, indigenisation and 'the lie of the land'*, blog, Africanarguments.org

[125] 'I'm making money in hunting - says Mahofa as she taunts Mzembi', *NewsdzeZimbabwe*, 9 September 2012

As is often the case, there is more going on below the surface, and a more in-depth analysis of political dynamics is needed. Such an analysis of lowveld land struggles is provided in a paper in *African Affairs*, "The new politics of Zimbabwe's lowveld: struggles over land at the margins"[126]. It explores the contrasting story of land struggles in the lowveld outside the 'fast-track' areas of Masvingo province, and draws conclusions on the implications for understanding the relationships between the state and citizens on the margins of state power: all issues highly pertinent to the rush of press commentary on the area.

The paper focuses on three high profile case studies – Nuanetsi ranch, the Save Valley and Chiredzi River conservancies and Gonarezhou national park. For each case, the article examines who gained and who lost out over time, from entrepreneurial investors to well-connected politicians and military figures, to white ranchers and large numbers of farmers who have occupied land since 2000.

In Nuanetsi ranch, controlled by the Development Trust of Zimbabwe, an ambitious plan to create a massive irrigated sugar plantation and ethanol plant was proposed by the notorious Billy Rautenbach, a staunch supporter of ZANU-PF. Yet, land invaders had occupied huge areas of land, and removing them was difficult. The paper documents the twists and turns of the story, as Rautenbach's investment plans shifted, and finally the informal settlers were granted the right to stay. Land invaders also moved onto the world-renown lowveld conservancies, but the major challenge to this white, elite enclave came from a high profile grab by politically well-connected politicians, military figures and traditional leaders, who were granted leases and hunting licenses. This elite grab was contested by the conservancy owners who rejected the claims that this was 'wildlife based land reform', but also local people who wanted to settle the land for farming and cattle rearing. Finally, in Gonarezhou national park, a group led by Headman Chitsa invaded an area that they claimed was a veterinary corridor. They were told to move, but stubbornly stayed put, arguing that this was their land, and it was linked to an ancestral claim. A stalemate persisted for more than a decade, and the villagers were seen to be a block to the realisation of the high profile Greater Limpopo Transfrontier Park, which promised infrastructural investment

---

[126] Scoones, I., Chaumba, J., Mavedzenge, B. and Wolmer, W. (2012) The new politics of Zimbabwe's lowveld: struggles over land at the margins, *African Affairs*, 111 (445): 527-550

and tourist income. In the end, again, the villagers' persistence won out, and they were granted permission to remain on what the parks authority finally agreed was indeed a corridor not the formal park.

In all cases, the paper identifies a dynamic of elite accumulation and control over resources, led by quite different groups, that has been resisted by shifting alliances of land invaders, war veterans and local political and traditional leaders. By documenting this struggle over time, we demonstrate that, in these marginal areas, outside the formal 'fast-track' land reform programme where more formal administrative-bureaucratic procedures came to operate, local communities retain the capacity to resist state power and imagine alternative social, economic and political trajectories – even if these are opposed by powerful actors at the centre, from the president downwards.

While much discussion of recent Zimbabwean politics has appropriately highlighted the centralised, sometimes violent, nature of state power, this is exerted in different ways in different places. A combination of local divisions within political parties, bureaucratic discretion within implementing agencies and local contests over land creates a very particular, local politics in the lowveld, at the geographic margins of the nation. This offers opportunities for a variety of expressions of local agency and resistance which temper the impositions of centralised state power, and suggesting diverse, as yet uncertain, future trajectories of land control.

CHAPTER 24

THE UNBEARABLE WHITENESS OF BEING: REFLECTIONS ON WHITE FARMING IN ZIMBABWE

The Unbearable Whiteness of Being is the main title of a 2012 book[127] by Rory Pilossof from the University of Pretoria and published by Weaver Press in Zimbabwe. The book documents the voices of white farmers in Zimbabwe through an analysis of the contributions to the CFU's magazine, *The Farmer*, especially in the period after the land invasions, a reading of the now burgeoning post 2000 literature by white Zimbabweans, and through interviews with members of the breakaway Justice for Agriculture (JAG)[128] group.

In addition to the brilliant title (although not the only use it seems[129]), it is a fascinating read giving a much needed account of this period from the perspective of those who lost land. The events that unfolded from 2000 with the mass invasion of farms, including outbreaks of, sometimes, extreme violence in places, are certainly very real. The tales told are harrowing and convincing: somehow more so than the journalistic accounts of Peter Godwin and co. They mix the mundane with the dramatic, and are set in life stories that are very peculiarly Zimbabwean. The appendix of profiles of those interviewed (mostly from Mashonaland) is particularly enlightening. Yet the unreal and strange is also there. These testimonies are from the twenty-first century, but with many views and perspectives belonging to the nineteenth.

As Pilossof recounts, farmers who were willing to speak (obviously a selective sample) were so caught up in the traumatic events that their prejudices were plain to see, and not hidden from an interviewer who, as someone with white skin, was assumed to be sympathetic and of similar views. To many outside the

---

[127] Pilossof, R. (2012) *The Unbearable Whiteness of Being: Farmers' Voices from Zimbabwe*, Harare: African Books Collective

[128] http://kubatana.net/html/sectors/jus002.asp?like=J&details=Tel&orgcode=jus002

[129] http://joesmall.net/section/198821_the_unbearable_whiteness_of_being.html

narrow, isolated social circles of white rural Zimbabwe, such views are shocking; what Pilossof calls 'condescending paternalism' and 'racist ramblings' in one book he reviews. Together these insights expose of course the extraordinary social and political separation that many in the white farming community got caught in, even 20 years after Independence. The cultural mores and political biases, and the racial tinge to everything are well documented in David Hughes' book[130], with its analysis of landscape, conservation and farming. But somehow this book is more direct. Pilosoff tries to be balanced, and clearly he is affected by many of the stories told, but he also is forced to comment on what he hears.

The pervasive 'white myopia', as Pilossof terms it, was upheld by a series of myths. These "served the important function of allowing white farmers to live at ease with the scale of their land holdings, and to believe that they had done no wrong by buying into a system that so obviously segregated black from white". This was bolstered by the view that farmers were apolitical, and that all they did was farm, despite for many representing the unfinished business of the liberation war. The book identifies a number of 'myths' of white farming: how farmers tirelessly struggled to tame an empty and unforgiving bush, how they had equally to control and discipline their workers who were lazy and deceitful, and how the productivity of white farming was the result of such disciplined hard work and investment. As he notes, no mention is made in the accounts of course of the massive government subsidies that kept most white farming afloat, nor the terrible conditions most farm labour suffered.

The accounts offer glimpses into a worldview overshadowed by patronising superiority. People emphasised how they loved and cared for their special servants and farm managers, yet despised and feared their land hungry neighbours, deemed to be 'gooks' and 'terrs'. There is no narrative of belonging or of equality, just one struck through with racial superiority. It is no wonder that most found the land reform utterly surprising and wholly reprehensible. It ran against all things they upheld. Despite being hard working and sometimes quite successful farmers, many simply did not realise that things had to change. The

---

[130] Hughes, D.M. (2010) *Whiteness in Zimbabwe: Race, Landscape, and the Problem of Belonging*. New York: Palgrave MacMillan; Scoones, I. (2012) *Whiteness in Zimbabwe*, blog, zimbabweland.wordpress.com

book shows the extraordinarily narrow outlook that many held. Pilossof concludes:

> "While many claimed to have changed their identity, to be Zimbabwean rather than Rhodesian, and to be 'white Africans', this is tempered by their use of the word 'African' to always and only to refer to blacks. As such, white farmers in Zimbabwe are 'orphans of empire', unable to progress past this state of being and thus 'become' Zimbabwean".

In some ways the book could be critiqued as unbalanced. Pilossof found it difficult to gain access to information, and many people would not speak, so charged was the atmosphere in the mid 2000s. His interviews are with an extreme group – JAG – which many would say was not part of the mainstream, although it was plentifully supported by foreign donors. He also interviewed people in the heart of Mashonaland where the land invasions were most contested, and where violence was most prominent. Also, after 2000 *The Farmer*[131] was in its dying days, when it was most shrill in its criticisms of the land reform, rejecting the more conciliatory stances of some within the CFU. He also uses the sometimes bizarre white memoirs and biographies as sources, which many would argue offer particularly odd interpretations of white Zimbabwe. He therefore did not speak to those realists and pragmatists who perhaps saw the land reform as the 'writing on the wall', something that was inevitable and that had to be accommodated. He did not discuss with those who did not have an escape route to town, with alternative non-farm businesses, and so did not speak to those who sought compromises and accommodations on their farms [chapter 15]. And he did not speak to those few who actually supported land reform, even if not the form it took. This is another dimension of white farmers' voices that needs to be told, and awaits another book.

But such gaps do not undermine the value of the book, as the array of perspectives garnered, while showing variation and lack of clear consensus, definitely shows a particular and well recognised discourse. As a documentation of the perhaps inevitable end of an era spawned by a brutal form of settler colonialism it provides a rather sad and telling doorstop to a troubled period.

---

[131] http://www.swradioafrica.com/mike-rook-the-truth-behind-the-forced-closure-of-the-farmer-magazine/

CHAPTER 25
A MEDIA GLASNOST?

The international media has had an appalling record of balanced reporting on Zimbabwe. A single narrative, repeating the myths we attempted to demolish in our book is endlessly repeated. All is disaster, the land reform was a catastrophe and punitive sanctions are the only route to punishing Mugabe's rogue regime. Even the move to a coalition government and the stabilisation of the economy gets barely a mention.

Journalists complain that getting stories accepted on Zimbabwe is really difficult, especially if they run against this storyline. One well-known reporter commented that the British newspapers they send articles to will only accept 'white farmer' stories, ones which take an explicitly racial angle on the land issue. Another observed that editors get worried when a deluge of negative comments gets attached to articles which even hint at a different story. When our book came out journalists were astonished that there was another perspective. They had no hint of an alternative from their local contacts, and our findings were genuinely news to them.

We can see quite easily how distorted media coverage emerges. Local contacts are not hooked into research networks and repeat what their paymasters expect to hear. Journalists are always up against copy deadlines and most international news outlets do not have the resources for special field investigations. Editors avoid contentious issues if this has the potential to bring trouble. And repeating the standard line brings in the money for the stringers and freelancers. Of course in Zimbabwe, strict government control of international media reporting, at least until recently, didn't help, and added to the problem, fuelling misperceptions.

This international media coverage, especially in the UK, has created a particular view of Zimbabwe, often way out of kilter with ground realities. But is this now changing? Is there a new media glasnost emerging around reporting on Zimbabwe? In mid-2012 two major articles by two very different but well respected journalists appeared: one in the UK Daily Telegraph and one in the New York Times[132].

The first by Peter Oborne argued that it's time Zimbabwe needs to reassess the UK position on sanctions. He argued that the UK Foreign Office under William Hague is developing a pragmatic approach to Zimbabwe, and showing a clear shift from the shrill diplomacy of earlier periods under the Labour regimes. Echoes of that were evident in the House of Parliament in an intervention by Peter Hain, arguing for yet more sanctions. By contrast, around the same time, the Foreign Office was beginning to realise (belatedly) that the sanctions serve no diplomatic purpose, and even have the opposite effect [chapter 44]. Zimbabwe, Oborne argued, needs to be 'brought in from the cold'. Even the language used is from the Cold War era. Glasnost indeed. The second piece appeared on the front page of the New York Times (remarkable enough for any African story), and was penned by the NYT Johannesburg bureau chief, Lydia Polgreen. It is based on some field visits to tobacco farms and auction floors in Zimbabwe and suggests, following the argument of our work, that there is a 'golden lining' to the land reforms, as many thousands of small farmers are benefiting, even if there have been some important downsides. The case of the booming tobacco sector [chapter 2] is used, but the wider argument is made forcefully that a rethink is required.

These two articles have attracted plenty of commentary, much of it negative, but they show a brave approach to critical journalism often shied away from by others. To their credit the BBC have engaged with our work, both through interviews and articles, and with a field visit, resulting in a *Crossing Continents* programme[133]. What makes these two articles stand out is their timing (around renewed debates about 'sanctions'), their location (the NYT and the Daily Telegraph) and their positioning (an unequivocal stance which challenges the status quo view). The media glasnost is to be welcomed. Let's hope the old Soviet-style era of controlled storylines on Zimbabwe is over and a proper debate can begin.

---

[132] Oborne, P. (2012) 'We must have the courage to bring Zimbabwe in from the cold', *The Telegraph,* 18 July; Polgreen, L. (2012) 'In Zimbabwe land takeover, a golden lining', *New York Times*, July 20

[133] http://www.zimbabweland.net/Media.html; http://www.zimbabweland.net/CC.html

SECTION D
LAND

There have been three big debates about land following the 2000 reform: who got the land, was the land reform legal and what should be the basis of ownership? These issues are discussed in the chapters in this section, largely in response to a well-rehearsed narrative that took hold that the land reform was a 'grab' by a political elite, benefiting a narrow group with close links to ZANU-PF higher echelons; that the land reform was illegal, contravening international law, as specified in the SADC Tribunal's most celebrated case; and that the reform was a fundamental challenge to private property rights, that these should remain sacrosanct, and should be the basis of any new land ownership and tenure regime. There has been a huge amount of commentary on these issues, driven in particular by those who had lost land during the reform, plus a group of human and land rights activists allied to the MDC.

In chapter 26, I look at the question of who took the land and what has been dubbed the 'crony debate'. This discussion took a particular form following the publication of what turned out to be a set of unverified data on land acquisitions by 'cronies' of ZANU-PF. While elements of this were clearly true, the overall story was not. The facts simply did not add up (chapter 28). This did not seem to worry a whole set of respectable newspapers, journalists and commentators who took these figures to spin an argument about political capture. The story, as ever, is of course much more complex. While of course the situation is different in different areas of the country, our research in Masvingo showed very clearly that in our sites (broadly representative of the province), only 5% of beneficiaries, occupying around 10% of the land mostly in A2 sites, could be regarded as 'cronies' (closely linked to ZANU-PF, and benefiting directly from its patronage). There were more outside our sample who acquired land particularly around the contested elections of 2008, but nowhere near the totals suggested by these media 'investigations'.

Others have argued that, while this may be true, connections to ZANU-PF were essential for gaining land, and that MDC opposition supporters were excluded. Certainly, party connections were important, but people came to the land reform sites from many locations, with many affiliations, and of course what people said they were may not be how they voted (certainly at least in 2008, this seems to be the case; although in 2013 there was some movement back to ZANU-PF[134]). Most research shows that for A1 sites at least, particularly those that were settled through the informal *'jambanja'* land invasion process, the majority of new settlers came from nearby communal areas or small towns, and these people were poor and land hungry and not 'cronies' in any sense at all.

The question of the legality of the land reform process has been much debated. At a superficial level, it was 'legal' as the law had been changed: a well known tactic of ZANU-PF to legitimise their actions. However, these moves have been disputed in other courts. The question of which law counts is a tricky one, as there is no clear hierarchy of laws across different courts and jurisdictions [chapter 29]. This lack of legal clarity has affected in particular the process of compensation, as the transfer of land to new owners and its release from formal ownership needs to be accepted before compensation can take place. Unknown to many, the government has been paying substantial sums in compensation to former white farmers [chapter 47], but others are holding out for larger deals, or reversals of the land reform. While this is very unlikely indeed, the continued legal confrontation creates confusion and uncertainty.

Debates about land and property rights reflect a wider controversy. The work of Hernando De Soto in particular has been deployed to argue that the only basis for land tenure that will allow for investment, collateral support and stability is freehold private property [chapter 27]. It is this form of tenure that is also at the root of the legal disputes over land, as titles were overturned during the reform, and the 'fast-track' programme only offered government-backed leases and registration documents ('offer letters'). These, some argue, do not provide security of tenure, and so undermine the capacity of settlers to be successful.

---

[134] See: http://www.theguardian.com/commentisfree/2013/aug/05/zimbabwe-inconvenient-election-truth and http://www.theguardian.com/world/2013/aug/05/robert-mugabe-zimbabwe-election-zanu-pf

The result, they argue, is that land becomes 'dead capital'. This argument has long been disputed, from many sources including the World Bank, and international experience shows that titling can be expensive, administratively cumbersome and provide no greater tenure security than other forms of tenure. In Zimbabwe, this debate has been on-going for years, and the recommendations of the 1994 Land Tenure Commission led by Professor Mandi Rukuni needs to be recalled: Zimbabwe is best suited to a multi-form tenure system, that can allow for tenure security, credit collateral and investment potential. Certainly the research from across Zimbabwe shows that current tenure systems are not preventing investments, although private banks remain reluctant to offer credit on the basis of offer letters and leases. This may however be more to do with the on-going political uncertainty and legal contests over land, than the particular tenure arrangements concerned.

The new Constitution, agreed in May 2013, was meant to deal with all this, and provide a firm, consensual agreement on all such core issues, supported by a referendum. The Constitution was overwhelmingly approved and, although it has problems as an inevitable political compromise, it provides an important benchmark, with some principles to guide the way forward (chapter 30). However, as discussed in chapter 31, there remain disputes about this too, with some arguing that elements of it need to be reversed.

Settling the legal basis for land reform, managing a fair form of compensation at least for land improvements, and ensuring equal and broad access to land in the future, overseen by a transparent and accountable Land Commission, supported by a land audit process, are all urgent priorities. Whether they will now happen with the new complexion of the Zimbabwean government, we will see.

However, all these debates about land, rights, access and compensation must be put in historical perspective. Law emerges from a context, and history is important, particularly around land in Zimbabwe. The final chapter in this section recalls a thesis written in 1968 by a then young student, one Malcolm Rifkind, who went on to become the UK Foreign Secretary. In it he argues that "a settlement which is opposed to the wishes of 95% of the population cannot be declared to be final and land will remain a vital problem". He was right, and it remains a vital, and as yet unresolved, problem to this day.

CHAPTER 26

WHO TOOK THE LAND? MORE ON THE 'CRONY' DEBATE

The debate continues to rage as to who were the beneficiaries of land reform in Zimbabwe. The standard international and Zimbabwe opposition media line is that the land reform is discredited as it was captured by 'cronies' – well connected party members linked to ZANU-PF, including politicians, senior security forces personnel, judges and others connected to them.

The main source of evidence is the report produced by a 'ZimOnline Investigations Team' in November 2010[135], coinciding with the launch of our book. The headline figure in this report – that half of the land was taken by top-level cronies – is repeated again and again, in all sorts of reputable places, from the *Guardian*[136] to the *Mail and Guardian* to the *Zimbabwean*. Professor Roger Southall[137] from the University of Witswatersrand, quoted it at great length (p. 93) in a largely favourable review of *Zimbabwe's Land Reform: Myths and Realities*[138] for Africa Spectrum. He concludes: "It would seem to offer a very different picture than that provided by Scoones et al". Arguing that the book may have missed an important political context for land reform, he goes on to ask rhetorically, "If… the *major* portion of land *has* gone to the political elite, is it not likely to shape their political behaviour?"

But what is the basis and source of the ZimOnline claims? When the ZimOnline report came out I tried to contact the authors via the website. I got nowhere. No documents were forthcoming. I wrote to the various newspapers who published

---

135 http://www.zimonline.co.za/

136 Smith, D. (2010) 'Mugabe and allies own 40% of land seized from white farmers – inquiry', *The Guardian*, 30 November

137 Southall, R. (2011) Too soon to tell? Land reform in Zimbabwe, Review Article, *Africa Spectrum*, 46(3):83-97

138 Scoones, I., Marongwe, N., Mavedzenge, B., Mahenehene, J., Murimbarimba, F., and Sukume, C. (2010) *Zimbabwe's Land Reform: Myths and Realities*, Oxford: James Currey

this data to enquire about their sources, but got no further, and only one published my letter [chapter 28]. Someone more cynical than myself commented that I was wasting my time, that this was propaganda and the data made up, and that no report or 'investigation team' existed.

Despite making it central to his critique, Southall does concede that "The accuracy of this study needs to be confirmed". But in practice, as I found out, the data is difficult to cross-check and verify. One set of data based on a decade of research (with all its readily admitted limitations) is thus set against another 'investigation' with no report on an online blog. Such data though is really important, as who got what and where is central to any discussion about land reform and the future of the agrarian economy and wider political behaviour and context, as Southall correctly argues.

Certainly some of the information is true, and there has definitely been a capture of land by high ranking officials through a combination of violence and patronage. The 'large-scale A2' category of farms that Sam Moyo describes in his detailed analysis of the emerging agrarian structure in Zimbabwe[139] is an important indicator of elite capture. But these are far fewer than claimed by the ZimOnline data, and the overall picture of a land reform dominated by small-scale and medium-scale acquisitions in the A1 and A2 schemes, most of whom are 'ordinary' farmers (a problematic category admittedly), still stands.

By 2013, the political wrangles over the constitution, the contested election and the on-going disputes over the ZANU-PF succession, the likelihood of a full-scale land audit happening receded. As Professor Mandi Rukuni explained in his contribution to the Sokwanele land debate[140], the technical capacity is in place to carry it out, but the political moment must be right. Earlier land audits by Utete, Buka and the 2006 A2 audit by the Ministry of Lands have shown a complex picture, with much variation between different parts of the country. But the overall picture is not hugely different to what we found, despite the on-going discussion about 'Masvingo exceptionalism' [chapter 57].

---

[139] Moyo, S. (2011) Three decades of agrarian reform in Zimbabwe, *Journal of Peasant Studies*, 38(3): 493-531

[140] Rukuni, M. (2012) *My perspective on the ongoing preparations for a national land audit*, Zimbabwe Land Series, Sokwanele

It is clear that, unlike the majority in A1 schemes, some A2 farmers gained access through patronage linkages. Application processes were manipulated and so certain people gained land when their qualifications were inadequate or their business plans were poor. These farms often still remain underutilised and undercapitalised, and some are effectively abandoned. But this is not the majority, the rest are building up their farms, slowly but surely, and it is interesting how these are linking into value chains in new ways. We cannot announce a success of the A2 farms yet, but there are more positive signs than a few years ago when the incentives and capacities to invest were so minimal due to the chaos in the economy.

But in addition to the standard A2 farms we also have the 'large-scale A2' farms, where whole farms were handed over. These are where the 'big chefs' reside, and where political patronage and cronyism of the sort described by ZimOnline is most prevalent. But again, these cases are limited and scattered, and in fact some are thriving – because funds from elsewhere (not always above board I am sure) are being invested. And then there are the conservancies [chapter 42], formally outside the Fast Track Land Reform programme, where an elite take-over has been attempted. However, much of this has stalled, as many such 'investment partners' have not been forthcoming.

Our findings from Masvingo show that the vast majority of land reform beneficiaries and land areas are being used by people who could not be classified as 'cronies'. There are however 'land grabs' on the margins which, while still small in overall numerical and area terms, are important politically. These peaked around the contested elections in 2008, and continue. A few remaining 'white farms' and wildlife areas have been targeted and taken over by politically and militarily connected elites. This is a pattern that is repeated elsewhere in the country and particularly dramatically in the high value land areas of the Highveld.

However, there is no decent research that supportsthe conclusions of the ZimOnline 'investigation', even if variations certainly exist across the country.

CHAPTER 27

DEAD CAPITAL: DE SOTO'S FALLACIES IN ZIMBABWE

A 2012 opinion piece in the *Zimbabwe Independent* by Eddie Cross[141], was titled "Land: Africa's greatest but still dead asset[142]". It very clearly picked up on Hernando De Soto's[143] ideas on 'dead capital' and the need for clear property rights on land and other assets in order to release their value.

Cross's article is extraordinary for its failure to engage with the substantial critique of this argument, presenting a simplistic and patronising perspective on 'tribal' (sic) tenure systems. It is doubly extraordinary as the author was the MDC-T's Policy Coordinator General and a member of the National Executive of the party, as well as being MP for Bulawayo South.

It demonstrates perfectly the poverty of understanding and debate on this subject in many quarters. The MDC's website[144] carries only a very general statement on land and agriculture, but if future policy is being informed by the sort of arguments presented in this article it is a tragedy. Even the World Bank rejects the simplistic argument that individual property rights are the solution to economic growth, and particularly around land where registration and titling approaches have long been shown to be costly and ineffective.

The article betrays a remarkable lack of understanding of African tenure and land governance systems, and offers a simplistic narrative peddled by right-wing think tanks, such as the Cato Institute (whose strap-line is 'Individual Liberty, Free

---

[141] http://eddiecross.africanherd.com/

[142] Cross, E. (2012) 'Land: Africa's greatest but still dead asset', *The Villager*, 6 February

[143] http://en.wikipedia.org/wiki/Hernando_de_Soto_Polar

[144] http://www.mdc.co.zw/

Markets and Peace'). Indeed, Cross himself wrote a Cato Institute paper on land reform[145] with this line of argument in 2009.

However, this perspective has been widely challenged. For example, Ben Cousins and colleagues at PLAAS produced an excellent briefing paper[146] a few years back that challenged the claims of De Soto and his followers. The central criticisms they focus on are "his oversimplification of the informal economy and associated property relations". The paper is short and well worth reading. They argue:

> "...many of de Soto's policy prescriptions may be inappropriate for the poorest and most vulnerable in our society, and have negative impacts on their security and well-being. More attention should be paid to supporting existing social practices that have widespread legitimacy. Features of 'extra-legal' property regimes provide a key to the solutions: their social embeddedness; the importance of land and housing as assets that help to secure livelihoods; the layered and relative nature of rights; and the flexible character of boundaries. The entire legal and social complex around which notions of 'formal' and 'informal' property are constituted needs to be interrogated more rigorously".

They conclude: "De Soto's ideas have mesmerised many policy makers and politicians, but a significant body of scholars and land reform practitioners are concerned that his policy prescriptions are highly misleading". Policy makers, they argue, "must resist the temptation to seek simplistic solutions to poverty of the kind offered by De Soto".

There is no strong evidence that there is an automatic causal relation between private property rights and economic growth and investment, despite the influential arguments of de Soto and others. Instead the relationship between property rights, investment and economic growth is much more complex, and is conditioned by wider factors, such as political stability, the investment

---

[145] Cross, E. (2009) *The Cost of Zimbabwe's Continuing Farm Invasions,* Economic Development Bulletin, 12, Washington DC: Cato Institute

[146] Cousins B., Cousins T., Hornby D., Kingwill R., Royston L., Smit W. (2005) Will formalising property rights reduce poverty in South Africa's 'second economy'? Questioning the mythologies of Hernando de Soto. *PLAAS Policy Brief,* 18. Cape Town: PLAAS, UWC

environment, local institutional arrangements for land access, and so on. Embarking on expensive cadastral surveys and land administration exercises is very often a big mistake, as study after study has shown. There are plenty of other routes to the same end that are more effective and cheaper. As Professor Rukuni (and many, many others) have long argued, a differentiated response is required that accepts multiform tenure, but does not go down the risky route of mass land titling.

Yet, virtually all the criticisms of de Soto and his ilk are repeated in almost pure form in Cross's piece. It seems Eddie Cross, like others, has been mesmerised. Let's hope the MDC does not come out with highly misleading and simplistic policy prescriptions too[147].

---

[147] Unfortunately, the MDC's land and agriculture policy produced in 2013 did indeed repeat some of these fallacies, see my commentary at:
http://zimbabweland.wordpress.com/2013/06/17/the-mdc-ts-agenda-for-real-transformation-art-why-the-land-and-agriculture-sections-need-more-thought/

CHAPTER 28
ACCURATE LAND FIGURES MATTER

Here is a letter I sent to the *Mail and Guardian* commenting on the publishing of unverified figures on land. The same figures were repeated in numerous media outlets, including the UK Guardian and The Zimbabwean. The M and G didn't publish the letter (perhaps they were embarrassed…), but the Zimbabwean did. I did try and contact the ZimOnline team many times to get a copy of their report, but it was not forthcoming. Someone commented to me that they thought it probably didn't exist!

Accurate land figures matter

Based on a report by ZimOnline, a news item 'Only the elite got rich in Bob's land grab' (December 6) claimed that a new elite controls nearly 5m hectares of land, close to half of all land taken through land reform since 2000.

It is of course critical that those holding multiple farms comply with the rules of the land reform programme and it is essential that a thorough and transparent land audit ensures that this happens. Identifying and listing in the public domain such contraventions is certainly a useful contribution. But to make the case that such capture by political-security elites is the dominant pattern of land reform in Zimbabwe is misleading.

Figures matter, but these simply do not add up. For instance, the list of 'Zimbabwe's top farm owners' in the article covers around 150,000 ha, only 3% of the 5m hectares of land claimed to be captured by elites. Even accepting that this list is only partial, how the huge headline-grabbing totals were arrived at is anyone's guess. Equally, the report contains important inaccuracies and inconsistencies in estimates of land areas transferred under the land reform programme, as well as the number of farms involved. I hope that the 'ZimOnline Investigations Team' who carried out this study will reveal themselves, and submit their detailed data to more thorough scrutiny. Around such a sensitive issue as land reform it is vital that media reporting is based on solid, verifiable facts.

Our detailed research into land reform in Masvingo province... shows that those who might be dubbed 'cronies' make up about 5% of all beneficiaries. By contrast, the vast majority were ordinary people, with half of all new farmers being asset and income poor families coming from nearby communal areas. In-depth studies from other parts of the country support this broad pattern. Our research does not deny that corruption, abuse and patronage have occurred, nor that land reform rules have been flouted. But our work offers a more balanced, rounded picture than offered by this report.

I hope in future that the *Mail and Guardian*, together with other respected media outlets, will interrogate their sources more thoroughly in order to encourage an informed debate about the future which is based on solid evidence, rather than spurious extrapolation.

CHAPTER 29

WHOSE LAW COUNTS? LEGAL CONTESTS OVER LAND IN ZIMBABWE

Much of the land debate in Zimbabwe has centred on a number of high profile legal cases. The most prominent of course is that brought by Ben Freeth and his late father in law, Mike Campbell. The SADC Tribunal[148] ruled in their favour, but the decision was rejected by Zimbabwe and the tribunal was disbanded[149], and is unlikely to regain significant powers despite a high profile campaign led by Desmond Tutu to have it reinstated.

So whose law counts? National, regional or international, and which courts can adjudicate on what? This is a fairly profound socio-legal conundrum, debated widely by those concerned with legal pluralism and the relationships between international law and national jurisdictions. The Zimbabwe case is thus far from new, but it is important, given the importance laid on 'the rule of law' as a building block of an effective economy and democracy. And more pragmatically, resolving the outstanding legal disputes over land ownership must be achieved, if Zimbabwe's agricultural economy is to move forwards.

In a piece contributing to the Sokwanele land debate, Dale Doré argues[150] that the last decade or so has seen an abrogation of legal principles by the Zimbabwean state, with laws made and broken seemingly at will. Certainly the flurry of legislation on land that has appeared justifying, usually *post hoc*, state actions is witness to this pattern. Whether the issue is compensation or compulsory acquisition, then a new law to suit the current situation was presented. Of course, the argument runs that this is what elected law makers do, and they are perfectly in their right to do so.

---

[148] Southern African Development Community (SADC) Tribunal (2007) *Mike Campbell and Others v. Republic of Zimbabwe, SADC (T) No. 2/2007*, Tribunal Judgement

[149] Ndlovu, R. (2012) 'Southern Africa: SADC Tribunal disbandment victory for ZANU-PF', *All Africa*, 22 August

[150] Dore, D. (2012), *A Law Unto Themselves (Part 1) : Making and Breaking the Laws of the Land*, Harare: Sokwanele

The question though is whether justice is being done, or whether this represented arbitrary, biased law making of the worst sort, without any underpinnings of natural justice. This is certainly Doré's main argument in his two-part contribution. And he clearly has a point. Following the rejection of the constitution in the 2000 referendum, the President insisted on inserting an amendment (no 16) allowing for compensation only for improvements, and while the High Court regarded the land invasions as 'illegal' in 2000, by December 2001, the Supreme Court ruled that Rural Land Occupier (Protection from Eviction) Act, giving rights to land invaders, was lawful and in line with the Constitution.

Clearly the law was a mess, and added to that the intimidation and clear political manipulation of the judiciary made much of this a sham. But to suggest that the law and politics and social processes, particularly in times of rapid change, are always separate is also inaccurate. Laws must reflect broad political choices, and more generally the people's will. If this was not the case, we would be stuck (as we often are) with laws that are outdated, regressive and anachronistic. New laws must though, as Doré argues, reflect the basic principles of fairness, natural justice and so on, but they also must be realistic and pragmatic, and appropriate to the social and political context of the time.

Probably the best way of resolving the detail is to look to the bigger picture. And this is where a Constitution can help. If this is agreed and broadly accepted, this can become the basis on which laws can be assessed. On land, the Constitution [chapter 30] is quite clear, supporting the 2000 position on compensation, and recognising, as the Global Political Agreement did, the irreversibility of land reform.

This is not to say that there aren't those who object. A *Financial Gazette* article entitled, "Draft constitution displeases displaced farmers"[151] reports on the position of the CFU and the views of Agricultural Recovery and Compensation manager Ben Gilpin, arguing that "The predicament of the former commercial farmers continues unabated as the draft constitution has failed to address the issue of compensation, stripping them of their rights to fair compensation as

---

[151] Mutenga, T. (2012) 'Zimbabwe: Draft Constitution displeases displaced farmers', *All Africa*, 10 August

indigenous Zimbabweans". The CFU has indicated that they will continue the struggle for full rights and compensation.

Yet, Doré argues[152] that the constitutional provisions are "conspicuously at variance with international law and offend natural justice". But this claim can be disputed. International law is not clear on land compensation, and compensations for improvements only are an accepted mechanism elsewhere, and probably the only feasible one for Zimbabwe. As for natural justice this rather depends on the wider consideration: clearly land reform was redressing longer term injustices due to colonialism, and striving for equity through redistribution must be seen as a commitment to justice too. Balancing individual human rights and narrow legal provisions created in another era, with wider commitments to rights, justice and redistribution is not easy, and in the end is a societal and political judgement. Overall, a national political consensus is clearly required on the land issue, and this will require compromises. Holding out on the basis of arguments around the 'sanctity' of private property is insufficient, and recourse to an individualistic rights discourse, ignoring the wider social-political context is also inadequate.

What then is the way out of this bind, where, as in the Sokwanele debate as in wider political discourse, the two protagonists talk past each other? A first step must be a new legal framework, based on a democratically agreed Constitution [chapter 30].

---

[152] Dore, D. (2012) *A Law Unto Themselves (Part II): The Rulings and Dissolution of the SADC Tribunal*, Harare: Sokwanele

CHAPTER 30
LAND AND THE CONSTITUTION

The draft Constitution[153] was released during 2012 and finally agreed in 2013, after long, hard negotiations. It has some interesting things to say about land. Some highlights are:

Access to agricultural land is seen as a 'fundamental right': "Every citizen of Zimbabwe has a right to acquire, hold, occupy, use, transfer, hypothecate, lease or dispose of agricultural land regardless of his or her race or colour". It notes that, following colonial occupation and the liberation war, "the people of Zimbabwe must be enabled to re-assert their rights and regain ownership of their land".

Amongst the general principles for land use, it argues that "the allocation and distribution of agricultural land must be fair and equitable, having regard to gender balance and diverse community interests" and that "the land tenure system must promote increased productivity and investment by Zimbabweans in agricultural land". Gender balance in land distribution is an interesting Constitutional principle, although nothing is specified about how it will be brought about, and the comment on 'tenure systems' again does not specify and particular form of property rights, as some have argued for [chapter 27].

Continued rights over land occupied under existing policies (presumably referring to the Fast Track Land Reform) are assured, and it emphasises the importance of tenure security (again not specifying what form of tenure) for those occupying land with the following statement: "The State must take appropriate measures, including legislative measures, to give security of tenure to every person lawfully owning or occupying agricultural land".

Compulsory acquisition of land, and transfer of title to the State, is allowed for public purposes including resettlement, but compensation on improvements

---

[153]'Draft Constitution of Zimbabwe', 17 July 2012, http://www.swradioafrica.com/ Documents/Final%20Consolidated%20Draft%20Constitution%2018%20July%202012.pdf. Final version: http://www.gta.gov.zw/index.php/documents/constitution-of-zimbabwe

[chapter 46], but not the land, must be paid. The draft goes on to note "the obligation of the former colonial power to pay compensation for land", but indicates that the Zimbabwean state has no such obligation. In other words, in practice there is no expectation of compensation for land, but only improvements, except for land protected by investment treaties and owned by foreigners (BIPPAs), where compensation for land and improvements is required.

The Constitution proposes the establishment of a Zimbabwe Land Commission which the government of the day will have a constitutional obligation to ensure that it "is able to exercise its functions efficiently and independently", and that the membership (specified in the draft) should act fairly and impartially. A key role of the Commission will be to carry out periodic land audits. The Constitution specifies the one farm policy quite precisely in the following statement: "The State may not alienate more than one piece of agricultural land to the same person and his or her dependants", suggesting that multiple farms held within a family (even under various holding companies) are unconstitutional.

Overall, these seem to me to be good constitutional provisions, and should help the country move forward, consolidating the land reform and dealing with the outstanding issues of tenure security and compensation in a clear and transparent manner. Having an independent commission to oversee audits will be important also. I am not a lawyer so cannot comment on the drafting, but if this is a cross-party consensus it looks to be a very positive step. There will be objections, and no doubt numerous wrangles about 'fair' compensation, and whether farms are owned legitimately and are sole properties [chapter 31], but it does provide a clear framework, although of course the details will have to be worked out.

CHAPTER 31

ZIMBABWE HAS A NEW CONSTITUTION, BUT DISPUTES OVER THE LAND PROVISIONS CONTINUE

On March 16th 2013, Zimbabweans voted on a new Constitution[154] in a national referendum. The voting was largely peaceful, and the turnout higher than expected, with over 3 million people voting. With all major parties supporting it, the result was a resounding 93% 'yes'. This endorsement was an important signal that a new commitment to moving forward had been reached, one that international donors agreed to respect with the removal of further 'sanctions' [chapter 44].

The Constitution is naturally a compromise document, one hammered out in parliament by all the parties. It involved wide consultation, with inputs from the public. Given Zimbabwe's immediate political past, it is in many respects a remarkable achievement. It is of course rough at the edges, and not everyone agrees with every section, but it now does exist, and should, in my view, by celebrated.

Of course one of the controversial areas has been the issue of land [chapter 30]. Some are very unhappy about the provisions, blaming the MDC in particular for conceding too much. Ben Freeth, the former farmer activist, is particularly outspoken[155]. In a slightly more considered contribution, Dale Doré asks[156], can the new Constitution bring about a just, legal and transparent land policy? He answers, "The prospects, unfortunately, look decidedly bleak. Chapter 16

---

[154] COPAC (2013) *Zimbabwe Draft Constitution*. Harare: COPAC Constitution Select Committee. And final version: http://www.gta.gov.zw/index.php/documents/constitution-of-zimbabwe

[155] Freeth, B. (2013) 'Why I cannot endorse Zimbabwe's new constitution', *Politics web*, 30 January

[156] Dore, D. (2013) 'The good, the bad, and the unworthy: Zimbabwe's draft Constitution and its implications for land policy', *Sokwanele*, 9 March

entrenches the outcome of land invasions and the seizures of farms and property. The draft Constitution also retains provisions under section 72 that are inimical to international law, human rights and the rule of law".

What then are Doré's complaints? He argues that the separation of provisions on property rights from rights over agricultural land is a big mistake, as the section on agricultural lands restricts rights, running against natural justice. He is particularly concerned about the long-talked about Land Commission, as he thinks it will not have teeth, and will be easily captured. He notes:

> "The most important retreat, however, has been to make the Land Commission an advisory body to Government rather than an independent parastatal organisation with executive authority. The Commission may make recommendations on a host of issues – including land tenure and compensation – but it lacks any real powers of implementation or teeth for enforcement. Decisions governing land remain firmly in the hands of the President and his appointed minister".

While Section 297(6) tries "to give the impression of independence and impartiality", he argues that this is not sufficient. This he worries will mean that a Land Audit, also a requirement in the Constitution, will not be fair, as it will be overseen by the Commission.

Overall he argues, that the section on land – Chapter 16 – "maintains all the discriminatory provisions governing farmland found in the current Constitution". He argues that there will be inadequate notice of compulsory acquisition and that compensation will be paid for improvements only, and not the full value of the land. He objects to the proposed dispute settlement mechanism, arguing runs against basic principles of 'rule of law', being an administrative not judiciary process. He argues that, as a result, the Constitution is not in line with earlier rulings by the now disbanded SADC Tribunal ruling. Yet, as I and others have commented before [chapter 29], this obsession with this particular ruling forgets that the proposed constitutional provisions are actually in line with much international practice, and perfectly compatible with 'the rule of law', as long as the rules and regulations are abided by. This of course is the critical point. The test will be in the practice, and the demonstrated impartiality and effectiveness of systems of land acquisition, compensation and dispute settlement. Given recent experience, Doré and others are right to be concerned, but have no real argument for rejecting the provisions as a whole.

Before jumping to excessively negative conclusions, we have to understand the political context for the new Constitution, in order to judge it properly. In a heated debate at the end of February 2013 on the new Constitution, chaired by Violet Gonda in the Hot Seat slot on SW Africa Radio[157], Professor Brian Raftopoulos commented:

> *"Well I think the first thing to point out is that this constitution was a central part of the mediation process. It was always therefore going to be a compromise document and part of a broader process of trying to establish the conditions for a free and fair election – which was the original objective of the SADC mediation. There's clearly things in the constitution which are problematic; there's also things which I think establish a very good basis for moving forward and I think that as part of a long term process of discussion between the parties which was established through the mediation, it's a step forward and one should look at it as that".*

On land, he notes:

> *"This land process has produced many contradictory results. As recent research shows, it hasn't been the complete failure people thought it was but at the same time it hasn't ended the land question. It's raised a whole series of new issues, which are going to confront Zimbabweans throughout – for the coming decades".*

Of course the land question is not going to be fully resolved by the Constitution. But hopefully the Constitution sets the basic parameters: the land reform is not reversible; rights to land are circumscribed by the state to avoid abuse; compensation for improvements are offered if land is acquired by the state; land administration and distribution is overseen by a competent authority in the Land Commission; and abuses are corrected through a transparent Land Audit. All of these provisions are actually good ones, and compatible with international practices, but will only work if the appropriate political and administrative

---

[157] Gonda, V. (2013) 'Hot Seat: Heated panel discussion on Zim draft constitution', *SW Radio Africa*, 21 February

conditions apply. Given recent experience, this is of course a concern, and why a wider political resolution of the on-going political impasse in Zimbabwe is so urgently needed.

However, given that it has now been approved by the referendum, and given that the Constitution represents an important moment in the mediation process to create such political conditions, surely its basic principles need now to be respected. Sure, there will be need for working out the details of the Commission, the Audit and the associated regulations to govern any land administration processes, but the overarching basis for these, surely, is now set.

Or is it? Dale Doré refers to a discussion with a 'senior MDC politician' who noted that: "The MDC had to make compromises. If it conceded to ZANU-PF on the land issue, he said, "so what?" Anyway, he added, land is not a major issue for the great majority. The issue of land and land policy was something the MDC could fix once in power". This seems more like a threat to unravel things that have been agreed, even as reluctant compromises. In an email exchange on Doré's piece as part of probably the most bizarre email list I am copied in to, Eddie Cross MP, the MDC's Policy Coordinator General (who supported a yes vote[158] with 10 reasons), commented on 10 March 2013, "Excellent as usual – but so long as everyone understands that this was the main focus of concession to the views of ZANU-PF in the negotiation and was a compromise – it is not the final word on the issue of agricultural land".

Yes the Constitution is a compromise. Yes it emerged through negotiation between parties that did not agree. And, yes, it is not the final word. As Brian Raftopolous pointed out in the SW Africa Radio discussion, "there are still a lot of issues around the land [issue] which wouldn't necessarily be dealt with simply through the constitution – issues which will have to be dealt with through legislation coming afterwards and through political and technical processes that need to take place in the aftermath of what has happened". But does this mean that the basic tenets of the Constitution should be dismissed? Technical and administrative details will be required of course, but should principles agreed through negotiation should not so easily be up for grabs. The new Constitution, with its inevitable flaws, now at last provides the basis for moving forward.

---

[158] http://www.eddiecross.africanherd.com/

CHAPTER 32
A PRESCIENT PERSPECTIVE ON LAND FROM 1968

In 1968, Malcolm Rifkind, then a 22 year old postgraduate student at the University of Southern Rhodesia wrote the following in his University of Edinburgh thesis, "The Politics of Land in Rhodesia"[159]:

> *"Today, (October 1968), land is a burning issue in Rhodesia, but only for the Africans. As far as the Europeans are concerned, the problem has been resolved – in their favour. ... However, a settlement which is opposed to the wishes of 95% of the population cannot be declared to be final and land will remain a vital problem, at least until the whole political system has changed".*

Well, 22 years later, in 1980 when Malcolm Rifkind was a member of Mrs Thatcher's government, the political system did change with Independence, but the land issue remained a 'vital problem', and continues to do so today. Malcolm Rifkind[160] of course later went on to become Britain's Foreign Secretary, and served in both Mrs Thatcher's and John Major's governments. A conservative politician, he is not usually associated with progressive views about land. But as a young student in Southern Rhodesia during the UDI period, his analysis of land issues showed deep insight and prescience.

Perhaps his successors at the Foreign and Commonwealth Office should have read it. Britain's appalling record of diplomacy with Zimbabwe has been repeatedly ill-informed. Of course the 'Clare Short letter'[161] was the pinnacle, but there have been so many other moments when inappropriate signals have been given and gaffes made. Informed British foreign policy on Zimbabwe in the coming years will be critical.

---

[159] Rifkind, M (1968), *The Politics of Land in Rhodesia.* Thesis, Edinburgh: University of Edinburgh

[160] http://www.conservatives.com/People/Members_of_Parliament/Rifkind_Sir_Malcolm.aspx

[161] http://politics.guardian.co.uk/foi/images/0,9069,1015120,00.html

SECTION E
LIVELIHOODS AND RURAL DEVELOPMENT

Our research in Masvingo province asked how have livelihoods changed after land reform? The analysis of livelihoods involves a complex piecing together of many pieces of a puzzle, taking account of patterns of social difference, relationships between people and places, and dynamics over time, and across generations.

Transferring land is one thing, but wider agrarian reform and rural development is another. This must encompass questions such as diversification of income earning opportunities off farm; the building of communities and social relations within new settlements; gaining access to services, including health and education; the way access to land and increased agricultural production translates into nutritional status, as affected by issues of sanitation; what happens to the next generations after the parents gain access to land; the relationships between new and old settlements – between the land reform sites and the communal areas, for example; the links to urban areas and wider circuits of migration, and the flow of people, goods and cash remittances back to the new farming areas; and the environmental and disease context of new settlement sites, and the implications this has for settlement patterns and livelihood opportunities.

The chapters in this section tackle all these issues. The section starts with a reflection of a piece of work that I was involved in over the span of 20 years in Mazvihwa communal area in Midlands province [chapter 33]. This longitudinal study shows how livelihoods are highly dynamic, with ups and downs, affected by contingency and chance, as well as longer term drivers of change. An interesting finding from this study was that those who got out of the communal area – to resettlement sites, both formal and informal - at various points over the 20 years, including under the fast-track programme, fared better than their counterparts who were left behind. Land reform however cannot be a one-off solution, as there are always next generation problems that follow, as chapter 34 shows. Chapter 37 delves into the changing role of young people in agriculture, and their own demands for land, and inclusion in agrarian reform processes.

The new land reform sites have created new communities: new people on new land, often from dispersed original locations, with diverse sources of authority. Much activity, including agricultural production, is reliant on social relationships – whether marketing, input supply, sharing equipment and draft power and so on. Building communities is an essential, but often unrecognised, part of a resettlement process, and chapter 36 reflects on this, with reference to work from Mazowe in particular. Churches, burial societies, kin networks, new development oriented institutions, as well as simple friendships built between neighbours, are all important.

Diversified livelihoods, involving a mix of on and off farm income earning, both local and broader, are usually a route to reduced vulnerability and greater resilience. Chapter 35 discusses changing patterns of livelihood diversification, with reference to our Masvingo studies. Relationships with others not living at the farm are also important, and always have been in Zimbabwe's migrant labour economy. However migration circuits have changed, as chapter 40 discusses. But yet again, the standard narrative that there has been a mass exodus from Zimbabwe has to be qualified. The figures on migration do not add up, and probably do not account for circular migration, with short visits for piece work, trading and so on, but with people firmly located at home in Zimbabwe. A deeper understanding of new patterns of migration and their effects on livelihoods is urgently needed, but, as with so many other areas, the data is poor and the standard policy narratives are found wanting.

New settlements were often in large farms that previously had little infrastructure and no social services to speak of. How then can large numbers of new school children be educated, and sick people be treated? The dilemmas of providing education services on the new resettlements are discussed in chapter 38, with reference to both Goromonzi and Masvingo. The failure of government to support these new settlements is a scandal. Equally, the shocking neglect by

UN agencies and others, despite the rhetoric of education or health 'for all', is highlighted as part of the wider discussion of 'sanctions' (chapters 43 and 44). Yet one of the achievements of these new communities has been to build schools and health posts, and attract teachers and health workers, often supported by community contributions.

One of the core provisions that people invest in first following settlement is clean water and toilets. However water and sanitation conditions on the new resettlements remain poor and underdeveloped; again because of the lack of external support. Chapter 41 discusses the complex relationships between food production, nutrition and sanitation around a particular puzzle. Why was undernutrition not worse in the period of Zimbabwe's crisis when calls on food aid occurred each year? A major nutrition survey showed that Zimbabwe was actually better off than many neighbouring countries. Yet despite this, stunting remains a major problem. Could this be due to what is called 'tropical enteropathy', the impact in early life of lowered nutrient absorption in the gut due to poor sanitation? The relationships are complex and poorly understood, but it challenges us to question the simple narratives around food and nutrition.

Some land reform settlements were in quite remote areas of the country, taking over marginal land on the edge of national parks and conservancies for example. These were inhospitable environments with very particular challenges for new settlements on the frontiers. Chapters 39 and 42 discuss two different threats to new settlers and their livestock: one from tsetse flies in the Zambezi valley and the other from elephants in the southeast lowveld. Both raise different questions about the trade-offs involved between resettlement and environmental conservation, and the challenges of clearing land not only from trees and bush, but from wild animals and disease-carrying vectors that are threats to humans and livestock. The contested visions of landscape from the point of view of settlers and conservationists are brought to the fore, with land reform being challenged, as potentially environmentally destructive.

Thus, this section argues overall, broader issues of livelihoods and rural development, encompassing all these issues and more, need to be brought within the ambit of agrarian reform, moving from a concern with land transfer to a wider process of long-term sustainable development.

CHAPTER 33
TWENTY YEARS OF LIVELIHOOD CHANGE IN SOUTHERN ZIMBABWE

In 1985 I first went to Zimbabwe, and to Mazvihwa communal area in Zvishavane district in particular, at the invitation of Ken Wilson and Cephas Mukamuri, the late father of Billy Mukamuri, now chair at the Centre for Applied Social Sciences at UZ. I was to start my PhD research on the ecology and economics of livestock production in the communal areas[162].

1985 was a time of hope and expectation. Independence had been achieved, investments were flowing (if rather slowly to the remote Mazvihwa), and everyone was expecting – including us idealistic researchers – a great developmental transformation. Yes there were challenges to this idealistic (naïve?) vision. Unknown to us then, the brutal massacres in Matabeleland were happening, and the political formation of the new Zimbabwe was shaky to say the least. South Africa was still under apartheid, and launched destabilising raids into what were then 'the frontline states'. But despite this, the future, to us at least, looked bright.

So what happened in Mazvihwa since? I have been visiting friends there over the for now nearly 30 years, and during the 1990s, I was involved in a project over the Runde river in Chivi which became the book, *Hazards and Opportunities*[163]. But it was not until 2004 when Josphat Mushongah wrote to me proposing a PhD at the IDS that I got to know what really had happened in the intervening years. Josphat had been the assistant district administrator in Zvishavane in the 1990s and knew many of the people I did. I suggested that he do a restudy for his PhD, asking what happened to people's livelihoods between 1986 and 2006.

---

[162] Scoones, I. (1990) *Livestock populations and the household economy: a case study from Southern Zimbabwe*, Doctoral dissertation, Imperial College London, London: University of London

[163] Scoones, I., Chibudu, C., Chikura, S., Jeranyama, P., Machaka, D., Machanja, W., and Zirereza, B. (1996) *Hazards and Opportunities. Farming Livelihoods in Dryland Africa: Lessons from Zimbabwe*, London: Zed Books

And this is what he did. A restudy is not as easy as it sounds. In the 1980s Ken Wilson and I only had a small sample of around 70 households. By 2006 many were still resident, although the older household heads had passed on. Some households had dissolved, and discovering when and why required some patient forensics. But tracing those who had left the area required the biggest challenge. Josphat travelled by bus, donkey cart and foot to the furthest reaches of the country, and located everyone. Tracing the next generation was also a challenge, as many had spread through the diaspora – from South Africa to Botswana to the UK.

His PhD[164] is a fascinating read, and a paper emerging from that restudy has just been published in the *Journal of Development Studies*[165]). In this paper we take the 'wealth ranking' analysis I did in the 1980s and the repeat Josphat did 20 years on, and explore, with survey data, livelihood biographies and so on, what happened to particular households – both those in the original sample, and their Mazvihwa resident offspring. It's an engrossing tale. Some have improved their lot, some have declined, while others have stayed much the same. The factors that have affected these changes are diverse. A sequence of poor harvests could push someone down; a death, illness or period of unemployment could have dramatic consequences. Equally, a windfall payout from a retrenchment or an inheritance of some animals could have the opposite effects. Chance, luck, and happenstance have as much to answer for as the relatively more predictable dynamics of social differentiation.

While only 11 acquired new land through resettlement – either through the formal resettlements in the 1980-90s, the informal movements to the 'frontier lands' of Gokwe and beyond in the 1990s, or the fast-track in the 2000s – the results of what happened to them are interesting. Nearly all of these households improved their lot, and only one who fled to the frontier areas showed a decline. Gaining land as an asset is an important form of social protection, and can help improve living standards.

---

[164] http://www.ianscoones.net/PhD_Students.html

[165] Mushongah, J. and Scoones, I., (2012) Livelihood change in rural Zimbabwe over 20 years, *Journal of Development Studies*, 48(9): 1241-1257

Overall, though, the great expectations and naïve hopes of the 1980s have not been realised in Mazvihwa. Despite the tarmac road, the new resettlement opportunities and the investments in schools and clinics, the place remains a backwater. Poor, isolated, and plagued by drought, few are making a significant living from farming alone. Off-farm opportunities are perhaps fewer than they were in the 1980s, and the prospects for the next generation are limited. Most talk of exit – getting educated, and getting out. For some this is to the new resettlements where there is land and some prospect of prosperity; for others it is out of the country, perhaps as border jumpers but ideally with a proper job.

CHAPTER 34

CHALLENGES AND PROBLEMS OF RESETTLEMENT: OVER A DECADE ON

What are some of the emerging challenges on the new resettlements? Here is a list of six generated during discussions on a trip to our field sites in Zimbabwe during 2011.

1. The next generation's demand for land for land is growing [chapter 37]. Those who were aged 16 at the time of the land invasions are now 27, maybe married and without a field. Some youth are mobilising and leading new invasions. Others remain discontented in the communal areas, or in the new resettlements. How to encourage turnover and new entrants, without the problem of eternal subdivision?

2. Boundary disputes while important from the beginning, are becoming more and more prevalent. With more people on the land, it is inevitable that boundaries are going to be contested. But who will resolve these as lines of authority in the new resettlements remain unsettled?

3. Markets for land are emerging, as demand for land continues to grow. These are illegal, underhand and not widely discussed, but are definitely happening, involving chiefs, *sabhukus*, local government officials and others. A clear and transparent land administration is an urgent policy priority. Land sales, leasing and exchange may well be part of the future, but it needs regulation and clarity in policy.

4. Soil fertility declines and the invasion of witchweed has been observed in some sites. Of course planting on virgin cleared land means for a few years, natural fertility can be made use of. But it does need replenishing. Fertiliser application rates remain low, and intensive manuring has not taken off, nor has effective crop rotation. It's maize, maize, maize and more maize. And now with witchweed taking over, rotations and improving soil quality is important. Just as Alvord, and all the extensionists that followed him, always said!

5. With improved production, comes the challenge of marketing. There are now increasingly large gluts of particular products – notably horticultural produce – with resulting collapses of prices and incomes. Greater diversification, and more sophistication in timing in relation to particular markets will be required. This will need better market knowledge, as well as improved infrastructure. In several of our sites, the intermittent train service for example has really hampered marketing to Masvingo and beyond.

6. One of the big demands for land was for grazing, and as we have documented, livestock populations grew rapidly with the new resources. But there are always limits, and particularly during drought times. At the end of this last dry season, animals were being moved to grazing reserves, but these are few and far between these days as the land is now occupied. In the past poach grazing on white farms was an option, but no longer. The management of drought cycles and grazing management in these dry areas is going to be an increasing challenge into the future.

CHAPTER 35
BEYOND THE FARM: GETTING LOCAL ECONOMIES MOVING

What happens beyond the farm is often as important to people's livelihoods as production on the farm. Ideally, the two interlink, with income earned from off-farm work being invested in farming, and farming providing sources of employment and income from value addition for diversified incomes. All livelihoods in the resettlement areas are made up of portfolios of different activities. The 'full-time farmer' is a myth; as it always has been (of course white large-scale commercial farmers regularly mixed their farming activities with other sources of income).

A new project is investigating the relationships between land ownership at different scales, markets and employment patterns. It is led by the Institute for Poverty, Land and Agrarian Studies at UWC, South Africa (PLAAS) and is called 'Space, Markets and Employment in Agricultural Development' and has field sites in Zimbabwe (Masvingo and Mazowe), as well as Malawi and South Africa. The project aims to address the critical issue of non-farm employment and the growth linkages [chapter 13] associated with agriculture, operating at different scales. The project's starting point is that "non-farm employment plays a vital role in ensuring broad-based, inclusive and sustainable development... Yet the impact of agricultural development decisions on non-farm employment is often disregarded by policymakers, who assume that those who do not find employment in agriculture can be absorbed into the economy in other ways".

The proposal argues that: "This is an issue of central importance for agricultural development policy: not only because there are many people in rural areas who are landless or not involved in agricultural production, and who will therefore not benefit directly from agricultural development; but also because, in addition, large-scale agricultural investment projects, and increases in the productivity and efficiency of agriculture may lead to people being displaced from land, 'shaken out' of farming, or to be otherwise induced to leave agricultural employment. Internationally, the existence of a large and growing population of landless and unemployed people, no longer involved in agriculture but unable to find a foothold in the non-farm economy, seriously compromises poverty reduction, food security, well-being and stability".

The problem is that, while widely recognised, the linkages between agricultural development and non-farm employment are poorly understood. In particular, the proposal argues that "not enough is known about the vital role of spatial relationships and linkages that can either support positive integration into markets, or lead to adverse incorporation or exclusion".

It is the spatial dimensions of economic relations (and with these of course social, institutional, political and other interactions) that are especially interesting. Land reform in Zimbabwe has radically reconfigured the spatial pattern of economic activity in rural areas, and with this, markets, value chains, trading routes, employment opportunities and so on. How can the economic potential unleashed from small-scale agriculture be amplified through off-farm linkage effects in the local rural economy? Can a territorial approach to local economic development help capture the benefits of land reform?

Zimbabwe of course inherited a century-old spatial structure based on a dualistic economy where large commercial farms and associated farm labour were separated off from small-scale 'peasant' farming areas. There were two economies, one deemed the mainstream, the other informal, marginal and ignored. The communal areas were supposed to act as labour reserves for the mainstream economy, and there was no real expectation of employment and growth within them. This has now changed, but this historical inheritance – and the mindsets that go with it – will be difficult to shift.

The project is in its early phases, and results are forthcoming. However, we did tackle this issue in Masvingo in our studies in the 2000s, at the height of Zimbabwe's economic crisis. This is how we concluded the chapter of our book dealing with livelihood diversification and off-farm income earning:

"First, in the past decade we have observed a shifting geographical relationship between the rural spaces of the new resettlements and the wider national, regional, even global, economy. Links between the rural and urban economies remain vitally important, but this relationship is different to the classic rural-urban dynamic observed in the past. In the context of the declining economy of

Zimbabwe in the past decade, movement across borders in search of a stable currency as a source of remittance has been critical. This has meant the establishment of new migration pathways and support networks. Very often such new livelihood opportunities have been illegal and involve high levels of personal risk.

Second, as the classic pattern of rural-urban migration has changed and new migration pathways have emerged, there has been an increasingly stark differentiation in opportunity and return. As the Zimbabwean economy contracted, those in low-paid jobs were the first to lose them. Educated, well-trained civil servants suffered too, as wages were transformed into a pittance due to hyperinflation. It was only those with access to foreign remittances sources who were able to weather the storm. And even in this group this was not easy, given the low pay, poor conditions and often serious abuses and xenophobic attacks that were the context of low-paid, unskilled work in South Africa in particular[166]. It was thus only those with relatively stable, higher paid jobs abroad who were really able to contribute to the remittance flows in any regular and substantial way.

Third, in the context of economic collapse in Zimbabwe there has been a substantial shift in economic relationships between town and countryside. Flows of food from the new resettlement farms to support urban migrants in Zimbabwe have emerged as a new phenomenon. While in the past few decades, food from the rural areas was sent to urban-dwellers as luxury goods (some bambara nuts, some green mealies or a special delivery of millet flour), the sending of food for survival has not been common, at least since the 1920s and 1930s when the former reserves kept the new mineworkers in food.

Fourth, the new settlers are definitely not full-time farmers. All livelihoods are made up of a portfolio of on and off-farm activity. This helps confront risk, smooth income and diversify options. Since rainfall-dependent agriculture is an inherently risky enterprise, especially in the dry zones of the country, expecting a full-time farming commitment of new settlers is clearly foolish. However, many strategies have involved survival diversification - wild fruit collection or gold panning, for example – and illegal, risky migration, such as border-jumping.

---

[166] http://news.bbc.co.uk/1/hi/world/africa/7414214.stm

Notably absent has been policy thinking supporting opportunity and growth-oriented livelihood diversification, both in the past and today.

Fifth, while household livelihood portfolios show substantial diversification, at the individual level people may be quite specialised. This is often highly gender and age dependent, as different people develop particular business, trading, craft or trade skills and markets. These specialised occupations – whether basket-making or building, hunting or cross-border trading – require the building up of customers and market connections to make them viable enterprises. This certainly requires specialisation and investment, and, yet again, such efforts suffer from a severe lack of support.

In sum, the past decade has seen a fundamental change in the relationships between town and countryside, between the farm and other employment and between the rural areas of Zimbabwe and the wider world, within and beyond the southern African region. While off-farm income sources and remittances remain vital, and the new settlers are not full-time farmers in the sense constructed in some policy discourses, the opportunities in the new resettlements are very real. The new resettlements have proved highly attractive to a wide range of people, as we have shown. In the past, the rural areas – and certainly the communal lands – were seen as places to retire, somewhere where family rituals took places, and where people should be buried. This remains the case, and indeed most new settlers in the new resettlements regard their communal homes as 'home' (*kumusha*). The new resettlements are regarded, instead, as places of economic opportunity, much in the same way as the urban areas and off-farm employment were once seen.

[Such] opportunities are very real, but to be realised they require hard work, ingenuity and persistence. Livelihoods have to be constructed anew, and diversificaiton is essential – everyone produces some maize and vegetables on a plot somewhere these days, as well as often having different businesses; and for some all of this is carried on at the same time as attending a job, even if the pay is paltry. The period of economic collapse has changed people's outlook. Diversification, entrepreneurialism, hedging bets, building portfolios has become a necessary part of survival – for everyone, and not just the poor. Survival means resourcefulness and a reliance on the state, NGOs or development projects has been futile.

How then should we interpret this data on livelihood diversification? Are we seeing a crisis of employment, where livelihoods are squeezed through people's inability to reproduce themselves through agriculture, and with this a process of deagrarianisation and increasing rural impoverishment[167]? Or are we seeing a new livelihood dynamic, where new, productive diversified livelihoods, rooted in agriculture, are possible because of the new opportunities for growth and enterprise on the new resettlements? With land reform there have been more people shifting to land-based livelihoods, the opposite of deagrarianisation. But will this be sustained? As the economy recovers, there may be a rebalancing of people's livelihood portfolios, and some may yet leave the land in search of better returns elsewhere. Certainly some people's livelihoods are highly precarious and survival diversification is widely evident. But, in parallel, as new farmers continue to 'accumulate from below' through successful agriculture, links to off-farm enterprises, providing services and consumption goods, are increasing, in a potentially positive spiral. Thus broader economic growth, rooted in smallholder production, but involving significant livelihood diversification, must be fostered as part of new policy thinking".

These findings from the late 2000s will act as important baselines for the new work that will look at what has happened after dollarization and the stabilisation of the economy, exploring how non-farm economies have changed, and with them livelihood opportunities.

---

[167] See, for example, Bernstein, H. (2004) "Changing before our very eyes': agrarian questions and the politics of land in capitalism today', *Journal of Agrarian Change*, 4 (1 – 2): 190 – 225 and Bryceson, D. (1996) 'Deagrarianisation and rural employment in sub-Saharan Africa: a sectoral perspective', *World Development*, 24 (1): 97 - 111

CHAPTER 36
CREATING COMMUNITIES

In 2012 I examined Mabel Hungwe's PhD thesis *"In search of community in Zimbabwe's fast-track resettlement area of Mazowe district"* at Lund University in Sweden. A huge amount of fascinating empirical material is encapsulated in a series of case studies collected during 2006-07. This was of course at the peak of the collapse of the economy and in the run-up to the highly contested elections of 2008. It was not an easy time to do fieldwork – especially in Mazowe.

The stories however are incredibly revealing, both about how people coped during this tough period, but also the alliances made as different groups came to form 'communities'. Of course the term 'community' itself is highly contested, and the thesis examines different definitions and interpretations very well. But what comes over very clearly is that in the 'melting pot' that is Mazowe district many of the same processes and outcomes we observed in Masvingo were occurring. Some people were doing well, others were dropping out. Some farms were being captured by elites, but others were being well used by new farmers. Former white farmers and farm workers were still present, often seeking new arrangements. It is a complex story, but again not all doom and gloom.

Mazowe is of course different to Masvingo. It is close to Harare, and has high agroecological and market potential. There were fewer small-scale A1 farms overall, with a greater proportion of A2 farms. The contrast between farms which were invaded by people from nearby communal areas, and those which were allocated by administrative and political processes was very apparent. And with such high value farms, often with significant infrastructure, this attracted the attentions of the political-military elite – some of whom did not invest, but some, perhaps surprisingly, did, often with the (hidden) support of former white farmers.

In such a volatile and contested setting, forming 'communities' is of course challenging. Those that succeeded were those who had former ties. Being part of the invasions certainly helped. Those who arrived to new A2 farms with resident farm workers who had not been paid for months had real difficulty.

Especially in the A1 sites, the Apostolic church was seen to be really significant, binding people through religion, land access strategies, commerce and marketing.

Of course the thesis covered only a narrow time period, and it will be really interesting to see who has succeeded and who has dropped out five or more years on. Contrary to the standard narrative that the land lies abandoned in the Highveld, there is clearly much going on.

CHAPTER 37
YOUNG PEOPLE AND AGRICULTURE

The Future Agricultures Consortium's[168] annual conference in 2012 had a focus on youth and agri-food systems[169].   The big question was how is the next generation going to engage in agriculture? Will they repeat what their forefathers did and take over (part of) the family farm? Or will they abandon farming, seeing a brighter future in the city, working in industries or the civil service? Or will they engage in farming and food systems in new ways, not replicating what their parents did, but using their improved education, their technological skills and their business acumen?

There were no clear answers to these questions across the papers presented[170]. Of course, it all depends. But the debates did highlight some important issues for the Zimbabwe context.

- How does education help young people gain skills for engaging with agriculture?

- What type of technology development will allow for added value creation?

- How can agriculture maintain a labour-absorbing role in growing economies?

- Will the consolidation of farms in large scale units create more opportunities for skilled labour for young people, compared to small scale farming?

- How can young people gain access to land in settings where land is scarce and controlled by the older generation?

---

[168] http://www.future-agricultures.org/

[169] http://www.future-agricultures.org/events/young-people-farming-a-food

[170] http://www.future-agricultures.org/conference-programme

- How are gender relations changing in the next generation, and how is this affecting demand for land and engagement in agriculture.

- If agriculture does not provide gainful employment/livelihoods what are the risks of conflict?

Examples from across Africa highlighted the dangers of not addressing youth employment. The consequences can be dire, including mass violence exacerbated by ethnic and political conflict. We have seen this in Sierra Leone, where the youth joined armed gangs which helped foment a civil war. The election violence in Kenya many agree was also linked to youth dissatisfaction and land issues. Yet also the conference highlighted the opportunities unleashed by young people, with new skills and capacities, getting engaged in agriculture.

A review of policy issues from across Africa[171] shows that, while everyone is happy to talk about 'youth' as a category, there are virtually no policies directed to the relationship between agriculture and food systems. The wider social, economic and political dimensions are simply not addressed. And young people's own views, perceptions and aspirations are rarely taken into account.

What of Zimbabwe? In our Masvingo study[172], we found that younger people were critical in the land invasions of 2000. They were the people that were able to leave home, join the *'jambanja'*, set up camp at the bases, and endure the hardships that the land occupations entailed. The result was that the A1 farms had overall a younger, better educated profile than the nearby communal areas. The A1 small-scale farms contrasted too with the A2 farms which tended to have older households, as they gained land through application (and patronage) and were not involved in the invasions.

The A1 farmers demonstrate that there was certainly a demand for land among younger people living in the communal areas. Many had inherited vanishingly small plots from their parents, and were finding it difficult to make a living. Many talked of the difficulty of continuing to be reliant on parents, only having a

---

[171] te Lintelo, D. (2011). Youth and policy processes. *FAC Working Paper*, 25. Brighton: Future Agricultures Consortium

[172] Scoones, I., Marongwe, N., Mavedzenge, B., Mahenehene, J., Murimbarimba, F., and Sukume, C. (2010) *Zimbabwe's Land Reform: Myths and Realities*, Oxford: James Currey

hectare or less to farm, and the challenges of establishing a family (or even getting married). With the economy in decline, and options for jobs in town or in the mines shrinking, joining the land invasions made much sense. A new, if uncertain and risky, opportunity opened up, and they grabbed it in large numbers. And it was not just young men who joined the invasions. Younger women were also part of the invaders, eager to stake their claim to land as independent farmers. In the communal areas, the patriarchal institutions of land allocation and inheritance often only allowed them land through marriage. But those who sought greater independence, or who had separated or divorced, could seek opportunities in the new resettlements with their young families.

However, A1 farmers who established homes in 2000 may have been in their 20s, but now are in their 30s. With many 'accumulating from below' they have invested in social reproduction and accumulated assets. There is now a further generation wanting land. New land invasions in the past years have often involved younger people, eager to gain land before it is too late. Sometimes, it is reported, their parents have invaded land on their behalf, staking a claim for the next generation. With the youth absent, perhaps border jumping to South Africa or in a temporary job in town, those who are resident can take the opportunity and join a new invasion.

But there are clear limits to this process. There are fewer and fewer opportunities for further redistribution of land, and the government keeps insisting that the process of land invasion must cease (although larger scale land grabs continue). The police are sent and evictions occur. So what hope is there for the new post-land reform generation, and the generations that will follow them? Are there new opportunities as new value chains are created, and new linkages between farm enterprises are made.

In our book, we argue that in the new rural economy, there has been a radical reshaping not only of land ownership and use but economic relations. This offers many opportunities for value addition, marketing, transport and service support for the new agriculture. Also, with a new rural economic geography, there are real additionalities to be gained by the connections between A1 and A2 and the new resettlements and the old communal areas. Trade, exchange and business opportunities can open up if a territorial approach to economic development takes place [chapter 13]. This is happening at the margins, but needs greater support and impetus.

Perhaps it is in this context of a reconfigured pattern of economic growth that in the longer term 'youth' will make the greatest contribution. For, even if they do not own land, they can engage in a revitalised agricultural economy that is not controlled by large farms and enterprises and where value chains exist where new entrepreneurs with new skills can enter. To make this happen, not only must investment in economic planning and growth occur at territory level, but education and support systems for youth must be fundamentally regeared.

Here, then, is a fantastic opportunity for the reevaluation of aid efforts [chapter 45] in Zimbabwe.

CHAPTER 38
EDUCATION ON THE FARMS

In a 2012 article in the UK's Guardian newspaper[173], Alex Duval Smith reports from Goromonzi on the challenges of educating children in the new resettlement areas. She describes how in Dunstan farm the former farm house is used as a 'satellite school' for nearly 300 pupils. But while there is a building and some teachers, there is little other support. And this 12 years after land reform.

The donors, she explains, still refuse to support development in the 'contested areas'. DFID [chapter 43], despite offering a new tranche of funding to the education sector will not support the resettlement areas. And UNICEF, who has a global responsibility for children, seems unable to respond without the blessing of the donors. This story is repeated again and again across the new resettlement areas.

Indeed the conditions on Dunstan farm are rather better than other places. Here the war vets vacated the main farm house and now every room is used as a classroom or for teachers' accommodation. Even the former tennis court has been cultivated to provide maize. In Masvingo there was less building infrastructure as the farms were so huge, and many schools still operate outside under trees. In Zimbabwe, people are deeply committed to education. The new settlers often represent the generation that benefited from the post-Independence expansion of educational opportunity in the rural areas during the 1980s. They want the same for their children.

A variety of strategies are followed across our study sites. Some maintain split households, with children still resident in the communal areas where they can attend schools, often resident with grandparents or other relatives. Otherwise, often ramshackle schools are built by the community - from poles and mud, or in old farm buildings and sheds. Considerable effort has been invested in creating these new schools, demonstrating the capacities for local level investment through community-based effort on the new resettlements.

---

[173] Duval Smith, A. (2012) 'Zimbabwe's resettled farmers struggle to educate their children', *The Guardian,* 24 April

Once registered as 'satellite schools', teachers have been allocated by the Ministry. Across Masvingo province, there are 162 satellite primary schools (out of a total of 849) and 83 satellite secondary schools (out of a total of 335), with each school accomodating several hundred students. Nearly all satellite schools are in the new resettlements: the scale of neglect is very clear.

For example, in Uswaushava, an area which was invaded and settled in 2000, but only became formally recognised as part of the 'fast track' programme in late 2011, there are two schools. The satellite primary school was established in 2002 and has the authorised staff complement of 16 certified teachers with over 650 pupils attending (328 boys and 331 girls), according to Ministry of Education data from February 2010. Uswaushava satellite secondary school was established in 2004 and has 120 boys and 110 girls. Again, in 2010 a full complement of 10 teachers was in place. However the schools were built by the community and there has been no accommodation for teachers built to date. Most teachers therefore commute daily from Triangle some 20 km away.

While educational facilities exist today on the A1 resettlements (although much less on the A2 farms), the quality of the facilities is grossly inadequate. Teaching and learning under such conditions is far from ideal, and there is no equipment and resources in the absence of donor support. Many teachers remain deeply committed to teaching in the rural areas, but low pay, poor conditions and lack of support mean that others give up and leave.

Some children have experienced their whole school career under such conditions. A whole generation has missed out on effective schooling. As the donors contemplate removing 'sanctions' [chapter 44], then perhaps improving the education infrastructure on the new farms could become an important early priority.

CHAPTER 39
FIGHTING THE FLY: DRIVERS OF DISEASE IN THE ZAMBEZI VALLEY

The battle against the tsetse fly in the Zambezi valley is a long and continuing one. The fly is the source of both animal and human trypanosomiasis – *nagana* in cattle, sleeping sickness in humans – and is one of the reasons why the valley has been only sparsely inhabited until recently. But the relationship between the fly, livestock, wildlife and people appears to be changing, with new transmission dynamics unfolding, potentially with dangerous consequences.

Conquering the fly and pushing back the fly belt was seen from the colonial era as one of the great civilising efforts of colonial development. Tsetse control was seen as a prime reason for intervention: clearing vegetation, exterminating wildlife, moving people, often in draconian ways. Yet others see the fly as the saviour of wilderness, and key to conservation of remote, biodiverse landscapes, protecting such areas from encroachment by people and their animals. The fly in other words is at the centre of the classic tussle between visions of civilisation and modernity and conservation and preservation, reflecting conflicting values, perceptions, politics and interests.

The social, ecological, political and economic consequences of the tsetse fly are therefore profound, raising fundamental debates about how people and disease interact in complex ecosystems. In his classic book, *'The Role of Trypanosomiases in African Ecology: A Study of the Tsetse Fly Problem*[174]*'*, published in 1971, John Ford – a scientist centrally involved in colonial control efforts - explored some of these debates, and challenged what he described as the 'colonial doctrine' of tsetse control, based on an ecological understanding of disease dynamics. Forty years on, the dilemmas of fly control persist today, with some important new contexts.

---

[174] Ford, J. (1971) *The Role of the Trypanosomiases in African Ecology. A Study of the Tsetse Fly Problem,* Oxford: Oxford University Press.

In our study area in Hurungwe district[175], a number of cases of human sleeping sickness have been confirmed. These are unusual in Zimbabwe, although reporting is often poor, so official data is misleading. When people become sick and die, the usual diagnosis is malaria. Scientists are wondering has something occurred in the ecology of the area to increase human infections? There are other puzzles too. Dissections of tsetse flies at the government's Rukomichi research station, in the heart of the tsetse belt in the Mana Pools National Park, show very few *T. brucei rhodesiense* trypanosomes, the ones that cause the disease in humans. Yet blood samples taken from cattle outside the park, show much higher incidence. And now humans are dying too. What is going on?

A new research project is trying to investigate. Is it changes in rainfall and climate patterns affect fly distributions and behaviour? Is it changes in vegetation and land use, influencing livestock-fly interactions? Is it changing settlement patterns, with people moving into wildlife areas, and coming into contact with wildlife disease hosts and fly vectors? Is it changes in wildlife movements, as they seek water and grazing outside the park? Is it changes in human behaviour and susceptibility as new people come to the valley in search of farm land for elsewhere in the country?

Unfortunately, we simply don't know the answers to any of these questions, and so cannot suggest what disease control strategies might work. There has been, of course, masses of work on tsetse and trypanosomiasis in Zimbabwe, part of long-term research and development programmes. But much of this has been very targeted – on fly behaviour, chemical control and trap design, for example. While this has been enormously important in developing effective, low-cost control approaches, it has often not looked at the underlying ecological, social and economic drivers.

This holistic, integrated, cross-disciplinary perspective is of course not new. John Ford was a great advocate of this from the 1960s, but it is only recently that a 'One Health' approach to emerging infectious diseases has become central to policy debates. The tsetse and trypanosomiasis challenge is difficult, but one that requires dedicated cross-disciplinary science to tackle.

---

[175] http://steps-centre.org/project/drivers_of_disease/

CHAPTER 40
MIGRATION MYTHS

How many times have you heard that over three million people have fled Zimbabwe, migrating to South Africa or elsewhere? The figure varies, but it's always big. But where does it come from and is it true?

This is a question asked by Jonathan Crush and Daniel Tevera in their edited book, *Zimbabwe's Exodus: Crisis, Migration, Survival*[176] published in 2010. They trace the earliest use of the three million figure to South African media reports in 2003, and to comments made by Thabo Mbeki who claimed there were this number of Zimbabweans in South Africa. The figure has been repeated since, yet the media reports keep presenting a picture of people continuously 'flooding' across the border to South Africa. The figures just do not add up. You would think that there would be nobody left, beyond Mugabe and his cronies, if you believed everything you read!

Crush and Tevera point to the political nature of these figures. They argue that "The South African media and officialdom have a history of making up numbers about migration to the country. These numbers, often highly exaggerated for alarmist effect, acquire a life of their own once they enter the public realm. Tracking down their source usually reveals that they have no sound statistical basis". They are, in other words, myths, and ones repeated by many who should know better.

Indeed the book shows there is no way of knowing the actual facts. No-one on either side of the border keeps proper records, people move back and forward between countries in the region with a high frequency and much movement is illegal in any case. The book offers some clues, however, and usefully compiles what statistics there are, but the authors are at pains to point out the difficulties of precise numbers particularly in the context of circular migration patterns. Circular migration – to places of work and back to home – has been part of southern Africans' livelihoods for the best part of a century, as Debbie Potts

---

[176] Crush, J. and Tevera, D. (2010) *Zimbabwe's Exodus: Crisis, Migration, Survival*, Cape Town: Unity Press

points out in her book[177] focusing on Harare. Yet, as Crush and Tevera point out, this history is often forgotten in contemporary policy discussions, framing current events as new, dramatic and with movement in need of containment. It is of course a familiar story for those of us who live in 'fortress Europe'.

But have things changed as a result of the crisis in Zimbabwe? Has there been a greater movement of people and have patterns changed? The answer is of course, yes. There are some excellent new works on the Zimbabwean diaspora which tell us lots about who the diaspora are, where they come from and how they relate to 'home'. Crush and Tevera concentrate on South Africa, while Joann McGregor and Ranka Primorac[178] focus on the UK, for example, and the chapters in these books contain plenty of fascinating cases. As we show from data from Masvingo, patterns of migration have changed significantly in the last couple of decades, particularly from 1990s and the period of structural adjustment. The 'classic' movement to the farms or mines within Zimbabwe for a period followed by return to the communal areas on retirement has shifted. There are now new migrants, including youth without land or the prospect of land, the border jumpers; there are more women migrants, tapping into regional trade networks, and there is greater transnational migration, to other countries in the SADC region, but also significantly to the UK.

Each of these migrant groups (and there are of course others) link to home in different ways, sending remittances in different amounts and forms. In the 2000s, when Zimbabwe's economy was in meltdown, these flows of remittances were crucial, especially if they could get into the country in foreign exchange. Work by Sarah Bracking and Lloyd Sachikonye[179] offers some insights into these relationships, but a deeper understanding of how such external players interact with local economies is always difficult to grasp.

---

[177] Potts, D. (2010) *Circular Migration in Zimbabwe and Contemporary Sub-Saharan Africa*, Oxford: James Currey

[178] McGregor, J. and Primorac, R. (2010) *Zimbabwe's New Diaspora: Displacement and the Cultural Politics of Survival* (Vol. 31), Oxford: Berghahn Books

[179] Bracking, S. and Sachikonye, L. (2008) Remittances, poverty reduction and informalisation in Zimbabwe 2005-6: a political economy of dispossession?, *Brooks World Poverty Institute Working Paper*, 28

In a review of the Crush and Tevera book, Terry Ranger asks[180]: "Perhaps the most important question is not why so many Zimbabweans have left, but why – and how – so many have stayed". This is an intriguing question because if as Crush and Tevera point out 'a few hundred thousand' have left, then most people have remained, even if they leave for periods and return. Given the crisis at home, why? We know much about the push factors, but what about the factors that keep people at home? There are of course the natural bonds of family and home that are valued, the importance of familiarity and the support networks that exist. These are big factors especially when contrasting with the xenophobia experienced by migrants in South Africa, for example.

But there is also one hypothesis that is not explored in these works, one perhaps too difficult to contemplate. Perhaps for some, things were not so bad at home; at least not as extreme as sometimes portrayed. The Zimbabwean economic crisis hit the still relatively small middle classes much harder than others. Others gained land, and some returned from abroad to gain access during the land reform. With no jobs at home and few in South Africa or elsewhere except for the connected and skilled, farming at home was perhaps a better option in this period. Certainly remittances have, as they have always done, offset the worst of the crisis, but perhaps land reform, although precipitating some migration from those dispossessed, including farm workers and white farmers, acted to provide a cushion for others. And, for significant proportion of new farmers in Masvingo province, particularly on the A1 plots, they actually fared rather well, and would not dream of leaving, and heading off to the uncertainties and vulnerabilities of the diaspora.

---

[180] Ranger, T. (2011) Zimbabwean diamonds, *Africa: The Journal of the International African Institute*, 81(4): 649-661

CHAPTER 41
NUTRITION PUZZLES

What is going on with nutrition in Zimbabwe? Many thought that the economic crisis of the 2000s, combined with land reform, would have resulted in a major decline in nutrition levels in the last decade. This does not seem to have happened. The big question is why?

Many of the international donors clubbed together in 2010 to fund a major nutrition survey across the country, involving a massive sample of around 40,000. This complemented earlier surveys carried out on and off since Independence. Over US$1m was spent on the survey, but the results were not as some expected[181].

Rather than a dramatic jump in poor nutrition indicators, they actually went down over this period – especially indicators of underweight children (low weight for age, an indicator of both chronic and acute under-nutrition) and wasting (low weight for height, an indicator of acute under-nutrition). Levels of stunting (low height for age – an indicator of chronic under-nutrition) remained constant, but with an increase in recent years, while other indicators declined. Aggregate patterns in Zimbabwe are not out of line from the rest of the region. Indeed indicators are somewhat better than other neighbouring countries.

Perhaps Zimbabwe's food crisis was not as bad as some had feared? Perhaps food imports saved the day and avoided mass undernutrition? Perhaps production of food was higher than many had estimated? We don't know. My suspicion is that agricultural production underestimates are a big part of the story [chapter 58]. People moved from reliance on formal supplies to local self-

---

[181] See: *ZIMBABWE NUTRITION SURVEY* 2010_Draft2:Layout 3.qxd; http://www.sadc.int/ fanr/aims/rvaa/Documents/Zimbabwe/Zimbabwe%20Nutrition%20Survey %202010%20Report.pdf; http://www.unicef.org/zimbabwe/media_5965.html; http:// www.sadc.int/fanr/aims/rvaa/Documents/VAA_Dissemination/2011/SADC%20RVAA %20Dissemination%20Forum%20Proccedings%20report-%202011.pdf

provisioning to avoid any major food shortages. This included informal (illegal) imports, and local sharing, bartering and exchange outside the market.

But why is chronic under-nutrition still so prevalent if people are feeding themselves? And why has it increased while other indicators declined? This is yet another puzzle, and no-one seems to know why. Poor absorption of nutrients in the early years is a potential cause of stunting, and some argue that a condition known as 'tropical enteropathy' may be part of the explanation. In a 2009 article in the *Lancet*[182], Jean Humphrey, working in Zimbabwe, argues that a combination of poor sanitation and poor nutrition can have major effects, resulting in effects on growth, even though nutritional intake remains high. What about the distribution of undernutrition across the country? According to the survey data, underweight children were concentrated in certain districts in 2010, but there are no clear reasons why – as these include very low potential areas (e.g. Binga) and some high potential ones too. And other districts, such as in Chiredzi for example, seem to have low levels.

The major donor funded nutrition report did not get much publicity. It didn't produce the results that were expected, and so did not justify major interventions. But it does raise some important questions and profound puzzles about underlying causes.

The hidden story of nutrition in Zimbabwe – and its complex interactions with sanitation – is one that requires much more research and evidence.

---

[182] Humphrey, J.H. (2009) Child undernutrition, tropical enteropathy, toilets, and handwashing, *The Lancet*, 374(9694), 1032-1035

CHAPTER 42
ELEPHANTS AND PEOPLE

During 2011, I received an email from the Britain-Zimbabwe Society list that had the subject line: PLEASE VOTE: URGENT SUPPORT FOR ZIMBABWE ELEPHANTS NEEDED – YOUR VOTE CAN HELP THIS ENDANGERED HERD. Yes it was in capitals. I read on. There were photos of dead elephants and a passionate plea to save the herd. And where was this? In the Chiredzi River Conservancy[183], where I had been a few weeks before.

The conflict between people and wildlife, always a hot topic in Zimbabwe, is accelerating, as more and more people come onto what was previously 'white-owned' land through the land reform. Elephants, lions and people just do not mix. This is presenting many dilemmas for conservationists, national parks rangers and ministry of lands officials alike. In the 1990s large areas of former ranch land were combined in the southeast lowveld to form conservancies. Fences were pulled down and the world's largest continuous private game reserves were formed. Save Valley Conservancy alone covers 3200 square km. These offered lucrative business opportunities, and investment from within and outside Zimbabwe flowed. Hunting opportunities, high-end safari lodges and game farming flourished. The argument was that the lowveld ecology was not suited to cattle ranching, which had been hit by economic problems combined with a devastating drought in the early 1990s. Whether it was to be cattle, wildlife, both or neither was a hot debate in the 1990s, and continued post land reform[184].

Privately, game ranchers admitted that conservancies were a better protection against land reform than individual ranches. Concessions to local communities surrounding these areas were made, and various 'community outreach' schemes

---

[183] Bell, A. (2011) 'Zimbabwe: Elephants Under Threat By Land Invaders', *All Africa,* 1 September

[184] Wolmer, W., Chaumba, J. and Scoones, I. (2004) Wildlife management and land reform in Southeastern Zimbabwe: a compatible pairing or a contradiction in terms?, *Geoforum* 35.1:87-98

and CAMPFIRE concessions were brokered. These were small sops in the bigger scale of the economic ventures concerned, but for a while these seemed to offer some protection, and deals were made with key headmen, chiefs and local leaders. Even grander schemes were proposed under the aegis of the Greater Limpopo Transfrontier Conservation Area[185], where southern Mozambique, Kruger National Park in South Africa and Gonarezhou National Park and the conservancies in Zimbabwe were to be connected in one massive sweep of conservation estate. If the hype was to be believed, this was to bring great riches – for the national economy and for local communities alike, and was to revitalise the tourism economy of the country.

Certainly the lobbying of the conservation groups seemed to work, and the conservancies were seen to be outside 'fast-track' land reform. Instead of being overseen by the lands ministry, the ministry of environment was the government authority. Even the president gave his backing. But on the ground things looked different. In 2000, to great outcry in the national and international press, the conservancies were invaded. This process has continued, with many areas now being farmed, and wildlife, now seen as a pest, hunted out. This has brought outrage from many quarters. But others pose the question bluntly: should it be animals or people who have the priority? This traditional battle between elite (often white) conservation hunting interests and poor local livelihood needs has been complicated by another set of interests in these areas. Smelling a business opportunity, a series of politically well-connected 'partners' have been imposed on the existing conservancy owners, as part of a supposed 'indigenisation' programme. The reported roll call[186] of those involved lists the top echelons of the political-military elite, with a number of local leaders and well positioned chiefs offered a slice too. Add into this mix some fairly ruthless poaching syndicates who have made use of the uncertainty allegedly to create alliances between political-military figures, Asian buyers and local hunting groups. This has all added further complications to the already tense stand-off in the conservation areas of the lowveld.

The elephants who we were urged to vote for through the BZS site sit in the middle of this political tussle over resource access and control. Their watering

---

[185] http://www.peaceparks.org/tfca.php?pid=19&mid=1005

[186] 'ZANU mafia in lowveld land grab', *The Zimbabwean*, 8 September 2009

holes are now being used by cattle. Their territories are increasingly being farmed. And they are being shot and snared by local people who regard them as pests, or valuable for the illegal ivory trade. The land on which the elephants roam is contested, between the 'owners' and the new 'business partners'. And confusion between government departments and local government authorities over who has jurisdiction over what just adds to the complexity.

The lowveld is a site of ongoing contestation over resources, and particular politics [chapter 23]. Wildlife is at the centre of this, as an important economic asset at the centre of a once booming but highly elite hunting and tourism industry. The elephants, unfortunately, are stuck in the middle of this tussle for control.

SECTION F
AID AND
DEVELOPMENT

Since the land invasions of 2000, there has been a diplomatic stand-off between Zimbabwe and the West, and particularly Britain. This had been building of course, and the infamous 'Clare Short letter' of 1997 added fuel to the flames[187]. Various sanctions – or in polite parlance, 'restrictive measures' – were put in place, mostly focusing on targeted travel bans on senior ZANU-PF politicians and their associates. However the dispute had much wider ramifications on investment flows, credit ratings and overall confidence in the economy. Although the nose-diving of the Zimbabwean economy in the mid-2000s was in part of the government's own making, these wider factors did have a significant impact.

The debate about 'sanctions' became a political touchstone for much of the decade [chapter 44]. ZANU-PF claimed that this was the result of the exertion of imperial power by the west, and that Zimbabwe, as an independent, sovereign nation, should resist. The opposition argued that basic human rights must be upheld and that sanctions were thoroughly justified. However as the stalemate progressed, the political impact of sanctions, aimed at applying pressure on ZANU-PF, was beginning to have the opposite effect. Sanctions, even though formally narrow and limited, were a propaganda tool for ZANU-PF, and the MDC in particular realised this, and began to argue for a progressive softening of the hardline stance.

By 2013, relations had improved substantially, especially after the successful referendum on the new Constitution. A high-level meeting of western governments occurred in London which was attended by senior ZANU-PF

---

[187] http://politics.guardian.co.uk/foi/images/0,9069,1015120,00.html

officials, as well as their coalition partners[188]. This seemed to be the start of a new, more positive engagement, one that became feasible both through changes in Zimbabwe, but also through the more pragmatic stance of the Conservative-led coalition government in London. After the contested 2013 elections, diplomatic relations with the west took a turn for the worse, but there does seem to be a more general commitment to engagement and dialogue, especially given the SADC and AU endorsement of the ZANU-PF win.

Although there has been much to-and-fro rhetoric about sanctions, there has actually been a lot of aid to Zimbabwe. The UK has committed £88m per annum, for example [chapter 45]. This has not come through government channels, except for some targeted programmes, and has mostly been channelled through UN agencies, NGOs and others. Much of it has come under the label of 'humanitarian' aid, and focused on food relief, HIV/AIDS programmes and so on, and so has not been focused on broader development issues. These aid flows have been important, however, particularly in the period when Zimbabwe's economy was in severe crisis and support to really vulnerable people was essential. However, such *ad hoc* support, working outside government systems, is often less accountable, is implemented in inconsistent ways and is sometimes prone to donor project fashions, without building real capacity and long-term solutions.

Because of the on-going contention around the land reform, new resettlement areas were excluded from such aid programmes. Sometimes escaping donor fads[189] is a good thing, but there are real investment needs in the new resettlements. The ban on working in new resettlements has therefore meant that, in the continued absence of substantial government support, the basic infrastructure has not been built: schools and health posts are limited and basic, roads are poor and dip tanks, wells and irrigation schemes are few and far between. This lack of investment has constrained the ability of the resettlement areas to grow and prosper. 'Sanctions', then, have had an impact, and in some instances on very poor and vulnerable people, including the sick and children.

---

188 Scoones, I. (2013) '*Making friends in London: is a new rapprochement on Zimbabwe occurring?*', blog, http://zimbabweland.wordpress.com

189 Scoones, I. (2012) '*Conservation agriculture: the problem of donor fads*', blog, http://zimbabweland.wordpress.com

One of the biggest, outstanding issues that hangs over Zimbabwe is the question of the national debt [chapter 46]. This has spiralled in recent years, reaching levels that are impossible to pay back in any reasonable timeframe. How to deal with the debt is again very contentious. Some argue against going down the route of the HIPC (Highly Indebted Poor Countries) mechanism, supported by the IMF and the World Bank, because of fears of extreme conditionalities. Others meanwhile argue that a debt audit is required to hold those responsible for accumulating it accountable. Tentative moves have been made towards a HIPC solution, but this may be upset by the outcome of the 2013 elections, and once again strained diplomatic relations.

Some resolution of the debt arrangements could also be a route to dealing with compensation for land acquisition [chapter 47]. Estimates vary hugely as to what compensation is due, even under the more limited provisions of the Constitution, focusing only on 'land improvements'. Sensible estimates seem to be in the order of US$2bn. This is way beyond the government's means, although payments continue to be made from a limited allocated budget. A full resolution of the compensation issue however is essential for the long-term settling of the land reform debate. Although on-going legal disputes will inevitable occur [chapter 29], a broad resolution will provide much needed stability. Rolling in the compensation requirements as part of the wider national debt makes much sense and, although there are technical complications, this may be a real option for land acquired for A1 farms, while making sure that compensation funds are raised from A2 farmers from leases, land taxation and other mechanisms [chapter 47].

The aid and investment environment is however changing, with western donors, development banks, companies and governments no longer being the only show in town. In the period of diplomatic fallout, Zimbabwe turned to its friends elsewhere, developing a 'Look East' policy [chapter 48]. China of course was the main player, and it has become involved in virtually every sector, from mining to agriculture, but also the security sector, transport and so on. Long-term relations, based on liberation war solidarities, provided a firm base for discussions, but the Chinese were also interested in access to Zimbabwe's resources, and Chinese companies have made a tidy profit from exporting tobacco produced from Zimbabwe's new resettlement farms [chapter 48], as well as of course a variety of minerals given their increasing stakes in key mines.

China, India, Brazil and of course South Africa are all investors, some with 'development cooperation' programmes, and none has the same diplomatic disputes with Zimbabwe.

The result is a new form of 'development encounter'[190] based on new rules. While some believe Zimbabwe is selling itself cheap, the result is some investment and support in the absence of sources elsewhere. This provides an important bargaining counter with the west, as western powers are keen not to lose their foothold in Zimbabwe to the Chinese or others.

---

[190] Scoones, I., Cabral, L. and Tugendhat, H. (eds.) (2013) New Development Encounters: China and Brazil in African Agriculture. *IDS Bulletin*, 44(4).

CHAPTER 43

AID TO ZIMBABWE: TIME FOR A RETHINK

In a 2012 article in the Guardian[191], Alex Duval Smith argues that aid to Zimbabwe must support resettled farmers on so-called 'contested areas'. These are the 8m or more hectares taken over as part of the 'fast-track' land reform programme from 2000. Around 180,000 households, about a million people live in these areas, yet aid – development and humanitarian – is not offering support despite the clear needs and challenges.

Many argue that the UK government and others should boycott such areas, as they are under dispute – sometimes with legal cases in Europe and elsewhere. The Zimbabwe Vigil[192] group, based in the UK, is vehement that sanctions should be retained. The EU argues[193] that the 'targeted measures' (notionally focused on individuals, but actually much broader in effect) should be sustained. But it has been years since the land invasions and the challenges are very real – whether in the area of agricultural production, social services, health and education.

I offered a brief contribution in response to the (yet again) rather ill-informed comments being made on the Guardian's website:

"Alex Duval Smith is absolutely correct to argue that Zimbabwe is missing out on the benefits of land reform by failing to invest in the 'fast track' resettlement areas. For sure some areas are not being fully utilised, but our decade-long research study in Masvingo province showed[194] how, particularly in the A1

---

[191] Duval Smith, A. (2012) 'Aid to Zimbabwe must take account of resettled farmers on contested land', *The Guardian,* 4 September

[192] http://www.zimvigil.co.uk/the-vigil-diary/396-uk-paper-urges-aid-to-mugabe--zimbabwe-vigil-diary-5th-may-2012

[193] 'EU won't lift sanctions on Mugabe until free and fair elections in Zimbabwe', *Voice of America,* 11 May 2012

[194] http://www.zimbabweland.net/Home.html

schemes, most new farmers are producing, selling, investing and accumulating. Most new farmers in these areas are not 'cronies', linked to the ZANU-PF elite, but ordinary farmers formerly from nearby communal areas or towns.

But equally, as Alex Duval Smith correctly points out, such farmers cannot do everything by themselves. They need support – from government, as well as donors. Their predecessors, the white farmers who occupied the land from the colonial period, received massive support over many decades, and new farmers need this too if the restructured agrarian economy is to thrive. Investment in schools, roads, irrigation, extension services, markets and so on are all essential.

Of course the situation across the country varies enormously, as the array of studies now available[195] shows, and thus it will be necessary to tailor support accordingly. But 12 years since the land reform, it must be time to reconsider the aid boycotts and 'sanctions'. These provide political succour to elements of ZANU-PF, and all sides concur they do more harm than good.

Everyone agrees that land reform in Zimbabwe was necessary and, although the manner in which it happened resulted in unnecessary violence, disruption and loss, today Zimbabwe, and its development partners, must look to the future, accepting the need for some compensation for those who lost out, but also supporting the new farmers. A more informed debate about Zimbabwe's land reform is urgently needed, and this article is an important and timely contribution."

A rethink of 'sanctions' [chapter 44] is clearly needed. Unfortunately the UK continues to sit on the fence. According to reports in 2012[196], the UK High Commissioner, Deborah Bronnert indicated that the UK government had no intention of changing their tune on land reform. "At some point I think we are likely to...support a future settlement but I think we are a long way from it and it will require quite a big political shift and a political settlement here for that to be taken forward," she said. Farm families on the new resettlements may have a long wait for education and other services [chapter 38].

---

[195] Scoones, I. (2012) *JPS Special issue on land reform outcomes – just released*, blog, zimbabweland.wordpress.com

[196] 'UK won't fund land reform now', http://www.theindependent.co.zw/

CHAPTER 44
SANCTIONS STAND OFF

The issue of 'sanctions' (or 'restrictive measures'[197] if you prefer) has become a political football in Zimbabwe's painful political transition. The US and Europe insist they are essential, but regard them as only limited and targeted. Meanwhile, ZANU-PF argues that they are undermining recovery and preventing unity. And various opposition groups, although not the MDC formations, argue that they are an important lever in negotiations around the constitution, addressing human rights abuses and so on.

The problem is that when discussing 'sanctions', different people talk about different things. For sure there are highly restrictive measures applied to particular people, including many close associates of the President. These prevent travel, financial transactions and more. But actually the effect of the diplomatic stand-off, now over a decade old, is much wider, with diverse knock-on effects. It affects the way aid funds are spent [chapter 45], with the channelling of funds away from government and through NGOs. It influences the ability of Zimbabwe to gain credit lines internationally, pushing the government and the private sector towards Chinese sources, for example. It undermines the relationships with the international financial institutions (the IMF and the World Bank), and so the ability to secure loans and seek debt relief [chapter 46]. And of course with diplomatic relations strained, normal interactions on the international stage are affected. While perhaps not formal sanctions, the effects are the same – and these are shaping Zimbabwe's economy and politics not just now, but perhaps for the long-term.

This may be the desired effect. Isolation, and the creation of a pariah state, reinforced by a narrative about the evil of Robert Mugabe, may be the diplomatic aim of US and European foreign policy. But does this really make sense? Many think not. Certainly SADC has long argued for the removal of sanctions. The MDC

---

[197]http://eeas.europa.eu/delegations/zimbabwe/eu_zimbabwe/political_relations/restrictive_measures/index_en.htm

also regularly make this plea. Alois Mlambo and Brian Raftopoulos[198] argue: "The future of the democratic forces in Zimbabwe depends, in important ways, on its capacity to lead an economic recovery programme that will strengthen the country's social base. The assumption that a deepening crisis and continued sanctions will be advantageous to the opposition is a dangerous fallacy". In other words, sanctions can act to undermine democracy, strengthening the hand of the nationalist hawks, while undermining any alliance of democratic forces in the MDC and beyond (including in ZANU-PF). Economic recovery – and with this must be the restructuring and revitalisation of agriculture following land reform – goes hand in hand with the growth of democracy.

This is a view reinforced by an insightful briefing by the International Crisis Group, 'Zimbabwe's Sanctions Standoff[199]'. Reviewing the fragile political situation in the lead up to the 2013 elections, the briefing argued that: "ZANU-PF manipulates the issue politically and propagandises it as part of its efforts to frustrate reform and mobilise against perceived internal and external threats to national sovereignty". Evidence, the briefing says, indicates that: "the existence of sanctions has strengthened ZANU-PF hardliners against more reformist elements and the MDC-T and provided an ostensible justification to block reforms".

The problem is that removing sanctions, even flexibly and incrementally, is seen as a sign of capitulation and victory of the hardliners. Not only has the issue become a contest between different political groupings within Zimbabwe, it has also been a contest between Harare based diplomats and their superiors in Washington, London or Brussels. Sanctions, as the ICG briefing suggests, has become a diversion, and the underlying political challenges that need to be addressed – most notably accountability of the security services – are not on the table. The international community has failed in the past to seize the opportunity to exert influence, preferring to maintain a simple, politically pure hardline stance, but this positioning has not helped. Indeed, according to many analysts, it has made things worse.

---

[198] Mlambo, A. and Raftopoulos, B. (2010) Zimbabwe's multilayered crisis, *CMI Brief*, 9(3)

[199] International Crisis Group (2012) Zimbabwe's sanctions standoff, *Crisis Group Africa Briefing*, 86

CHAPTER 45

THE UK AID PROGRAMME IN ZIMBABWE

The UK's Department for International Development (DFID)[200] is one of the largest aid donors in Zimbabwe. It plans to spend £88m per year[201] in the period to 2015 – and more if a political transition acceptable to the British government happens. The 'value for money' rationale, the Operational Plan for 2011-15[202] states:

> "Political conditions permitting, there is a compelling argument for making development investments now, in order to repair the damage resulting from many years of under or mis-investment in Zimbabwe. Rather than making investments later to build again from scratch investing now has the potential to deliver significant VfM [value for money]. The relatively high levels of human capital, the latent – albeit dilapidated – quality of the infrastructure stock, the abundant natural resource base and the geographical position in a stable region, all suggest strong potential for significant and rapid developmental bounce-back if the political and economic transition in Zimbabwe is managed successfully".

Much of the plan is centred on the need for a 'political transition'. It is clear that for DFID the Government of National Unity (GNU) was unacceptable as an aid recipient. Whether the ZANU-PF government that came into power in mid-2013 will be remains an open question[203]. The UK government-imposed restrictions on aid delivery therefore mean that most support must be directed outside government. The plan states:

---

[200] https://www.gov.uk/government/world/zimbabwe

[201] DFID (2012) *Summary of DFID's work in Zimbabwe 2011-2015*, London: DFID

[202] DFID (2012) *Operational Plan 2011- 2015*, Harare: DFID Zimbabwe

[203] http://africanarguments.org/2013/10/24/on-zimbabwe-britain-must-avoid-the-misplaced-patronising-stance-of-the-past-by-ian-scoones/

"The political context for our work in Zimbabwe restricts our current choice of aid instruments. At the moment all DFID resources are channelled through third parties: multilateral organisations, the private sector and Non-Governmental Organisations. We anticipate that following a successful political transition our choice of aid instruments would widen. We are investing now in activities which prepare the ground for the day when we can consider alternative delivery options, such as improving public financial management systems. We could then consider channelling money through Government systems and once the conditions were right, to provide budget support either generally or by sector".

This reliance on the UN and NGOs for delivery means that sometimes aid quality is poor. The example of the DFID support to 'conservation agriculture' as part of (conditions of) input programmes was highlighted [chapter 8]. In addition, aid flows are not supposed to flow to the new resettlement areas. Most NGOs boycott these areas too. This means that 'investing now in activities that prepare the ground' for future support does not happen, and support to agriculture remains part of what is essentially a relief effort (formerly the 'Protracted Relief Programme' – see DFID project overview[204] and details of recipients of the £49m of the second phase), narrowly focused on the communal areas.

The result of this aid focus is that donors, including the British who have a key role because of the size of the aid programme and the history of engagement with Zimbabwe, have often very little clue of what is happening on the ground. This is improving, but I have been shocked at donor meetings with some of the (mis)perceptions which are repeated – especially about the emotive subject of land reform. I am not sure what they get in the foreign office briefings, but a combination of the international press and the cocktail party circuit in Harare can lead to a very distorting perspective indeed.

Zimbabwe of course comes into the 'high risk', 'conflict', 'failed-state' category of the UK aid programme, and all that comes with that. Sometimes it gets bundled up with Afghanistan, Iraq or Pakistan. A 2011 DFID/FCO/MOD strategy, Building Stability Overseas[205], noted: "in a range of states, from Somalia to Zimbabwe and

---

[204] http://projects.dfid.gov.uk/project.aspx?Project=113871

[205] DFID (2011) *Building Stability Overseas Strategy*. London: DFID, FCO, MoD

Burma, weak and bad governance is entrenched". Rather different contexts I would suggest. On lists of conflict countries[206] Zimbabwe is always there – sometimes near the top – and according to criteria that often remain opaque. The World Bank offers a listing[207], for example, with a range of scorings.

The UK's bilateral aid review[208], announced by Secretary of State Andrew Mitchell in March 2011, encouraged a focus on such countries, as part of a wider security-governance and conflict prevention[209] agenda. This has its merits, but I wonder if this is the right perspective. Zimbabwe's problems are rather different to other conflict areas, and while engaging with the current government has problems, DFID has bilateral aid programmes with many worse [chapter 20].

Donors have missed many opportunities to influence the direction of Zimbabwe's development – in 1998 when a land deal might have been brokered or in 2009 at the beginning of the GNU, for example. Another opportunity exists following the 2013 elections. Thirteen years after the land reform, DFID should now be able to engage in a pragmatic and progressive way, without being burdened by the ideological overtones of 'sanctions' (or restrictive aid measures) [chapter 44] or the categorisation of 'failed' or 'conflict-affected' state, and all the often inappropriate baggage that comes with this.

---

[206] http://web.worldbank.org/WBSITE/EXTERNAL/PROJECTS/STRATEGIES/EXTLICUS/ 0,,menuPK:511784~pagePK:64171540~piPK:64171528~theSitePK:511778,00.html

[207] http://siteresources.worldbank.org/EXTLICUS/Resources/5117771269623894864/ Fragile_Situations_List_FY11_(Oct_19_2010).pdf

[208] https://www.gov.uk/government/news/the-future-of-uk-aid

[209] 'Building Stability Overseas Strategy', July 2011. London: DFID, FCO, Ministry of Defence.

CHAPTER 46
DEALING WITH THE NATIONAL DEBT

Zimbabwe has a massive national debt. In 2011 it was estimated to be US$7bn[210]; it has grown since. If Zimbabwe is to gain the necessary support from international finance institutions, commercial lenders and others, it has to deal with it. Of course some debt is perfectly acceptable, but it has to be serviced, and with debt exceeding GDP this is difficult, as debt servicing takes up too much government revenue. And of course when debt is not serviced, then confidence in the economy plummets and investment does not flow. It's a catch-22: ask the Greeks, Irish or Portuguese – and even the British and Americans. Dealing with the national debt is therefore crucial to national recovery.

With the catastrophic economic collapse through much of the 2000s, exacerbated by appalling fiscal discipline and accelerating hyperinflation to early 2009, the economy was in a real mess. So all credit to Tendai Biti in his role as finance minister until 2013 for getting things back on course. The change in currency (abandoning the Zim dollar) was critical, but so have been other measures. In 2011-12 growth was estimated to be 9%[211], and investment was flowing back into the country.

So what should be done about the debt? This is a crucial element of longer term recovery, and will allow government financing of key areas. There are two views as to what to do about the national debt. A Jubilee Debt Campaign report[212] reviews these options, and lays out the pros and cons. One option argues that a local solution should be found, whereby mineral revenues (which are large and growing) should be channelled towards debt write-off and external financing should come with no (or few) strings attached. When Zimbabwe's economy was at its low point, China continued to provide (tied) finance – for the fertiliser and tractor programmes of the Reserve Bank, for example. China's banking and loan

---

[210] 'Mutambara says Zim 'over-borrowed', *New Zimbabwe,* 2 July 2011

[211] 'Zimbabwe: economic growth prospects bright', *AllAfrica,* 29 December 2011

[212] Jones, T. (2011) *Uncovering Zimbabwe's Debt. The Case for a Democratic Solution to the Unjust Debt Burden,* London: Jubilee Debt Campaign

finance arms[213] are now widespread across Africa, and very active in Zimbabwe. But is this enough, and will the minerals tax take flow as smoothly as suggested towards debt repayments?

Another view is to go for an international debt write-off under the HIPC (Heavily Indebted Poor Countries)[214] mechanism. Under an international deal, the land compensation issue could be incorporated and calculated as part of the HIPC deal [chapter 47]. However, this would require adopting International Finance Institution conditions, and undertaking a poverty assessment to show that reform could be directed to poverty reduction. This is a route a number of African countries have gone down, including some now doing rather well, including Zimbabwe's neighbour, Zambia.

Some argue though that the HIPC route would be disastrous. Those making this case – as ever in Zimbabwe is a strange combination – include hardline ZANU-PF politicians who argue that this would undermine national sovereignty and debt relief campaigners who are worried about the conditionalities that would be attached. Should Zimbabwe suffer another ESAP period, just as things are looking better?, they ask. The Jubilee Debt Campaign report[215] argues:

> "*The Zimbabwean story highlights many dangers of basing economic development on the use of foreign loans. We support calls for poverty and inequality to be reduced primarily through mobilizing domestic resources and reducing the outflow of resources through illicit flows, tax avoidance and multinational company profits, as well as debt repayments.*"

The report argues against an immediate debt relief solution. Instead they argue that a first step must be a full debt audit to see who paid for what in past debt. While it is important that both the processes of taking on debt and writing it off should be clear, transparent and accountable, it is not that clear to me at least what the benefits of uncovering the rights and wrongs of all loans since 1980 would be.

_____

[213] http://english.eximbank.gov.cn/

[214] http://www.imf.org/external/np/exr/facts/hipc.htm

[215] Jones, T. (2011) *Uncovering Zimbabwe's Debt. The Case for a Democratic Solution to the Unjust Debt Burden*, London: Jubilee Debt Campaign

In the report a number of different past loans are highlighted. For example, the World Bank financing of the Forestry Commission in the 1980s is offered as a case of a 'bad' loan. The returns were not significant and the money was wasted it was suggested. Having been involved in forestry debates in this period, there is plenty to critique, but I am not sure that a World Bank loan was irresponsible, as the Commission was trying to regear itself to serve the whole country and had to concern itself with fuelwood and trees in the communal areas. Another example is the sale of land rovers to the Zimbabwean army. But again remember in the 1980s, the UK provided much support to the creation of a professional army following the war. All of these ended up with the racking up of debt.

But these were perhaps not the main economic misdemeanours that have led to the current crisis. This had its origins in the structural adjustment programme, and then a series of politically driven decisions which led to reckless fiscal indiscipline (from the war veteran payouts to Gideon Gono's frenetic printing of money), and a massive growth in corruption, linked in particular to mineral revenues.

While arguing for transparency and accountability in future financial dealings makes much sense, a long drawn out audit of the past probably doesn't, particularly if it delays yet further resolving the debt issue through a negotiated HIPC route (a solution which, while problematic on some counts, is definitely not all bad in my view). And there is no time to lose. The lack of finance in the Zimbabwe economy over the past decade has limited recovery and created poverty. As argued elsewhere, a lack of economic recovery also stymies democratic renewal. Addressing the debt issue must be a priority therefore. And, if linked to dealing with the resolution of the thorny compensation issue [chapter 47], then an array of tenure, finance and security issues can be dealt with in the agriculture sector, releasing the full growth opportunities of the land reform.

CHAPTER 47
COMPENSATION FOR LAND

In an important piece in the on-going Sokwanele debate on land entitled "The significance of land compensation for rehabilitation of Zimbabwe's land sector"[216], Professor Mandi Rukuni, former chair of the Zimbabwe Land Tenure Commission and professor of agricultural economics at UZ, offers his thoughts on the compensation issue. As ever it is a measured, pragmatic stance and one with much merit. He makes a number of key points and maps out a way forward. It is worth summarizing the highlights.

He points out that existing legislation (from 2000) allows for compensation for 'improvements' only. This has been confirmed in the Constitution, suggesting at least that the MDC agrees with this formula, although the Constitution allows for full compensation including for land for those farms governed by investment treaties. Around 125 farmers settled on this basis in the early 2000s before hyperinflation kicked in. Now others are contemplating this, among the former owners of the 1250 farms that have been surveyed and valued. Thus since the Fast Track programme, 210 farmers have been compensated for improvements. Compensation values which have been paid out vary from about US$200,000 to US$1.2 million, according to Rukuni.

But what would the total cost be? In order for the agricultural economy to move forward and for investment to flow, with confidence once again being restored, dealing with the compensation issue is a priority. Under the existing law, compensation and so 'quittance' must precede the issuing of any new lease. Without compensation then, especially for the larger A2 farms, lease arrangements are impossible, resulting in continued insecurity for existing farmers.

According to government, the total settlement bill on this basis would be US $1.5-2 billion. However, the Commercial Farmers' Union disputes the legislation, arguing that compensation values should include land, improvements, interest

---

[216] 'The significance of land compensation for rehabilitation of Zimbabwe's land sector', *Sokwanele*, 2 July 2012

and consequential damage. They estimate the total would come to between US $6 and US$10 billion. Clearly there is a big gap between the estimates. What then is a pragmatic solution? The fact that the government is serious about compensation is clear from the budget allocations up to 2014, over which period some US$30 million has been earmarked for compensation. This is clearly not enough, and other support, including from the international community, will be required to resolve this. So, what else needs to be done?

Rukuni identifies two things for immediate action. First, valuations must be speeded up. Currently over 5000 properties still need to be properly valued, and if valuations are disputed, they must be dealt with in the Administrative Court. Second, a Land Acquisition Compensation Fund needs to be set up to allow swift and complete payment of all compensation. The fund would be made up of contributions from the national budget, contributions from international donors and development banks, and from transfer fees and ground rents from A2 farmers once leases were issued. One suggestion is that A2 farmers pay 30% of the cost up-front into a fund, and the rest is paid off over time as part of land taxation.

Above all, Rukuni argues for a pragmatic and flexible process. While there are some who will stick out for a full settlement and will continue to pursue this in any court that will hear them, there are many others – perhaps the majority – who want an end to the uncertainty. For many the economic collapse, as well as the loss of their farm assets, has resulted in severe hardships, very often in a vulnerable period of retirement, given the age profile of most former white farmers.

Rukuni comments, showing his frustration with all sides: "...frankly the country needs a more proactive leadership from both government and organized farmers on this matter. It is better for government and farmers to face donors with a negotiated position than the current huge gulf in positions". In other words, he suggests, until there is a sense of joint movement on this donors, whose budgets are being squeezed in any case, are unlikely to touch the politically charged prospect of compensating a few thousand white former farmers, prioritizing them above other perhaps more pressing humanitarian and development needs.

Yet for the country to move forward some compensation deal, at least for the majority, is essential. This must emerge from a national consensus, driven jointly by former farmers and the government. This must represent a reasonable, not a maximum, claim, more likely in the ballpark of the government's estimate. As argued in the previous chapter, rather than expecting the constrained national budget and aid budgets to bankroll this, any compensation settlement must be wrapped up in a deal around national debt. Yet sadly on this too, there remains little consensus. So, while the administrative and legal mechanisms for resolution exist, the political commitment from key players must be there too.

CHAPTER 48

CHINA AND BRAZIL IN ZIMBABWE

There is much talk – and even more hype – about the role of the emerging economies – the BRICS countries – in development. Aid programmes[217] have been established by China, Brazil, Russia and South Africa, and others are following suit. In the G20 and in the Busan[218] meeting, a whole new modality for aid giving was hailed. A new way of doing development cooperation is in the offing, and the hegemony of the western powers will be offset, some argued.

Well maybe, but not yet. As Jonathan Glennie pointed out[219], the Gates Foundation, run by a few very rich US citizens, provides more aid than China. But it is of course not the volume of aid that matters, but what it does – and in particular how it is linked to other forms of investment. This is where aid – seen by some (mistakenly) as a pure form of giving – gets messy. Aid is always tied in some way, despite the disclaimers from the likes of the British government. It is always linked to trade interests, investment opportunities, security and foreign policy agendas. Of course it is. And if this is what the US or UK does, why not China and the rest?

China is of course fairly explicit about this. They have a keen interest in Africa's mineral resources to fuel their massively growing demand for primary resources. They will exchange access for aid, but it is often fairly transparent what the deal is. Brazil is of course different, but there are many who see Africa as a source for expansion of *Cerrado*-style agriculture and a source of investment for sugar, soy and other enterprises on other land frontiers away from the Brazilian Amazon.

But it is not all such brutal self-interest. Such relations are more complex and nuanced, and have to be understood in the context of history, as Deborah

---

[217] Rao, S. (2012) 'BRICS: Future Aid Superpowers' *Global Investing, Reuters*, 26 March

[218] Rogerson, A. (2011) *Key Busan challenges and contributions to the emerging development effectiveness agenda*, Background Note, London: Overseas Development Institute

[219] Glennie, J. (2012) 'Aid from BRICS countries is making a bigger splash' *Poverty Matters Blog, The Guardian*, 26 March

Brautigam[220] argues effectively for China's relationship with Africa. Both China and Brazil have an important sense of solidarity with Africa. This relates in China's case to long-standing support for liberation movements. This may translate into some fairly dodgy political affiliations in the contemporary world, but it comes from a genuine commitment to assist. Brazil of course dwells on the historic links with Africa via the slave trade, and the solidarity that emerges from the African connection. It also sees itself as linked geographically – part of the southern hemisphere, and a different zone of influence.

And of course both China and Brazil are proud of their achievements in reducing poverty and improving agriculture. And rightly so. China has seen the most dramatic decreases in poverty in human history, and they are keen to show others how to do it too. They have had big achievements in agriculture too, with real opportunities for sharing, as Li Xiaoyun and colleagues[221] explain in their book. Brazil is a world leader in agricultural technologies, and through its agency Embrapa, and wants others to benefit, so have begun to establish offices in Africa, with the first opened in Accra, Ghana[222]. Brazil has also created novel social welfare programmes (the *Bolsa Familia* being the most famous) that have lifted many out of poverty, creating employment and growth.

With many donors shunning Zimbabwe over the past decade, China and Brazil have been knocking at the door. Much Chinese support has been in the minerals sector, although they have interest in the financing of the tobacco sector, and some interest in cotton. Chinese finance has been critical in the rebirth of the tobacco industry following land reform, and has created a rebound no-one was expecting, with now small-scale farmers leading the way where once only large white-owned tobacco estates dominated. In 2011, a major loan was offered[223] by China, with US$342 earmarked for agricultural machinery. They have also built

---

[220] Brautigam, D. (2013) *'China, the US and Africa: how many embassies?'*, blog, http://www.chinaafricarealstory.com

[221] Xiaoyun, L., Gubo, Q., Lixia, T., Leshan, J., Zhanfeng, G. and Jin, W. (2012) *Agricultural Development in China and Africa: A Comparative Analysis,* Oxon: Routledge

[222] http://www.embrapa.br/a_embrapa/labex/africa/Escritorio_Africa#

[223] 'China's $700 - million loan aims to revive Zimbabwean economy' *China Daily,* 23 March 2011

an Agricultural Technology Demonstration Centre[224] at Gwebi College, opened by Vice President Mujuru. But, contrary to some NGO reports, they have not been involved in extensive 'land grabs'[225]. Meanwhile, Brazil has started an extensive exchange programme with agriculturalists in the ministry, with extension officials, researchers and policymakers travelling to Brazil to marvel at the achievements of Brazilian agriculture. Under their 'family farm' programme, support for mechanised agriculture involves the provision of tractors, and the support for mechanisation of smallholder agriculture, and a US$300m loan[226] was offered in 2011.

The Future Agricultures Consortium has started some research, funded by the UK's Economic and Social Research Council (ESRC) looking at the changing relationship between China and Brazil and Africa[227] in the context of new 'development cooperation' relationships in Africa. This work will include studies in Mozambique, Ethiopia, Ghana and Zimbabwe, and will focus on the details of the relationships emerging between African and Brazilian/Chinese players.

Clearly a diversification of support and a sharing of ideas make much sense. African countries have for too long been reliant on a narrow set of expertise channelled through aid and technical cooperation programmes from Europe and the US, or via the 'international' programmes of the CGIAR or the Gates Foundation, which replicate such perspectives. But with new players on the scene, does this now mean that African perspectives, local knowledge and located experimentation will have more chance of breaking through?

I wonder. The top-down, expert led stances of past development interventions – from colonialism to the western aid era – are being replicated. Aid is about power, and sadly in Africa this remains skewed to the outsider, wherever they come from.

---

[224] 'Adequately fund irrigation, fiscal authorities told', *The Herald Online*. 6 April 2012

[225] Brautigam, D. (2012) *"Zombie" Chinese land grabs in Africa rise again in new database!* blog, http://www.chinaafricarealstory.com

[226] 'Zimbabwe secures $300 mln Brazil farm loan: paper', *Reuters*, 27 October 2011

[227] http://www.future-agricultures.org/research/cbaa

SECTION G
COMPARATIVE
LESSONS

What are the lessons from Zimbabwe's land reform for elsewhere, especially other former settler economies in the region? And what lessons can Zimbabwe learn from countries that have undergone major transitions, influenced by land reform? Such comparative perspectives are useful, as long as the local specificities and contexts are borne in mind.

The Zimbabwe story has been a source of intrigue and not a little dread in neighbouring South Africa in particular. Commentators are asking 'is South Africa now like Zimbabwe in 1999', on the brink of a major upheaval provoked by a failure to deal with the legacies of colonialism and apartheid?[228]. The uproar in the South African press following Max du Preez's commentary on land reform [chapter 13] is indicative of a fear among white South Africans in particular of the Zimbabwe path.

The review of our book in South Africa's *Mail and Guardian* by Percy Zvomuya sparked another discussion [chapter 49]. He argues that South Africa needs to take the Zimbabwe experience seriously and think about land reform. One hundred years after the Natives Land Act was passed in South Africa, little has been done to transform the lives of the marginalised and dispossessed [229], a theme picked up in the important collection on agrarian change in South Africa reviewed in chapter 50. The challenges of the broader transformation of a

---

[228] Hartley, R. and Mills, G. (2013) Zimbabwe's election is also about our own political path. *Business Day Live*, 2 August

[229] Scoones, I. (2013) '*The people's declaration: land in South Africa*', blog, http://zimbabweland.wordpress.com

monopoly capitalist settler economy like Zimbabwe are tackled in Sam Moyo's book, *Beyond White Settler Capitalism*[230], offering important lessons for the region. Yet land reform in South Africa, as in Zimbabwe, can have positive effects, as the econometric analysis reviewed in chapter 51 shows. As Michael Aliber and colleagues[231] showed in Limpopo province of South Africa, it was the informal arrangements not the planned settlements that did best. If farmers are left to their own devices they seem to do better than if 'assisted' by the consultants, planners and advisers. This was an important lesson from Zimbabwe, and one that South Africa's land reform approach – and that of Namibia and elsewhere – could usefully take notice of.

What of lessons from elsewhere? The history of successful agricultural and economic development in many parts of the world has started with a redistributive land reform. Japan, Taiwan and Korea are the well known examples, but there are others too[232]. In chapter 52 I look at Thailand, but focus less on the usual questions of technology and economics, but on politics. For, as Andrew Walker argues, it was the creation of a vocal, and increasingly rich and independent, class of 'political peasants' that was crucial in Thailand's agrarian transformation. They were able to command support from the state in return for political loyalty, and the result has been an extraordinary change in fortunes over 40 years. The question for Zimbabwe is: what deals with the state will be struck by alliances of new settlers [cf. chapter 19]?

Africa, and Zimbabwe in particular [chapter 48], is looking outside the traditional western donors and investors for inspiration and support. Some regard the role of the BRICS in Africa simply as a return to imperial exploitation, but under a new guise. Others see new relationships being forged on a potentially more equal footing, with the potential for more firm negotiation around development options [chapter 53]. Certainly arguments for state-led, guided capitalist

---

[230] Scoones, I. (2013) *'Beyond White Settler Capitalism: Zimbabwe's Agrarian Reform'*, blog http://zimbabweland.wordpress.com

[231] Aliber, M., T. Maluleke, T. Manenzhe, G.Paradza, B. Cousins (2013) *Land reform and livelihoods. Trajectories of change in northern Limpopo Province, South Africa*. South Africa: HSRC Press

[232] Chang, H. J. (2009) Rethinking public policy in agriculture: lessons from history, distant and recent, *Journal of Peasant Studies*, 36(3): 477-515

development have much appeal, especially in Africa given the disastrous experience with liberalisation and structural economic reform imposed by the international financial institutions of the west. New models and ideas are now available, along with new forms of technical expertise, types of technology and sources of investment.

The final chapter in this section looks at the experiences of white farmers who left Zimbabwe following the land reform and tried to set up elsewhere. The exodus included moves to Zambia, Mozambique and as far afield as Nigeria [chapter 54]. There has been mixed success, and there are important lessons to be learned. While those who moved had undoubted skills and capacities, they often didn't make it, despite their former success in Zimbabwe. Why was this?

A key part of the answer is the role of state support and the wider policy environment. This was very favourable to large-scale commercial farming in Zimbabwe from the pre-independence period to the late 1990s. There had been a massive investment in basic infrastructure and subsidies continued at high levels for many years. Such farmers profited from the trade and export agreements negotiated after Independence, and the aid programmes that came with them (such as veterinary disease control).

In Nigeria, while they were welcomed with open arms and given significant start-up support, the social and political conditions were not as conducive, and with political change they were left out on a limb. Much the same happened in Mozambique, although in Zambia they have fared better, as they integrated into a more stable system with support both from other farmers and the state. In other words, the conditions for farming are crucial, and state support is vital. Successful farming, particularly on a commercial scale, is more than the image often portrayed of individual endeavour and hard work under difficult conditions. Although of course this is essential too, the state must also play an important role – a lesson also drawn from looking to the 'developmental states' of East Asia, as well as Brazil.

CHAPTER 49

ZIMBABWE'S LAND MYTHS EXPOSED - IMPLICATIONS FOR SOUTH AFRICA?

During 2012, Percy Zvomuya of South Africa's leading newspaper, the *Mail and Guardian*, published a review of our book[233] (the full text is below). He offers a very positive review and argues that every bureaucrat in the region should read it!

But not everyone wants to hear the story we tell. There were, as usual, a series of weird and wonderful comments on the webpage and on twitter. The comments – rather like the 169 added to the UK Guardian article[234] we wrote in 2010 – show how important it is to engage in this debate with some solid evidence and based on fieldwork, not ideologically charged hysteria. Some don't like engaging, but hopefully more will read the book and reflect on the facts as a result of this review (for other reviews, see http://www.zimbabweland.net/Reviews.html).

So who is reading the book? Probably not many of those who take time to comment on newspaper websites, but there are others. Miles Tendi[235] reflected on the readership among the political elite in Zimbabwe a while back. But exposure in the M and G helps spread interest in South Africa. Apparently at the World Bank land conference at the end of April in Washington DC, just after the review was published, the deputy minister of rural development and land reform of South Africa, Mr Lechesa Tsenoli, urged people to read the book. Perhaps, as Percy Zvomuya suggests, he will get his bureaucrats to read it too!

Of course, as we discuss in the book, South Africa is very different. But there are important resonances and implications of the Zimbabwe experience over the past decade. As Zvomuya's review says:

---

233 Zvomuya, P. (2012) 'Zimbabwe's land myths exposed', *Mail & Guardian*, 20 April

234 Scoones, I. and Mavedzenge, B. (2010) 'Don't condemn Zimbabwe', *The Guardian*, 8 November

235 Scoones, I. (2011), *Who is reading the book in Zimbabwe?*, blog, http://zimbabweland.wordpress.com/

"What is never hidden in South Africa's keen interest in the story about the country north of the Limpopo river is a fear framed both as a question and a premonition: Will we become like Zimbabwe?... So, unless South Africa's land issue is resolved, a Zimbabwe could be replicated here".

Perhaps that's why Mr Tsenoli is reading the book.

Zimbabwe's land myths exposed by Percy Zvomuya

Thirteen years ago the opposition Movement for Democratic Change, most urban Zimbabweans and the international media were shrill in their condemnation when peasants and war veterans, soldiers, public servants and elites invaded white-owned commercial farms. The Western media was hysterical in its criticism of Robert Mugabe's "land grab" that had transformed Zimbabwe from a "bread basket" into a "basket case".

It was in these charged and uncertain times that my father, a man who had somehow managed to remain apolitical and indifferent, sat me down and said words along the lines of: "My child, Mugabe might be a dictator. In fact, I do not care whether he stays or goes, but as far as the land issue is concerned, I think he has a point. I was already a young boy when the Rhodesian government moved us from our fertile ancestral land to this rocky wilderness. What Mugabe is doing is right. It is called justice."

A few other people I knew, born in the 1950s or before, shared my father's position. They were able to untangle the knots of the complex, confusing situation that unfolded daily. Given that April 18 is Zimbabwe's day of independence, it is apt to revisit a book that looks at the truths and lies surrounding the land reform process.

Zimbabwe's Land Reform: Myths and Realities (James Currey and Jacana, 2011[236]) was co-authored by six scholars: Ian Scoones, Nelson Marongwe, Blasio Mavedzenge, Jacob Mahenehene, Felix Murimbarimba and Chrispen Sukume.

They write: "The story [about land reform] is far more complex than the generalisations of the media headlines." Because Zimbabwe's land reform fatally

---

[236] http://www.zimbabweland.net/The_Book.html

intersected with its nationalist politics, one had to be really astute and attentive to know what was going on. And right up to the present, apart from truisms and clichés such as "Uncle Bob is mad", most people are not quite sure what really happened.

Disinformation and misinformation

Were the invasions spontaneous or were they planned by the country's intelligence agency? Did the ordinary villager benefit or did most of the farms go to ZANU-PF elites and their cronies? Yet, notes the book, "numerous reports, newspaper op-eds and consultancy documents have offered opinions about what to do. What is noticeable about most of these is their almost empirical lack of empirical data."

A direct result of the years of disinformation and misinformation (and whatever is in between) is "the generation of a series of oft-repeated myths … which have gained the status of truth". The five myths the authors set out to explode are "Zimbabwean land reform has been a total failure", "the beneficiaries of Zimbabwean land reform have been largely political cronies", "there is no new investment in the new resettlements", "agriculture is in complete ruins, creating food insecurity" and "the rural economy has collapsed".

In 250 pages, they examine and puncture each myth, finding most to be baseless and grounded in malice and ignorance. They conclude that land reform was "neither a populist revolution by the peasantry, nor a corrupt takeover by elites and political cronies". Ordinary men and women, elites and the working class, public servants and other "unclassifiables" are among those who benefited. Most of their research is based on Masvingo province, in farming regions three and four. This area, semi-arid and hot, receives less rainfall than the much-desired land on the highveld, the well-watered and fertile earth found north, west and northwest of Harare.

If I have reservations, it is mainly because Masvingo is not exactly prime agricultural land, which makes it difficult to use data from this province to dispel myth two.

But the book triumphs in going beyond the sensationalism and the myths and in the way the authors spoke to ordinary villagers and "new" farmers. The interviewees were not just a token few, but scores who talked about why they had invaded farms, whether their lives had improved (significant numbers said they had) and their hopes and aspirations. Even though data is notoriously difficult to get hold of in Zimbabwe, the authors are fanatical in their empirical approach.

Human touch

Yet their empiricism allows personal details, cultural idiosyncrasies and the lives of many ordinary folk to come through. The book does not have wodges of text written in technocratic speak, but writing in which human life lights up almost every page.

There are lessons for South Africa; after all, Zimbabwe is our tenth province. What is never hidden in South Africa's keen interest in the story about the country north of the Limpopo river is a fear framed both as a question and a premonition: Will we become like Zimbabwe? It is something the scholars address in the concluding chapter of book. "In the mid 1990s, no one thought that radical land reform might unfold in Zimbabwe." And look what happened. So, unless South Africa's land issue is resolved, a Zimbabwe could be replicated here.

It is a book that every bureaucrat in the region should read. It is a book that demands the attention of everyone who wants to know the "true", unfinished story of Zimbabwe's land reform.

Although the nationalists want us to think of the process as just revolutionary, which it was, much more happened that was reactionary — narratives with which these six scholars grapple. There was plunder, death and corruption and yet, for the one million ordinary people who benefited from the process, there was a sense of triumph, restitution and justice.

Zimbabwe's Land Reform: Myths and Realities is fascinating, exhaustive and immensely readable. It goes beyond the myths to try to tell the story of a province whose reality might hold true for the rest of the country.

CHAPTER 50

AGRARIAN CHANGE, RURAL POVERTY AND LAND REFORM: SOUTH AFRICA'S EXPERIENCE

An important special issue of the *Journal of Agrarian Change* was released during 2013 on Agrarian Change, Rural Poverty and Land Reform in South Africa since 1994[237]. It is in some ways an update of the earlier issue discussing post-apartheid transition, published in 1996, and edited by Henry Bernstein[238].

The new introduction poses some basic questions, asking "by what means, in what ways, and how much can agrarian reform address the processes that underlie rural and urban poverty and the increasing inequality that marks contemporary South Africa?" In framing the debate, the editors refer to the classic labour reserve theorists who provided a structuralist analysis of the way capital creates dualism, and so inequality and poverty:

> "They focused on the question of labour, and particularly on the pervasiveness, durability and eventual vulnerabilities of migrant labour.... They saw the constitution of the 'Native Reserves', both social and physical spaces, as central to the functioning of colonial capitalism. The account that they provided helped us to understand that the poverty and misery of black rural areas were not the residual result of an absence of development but, rather, manifested a particular pattern of capital accumulation on the back of land dispossession".

However, there are clear limitations to this theorisation, as it is too reliant on macro constructs and economistic thinking, forgetting the local, particular social dynamics and the wider colonial politics which have shaped current settings. The

---

[237] O'Laughlin, B., Bernstein, H., Cousins, B., Peters, P.E. et al (2012) Agrarian change, rural poverty and land reform in South Africa since 1994, *Journal of Agrarian Change*, Special Issue, 13 (1):1-1

[238] Bernstein, H. (ed.) (1996) The agrarian question in South Africa, *Journal of Peasant Studies*, Special Issue, 23 (2-3): 1743-9361

Issue editors comment, "...it is necessary to grasp the diversity and differences of the rural areas of Southern Africa, and the complex social dynamics, including divisions of class, gender and generation among their inhabitants. Their histories, both past and future, are not written by capital alone".

They also point to the important work by Mahmoud Mamdani, who argues in *Citizen and Subject*[239] that there has to be much better attention to the historical-political conditions of colonialism that gave rise to domination, and the 'bifurcated state'. Of course since the classic Marxist work of the 1970s, the migrant labour system has been radically reconfigured. 'Today there is "growing 'surplus labour', unemployment and casualization", with very different implications for livelihoods and land. This means new theorisations of land and agrarian change are needed, suited to contemporary situations. How this is done of course will frame what questions are asked, and what solutions are suggested.

The contributions to the Special Issue offer a diversity of perspectives. Andries du Toit, for example, argues strongly for a perspective centred on inequality, avoiding getting too hung up on ownership of land and resources. From this perspective redistribution may operate across a number of dimensions (up and down the value chain) and spaces (including both rural and urban), allowing new livelihood opportunities to emerge. A focus on labour offers another perspective. As Sender and Johnston[240] argued provocatively in 2004, an emphasis on improving the conditions of labour on commercial farms may be a more effective redistributive and emancipatory option, compared to redistributing the land itself.

Others focus on the potentials centred on local level accumulation from own agricultural production. The paper by Ben Cousins, for example, shows the potentials and limits of such 'accumulation from below' in KwaZulu Natal. A wider livelihoods perspective looks at how agricultural possibilities from land reform must be combined with assessments of income from other sources, as Mike Aliber and Ben Cousins show from a study in rural Limpopo province. Still

---

[239] Mamdani, M. (1996) *Citizen and Subject,* Princeton: Princeton University Press

[240] Sender, J. and Johnston, D. (2004) Searching for a weapon of mass production in rural Africa: unconvincing arguments for land reform, *Journal of Agrarian Change*, 4(1-2): 142-164

others point to perspectives centred on social development, and how access to education, health and social care may influence poverty levels in profound ways. And whether the focus is on inequality, labour, agricultural accumulation, livelihoods or distributive justice and social development, all are intersected by dimensions of differences affected by gender, age and ethnicity.

The Special Issue thus offers no clear-cut answers, nor any defined formula for the way forward – indeed there is no clear agreement on theoretical framing among the papers, and so a diversity of positions implied on the value (or otherwise) of redistributive land reform. This makes it a refreshingly pluralistic take on a complex issue, where different perspectives combine, challenge, contradict and complement in different ways. There is no one-size-fits-all version, as in the 1970s framing, but a diversity. This is helpful for productive debate, and this Special Issue is an important contribution, helpful for anyone seeking to understand agrarian change in Southern Africa, including Zimbabwe.

Where the authors do converge, though, is the urgent need to do something about deeply structured patterns of inequality, whose characteristics have barely budged since 1994. Henry Bernstein observes that "South African agriculture and agricultural policy since 1994 has done little, if anything, to 'transform' the circumstances of the dispossessed – rural and urban classes of labour – whose crises of social reproduction remain grounded in the inheritances of racial inequality". This is a shocking realisation, given the great hopes that were held up for a 'free' South Africa. As the centenary of the 1913 Natives' Land Act[241] was commemorated during 2013, it is a reminder that, as in Zimbabwe, the inheritance of a particularly divisive history is exceptionally difficult to shed.

While the Special Issue is focused on South Africa, Zimbabwe is frequently mentioned across the papers. The editors note the 'spectre' of Zimbabwe in public and policy discourse, as an impetus to address these stark poverty and inequality challenges. But perhaps Zimbabwe can also offer lessons on the potentials as well as challenges of redistributive land reform. The conditions and contexts are of course massively different, but some exchange of ideas and perspectives between South Africa and Zimbabwe may be productive, given the urgency of the challenge south of the Limpopo.

---

[241] http://www.ruraldevelopment.gov.za/1913-land-act-centenary#.UcszphJwbmQ

CHAPTER 51

THE CASE FOR REDISTRIBUTING LAND: EVIDENCE FROM SOUTH AFRICA

A paper by Malcolm Keswell and Michael Carter based on an analysis of land reform in South Africa[242] found that the land transfers boosted household living standards by 25%. It seems that even in South Africa land reform works for the poor.

A sophisticated methodology was used (and some quite complicated maths too…) using binary treatment effects for each case, allowing deeper insights into specific households' living standard trajectories across 1650 households participating in the government's LRAD programme.

Also, and particularly interestingly, the continuous treatment estimates "which exploit variations in the period of ownership of the redistributed land" show a pattern seen before in Zimbabwe, as argued by Bill Kinsey for the 1980s resettlements. Their results "show that living standards initially dip with the land transfers, but then after three years rise to levels that imply a 50% increase in living standards of the treated households who entered the program with poverty line standards of living".

So could land reform become a central plank of 'social protection' schemes so beloved of donors and government programmes across Africa? There is much talk of building assets for transformative social protection, yet so many assets offered by aid programmes are inadequate without land access. What can farmers do with tools if they have little land to farm, or livestock if they have no grazing? The other day, I asked Stephen Devereux, a leading expert on social protection in Africa, whether land transfers were being used in social protection programming. Apparently only one programme in Bangladesh has tried it – and with some success apparently.

---

[242] Keswell, M. and Carter, M. (2012), *Poverty and Land Redistribution.* UC Davis: Dept of Agricultural Economics

Our work under the Livelihoods after Land Reform[243] programme by Michael Aliber and colleagues[244] showed glimmers of positive news in South African land reform sites in Limpopo province, but not the more dramatic improvements in agriculture and livelihoods that we saw in the sister study in Zimbabwe, and we did not have the time series data to explore the sort of changes seen by Keswell and Carter.

But maybe our methodology was too crude. Our study was certainly more limited, and focused on a province with low agricultural potential. The most significant finding from the Limpopo study was that success was happening on the margins, outside the formal strictures of the land reform programme, through innovation and experimentation by different farmers with models of farming more suited to their needs, aspirations and livelihoods. The South African models for land reform, it seemed, were almost designed to create failure – creating unwieldy co-ops, forcing farmers to adopt business models borrowed from white commerical farming, and allowing schemes to become embroiled in complex planning, financing and consultancy driven design systems.

There was a substantial critique of the top-down nature of Zimbabwe's resettlement programme in the 1980s, including the assumptions about the need for new settlers to be 'full-time farmers'. In the post 2000 period, of course, Zimbabwe's land reform beneficiaries have been largely released from the strictures of top down planning and permit systems (although attempts have of course been made). This has unquestionably allowed more flexibility, innovation and responsiveness.

But the question raised by the new South Africa paper is whether land reform can be used more strategically as part of social protection and poverty reduction programmes in the future. Or will donors prefer to carry on handing out cash, food, and maybe a few tools and goats?

---

[243] www.lalr.org.za

[244] Aliber, M., T. Maluleke, T. Manenzhe, G.Paradza, B. Cousins (2013) *Land Reform and Livelihoods. Trajectories of Change in Northern Limpopo Province, South Africa.* South Africa: HSRC Press

CHAPTER 52

LESSONS FROM THAILAND? A NEW RURAL ECONOMY AND ZIMBABWE'S POLITICAL PEASANTS

I have just been reading a fascinating book about rural Thailand called *"Thailand's Political Peasants: Power and the Modern Rural Economy"* by Andrew Walker from ANU[245]. What on earth has this got to do with Zimbabwe, you ask?

Currently, a number of scholars are interested in the experience of southeast Asian countries in agricultural and rural development, and the lessons there may be for Africa[246], including an interesting research study looking at paired African-SE Asian comparisons[247]. Such countries – including Thailand, but also Laos, Cambodia, Malaysia and Vietnam – have seen rapid economic growth overall, driven in part by a strong agricultural sector. The result has been plummeting poverty levels, and rising prosperity including in previously extremely poor rural areas. Their agricultural sectors have benefited from sustained state investment, including substantial input subsidies, strategic infrastructure development and reduced taxation. Land and tenure reform has been part of the story too, as more equitable land holdings provided a strong foundation for growth. There has of course been differentiation, and this has created a new class of rural dweller: someone who farms successfully, often linked into quite specialised value chains, but also someone who has also diversified into a range of off-farm activities, creating vibrant rural economies with strong forward and backward linkages. There are those who have dropped out too, but growing economies mean potentials for absorption in gainful urban employment – or increasing rural employment as previously depressed rural areas boom.

---

[245] Walker, A. (2012) *Thailand's Political Peasants. Power in the Modern Rural Economy,* Madison: University of Wisconsin Press

[246] http://www.institutions-africa.org/page/initiating-developmental-regimes

[247] Van Donge, J.K., Henley, D. and Lewis, P. (2012) Tracking development in south-east Asia and sub-Saharan Africa: the primacy of policy, *Development Policy Review,* 30 (Issue Supplement s1): s5-s24

In each of these countries, there has been a different pattern, phasing and geographically specific set of impacts. Thailand's Political Peasants focuses on the fortunes of northeast Thailand. Andrew Walker describes[248] how:

> "Thailand's 21st century peasants have mobilised to defend the direct relationship they have established with the Thai state over the past 40 years. This is not the old-style politics of the rural poor, characterised by rebellion, revolution or resistance. Contemporary rural politics is driven by a middle-income peasantry with a thoroughly modern political logic. Their strategy is to engage with sources of power, not to oppose them."

Unlike other studies which focus on the economic factors, this book highlights the politics. The strong backing of Thaksin Shinawatra, often through highly corrupt, patronage arrangements, was an important factor. The rural population benefited from such investment, and backed Shinawatra and his party (and since 2011, Yingluck Shinawatra). In the regular tussle between the urban based elite monarchists, the orange shirts, and the rural based red shirts, the national political dynamic is laid bare. But rural constituencies matter when they are doing well, and no political party in Thailand can ignore them, no matter how much the urban, industrial boom continues.

As discussed in chapter 18, social differentiation unleashed by land reform in Zimbabwe presents a new, and potentially powerful, constituency, reconfiguring the national political landscape. The emergence of a strong, vocal, relatively economically successful middle farmer group is an important new political phenomenon. Here the parallel with Thailand ends, however. Agriculture and rural development has not received the backing by the state, or any political formation, in the same way, and as a result the type of upward spiral economic growth seen in Thailand has not emerged. Zimbabwe's economy is severely depressed so non-rural alternatives are not available, and the middle income country dynamic seems a way off yet.

But perhaps, just perhaps, there are more lessons. They are all big ifs right now, but what if a new political settlement centred on this new rural constituency, and political survival and rural economic growth became intimately linked? What if the new windfalls from mineral resources were invested in rural revitalisation?

---

248 Walker, A. (2012) 'Thailand's political peasants', *East Asia Forum*, 29 August

What if this resulted in the sort of agriculture-led economic growth that we have seen hints of already, with spin-offs into employment, rural markets and the growth of rural towns? It will require a new political settlement combined with a new economic vision, neither of which evident right now, but just maybe a shift in political forces in the coming years, driven by changes in class affiliations, motivations and alliances, will result in such a shift. In the 1970s, as Andrew Walker documents, no-one believed it would happen in Thailand; maybe in 20 or 30 years time Zimbabwe will look very different too.

CHAPTER 53

BRICS IN AFRICA: NEW IMPERIALISM OR A NEW DEVELOPMENT PARADIGM?

During 2013, Durban hosted the 5th BRICS summit[249] , with the heads of state from Brazil, Russia, India and China being welcomed by President Zuma of South Africa. After a stopover in Russia, the new Chinese president's first overseas trip was to Africa – first Tanzania and then on to South Africa. At the meeting, the BRICS leaders committed to creating BRICS bank[250] with at least a US$50 billion start-up fund, with a focus on infrastructure development.

This has been hailed as a new mechanism to support development, particularly in Africa, to rival the World Bank. The new BRICS facility would in turn usher in a new era of South-South cooperation, banishing the former colonial powers to the side-lines. But is this really going to be the case? China and Brazil certainly have significant and growing economic might. But South Africa is a mere 'briquette'[251], according to some commentators.

So what is South Africa's role in this new power bloc, given that its economy is dwarfed by the others? Is it just a convenient addition to add in Africa? Or is South Africa being used as the 'gateway' to new investment from the new global economic powers? Is this new configuration creating, as Patrick Bond claims, a new sub-imperialism[252]? And what are the broader implications for Africa's development, as the global geopolitical and economic contours shift? With Zimbabwe just north of the Limpopo, and in urgent need of investment, these developments have potentially important ramifications.   Bond rejects the potentials of a new development paradigm, and comments[253], "BRICS offer some

---

[249] Scoones, I. (2013) 'What are the BRICS building in Africa?', *Huffington Post*, 27 March

[250] Smith, D. (2013) 'BRICS eye infrastructure funding through new development bank', *The Guardian*, 28 March

[251] Smith, D. (2013) 'South Africa: more of a briquette than a BRIC?', *The Guardian*, 24 March

[252] Bond, P. (2013) 'Are BRICS 'sub-imperialists'?', *Pambazuka News*, 20 March

[253] Bond, P. (2013) 'Africa: Are BRICS 'sub-imperialists'?' *All Africa*, 21 March

of the most extreme sites of new sub-imperialism in the world today. They lubricate world neo-liberalism, hasten world eco-destruction and serve as coordinators of hinterland looting. The BRICS hegemonic project should be resisted".

Working with collaborators in China, Brazil and across Africa – including Langton Mukwereza in Zimbabwe[254] [chapter 48] – the Future Agricultures Consortium has been starting some work to look at how China and Brazil in particular are engaging in African agriculture[255]. While we don't buy the misty-eyed talk of South-South sharing and solidarity, we equally do not dismiss the new players completely. Clearly commercial business interests are at the heart of such engagements, and Chinese and Brazilian interests in agricultural machinery, agro-processing, ethanol production and so on are very evident in the new deals being struck with African governments. But such new development encounters are creating a new dynamic at the same time - that may offer some room for manoeuvre for African states, in negotiating new arrangements from both traditional donors and investors, and new ones.

Much recent work on 'the BRICS in Africa' has emphasized the geopolitical scale, as these new players engage in areas dominated in the past by western donors and companies. This often gives a very general picture of 'Rising Powers' or 'China' and 'Africa', for example. Yet behind these labels, China, Brazil and India -- for example -- have very different interests and priorities, and within these countries there are battles between different approaches, reflecting domestic political debates.

Of course, the 55 countries which make up Africa are also hugely diverse, and any new encounter arrives on the back of a very particular history, shaped by development interventions since colonial times. Each country has its own agrarian history and political economy. So depending on the context, similar interventions -- a commercial agricultural scheme, for example, or technical training -- will have very different consequences. From the initial negotiation to the daily running of projects that are set up, the results vary widely.

---

[254] Mukwereza, L. (2013) *Chinese and Brazilian Cooperation with African Agriculture: The Case of Zimbabwe,* CBAA Working Paper 48, Brighton: Future Agricultures Consortium

[255] http://www.future-agricultures.org/research/cbaa.

From the colonial era and through post-colonial development, African policymakers and technical experts have learned to negotiate around technology transfer, economic reform or loan agreements. 'Africa' has not just been a passive recipient in many of these cases.

The same applies to these new encounters. But with new players, carrying with them different discourses and practices rooted in their own recent development experiences, the room for manoeuvre by African states may be increased. Different players can be traded off against each other: western donors for welfare and social protection, China for large-scale infrastructural development, Brazil for agricultural technology transfer, for example. But the range of choice presents dilemmas. Should Mozambique, say, go down the route of smallholder agricultural production, and low input agriculture, promoted by many western donors and NGOs? Or should it aim for large-scale commercial, mechanised agriculture, modelled on the Brazilian *Cerrado* experience, or the large farms of northern China?

In many respects the arrival of new players on the scene in Africa has opened up the development game. The old, narrow conditions no longer apply, and African governments do not need to be constrained by the rules of Western development aid. Yet engagement never comes with no strings attached, despite the warm-sounding rhetoric of 'South-South cooperation', 'mutual benefit' and 'political solidarity'. China and Brazil need Africa, just as Africa needs them. Africa's resources, including its land, are critical both for longer-term global food security, particularly in the populous parts of Asia, and such low-cost resources, labour and market connections are vital for agribusiness and trade plans.

To understand the new encounters in development cooperation brought by the BRICS and others, we have to get to grips with the details, and the cultural, social and political relations at play, as well as the wider political economy that structures such engagements[256]. Whose interests are being served? Who wins and who loses? These questions will be keenly watched as Africa's farmers, food producers and politicians look to partners in the South for a new future.

---

[256] Scoones, I., Cabral, L. and Tugendhat, H. (eds.). (2013). New Development Encounters: China and Brazil in African Agriculture. *IDS Bulletin*, 44(4).

CHAPTER 54

THE NEXT GREAT TREK: FROM ZIMBABWE TO NIGERIA

To great fanfare, in 2004, 13 white farmers from Zimbabwe arrived in Kwara state, Nigeria at the invitation of the then Governor. Their arrival had been facilitated by the CFU and (apparently) the British embassy in Nigeria. They had been allocated around 200,000 ha of land in the 'Shonga farms' area, and had been feted as saviours of the agricultural sector in the state, and hailed as the source of 'modern agriculture' which would spread to others.

In addition to the land, they had been offered subsidised deals on inputs and they had unparalleled access to support through close political patronage. Although there was some local resistance, there was not huge displacement, and local people were offered promises of support, including a youth training programme for next-generation farmers. It looked like a good start. So what happened?

Joseph Ariyo and Mike Mortimore[257] have been trying to find out, as part of a research project linked to the land theme of the Future Agricultures Consortium. They also reported on the 'youth' dimensions at the FAC conference[258] in Accra (see also the *African Affairs* paper by Raufu Mustapha[259] on the Kwara farmers which sets the story in a wider context).

---

[257] Ariyo, J. and Mortimore, M. (2011). *Land deals and commercial agriculture in Nigeria: the new Nigerian farms in Shonga District, Kwara State.* Paper presented at Conference of Global Land Grabbing, Institute of Development Studies, University of Sussex, 6-8 April, 2011. Brighton: Future Agricultures Consortium

[258] Ariyo, J. and Mortimore, M. (2012) *Youth employment in agriculture: a development dilemma in Nigeria,* Paper presented at International Conference on Young people, farming and food in Africa, 19-21 March, 2012, Accra, Ghana. Brighton: Future Agricultures Consortium

[259] Mustapha, R. A. (2010) Zimbabwean farmers in Nigeria: Exceptional farmers or spectacular support?, *African Affairs,* 110 (441): 535-561

The results are mixed. Some farmers have done well, while others have struggled. Some 300-400 jobs have been created, but the spread of commercial farming to surrounding areas has been limited. There have been some spill-over effects, with soybeans being taken up widely in neighbouring areas, and local pastoralists have gained from access to milk processing facilities. Gaining access to credit through the arcane Nigerian banking system has not been easy, and financing developments has been stalled. With the governor who originally invited them now replaced, the future looks rather more uncertain.

In a policy feedback meeting in the state capital with senior government officials, the research team concluded that the experiment was worthwhile, and should be continued, but it was not replicable. If the Shonga experiment is to have a future – and indeed large-scale, 'modern' commercial agriculture more generally in the state, with or without white Zimbabwean support – then, in particular, the financial support system needs a dramatic improvement. Also, commercialised agriculture cannot operate without effective infrastructure – roads, electricity and so on – and this remains poor in the area. The Shonga farmers are not able to risk expansion of their cultivated areas beyond the current 50%, nor further investment under these circumstances.

The meeting concluded that such showcase projects may be helpful as demonstrations, and clearly they generate important political capital, but the investments made are not really justified by the returns. For the longer term, a focus on creating a new generation of commercial farmers among Nigerian youth was emphasised, perhaps drawing inspiration from their Zimbabwean neighbours, but not focusing so much effort (and public resources) on a small group of high-profile farms.

SECTION H
RESEARCHING LAND AND AGRARIAN CHANGE

Researching the process of land reform and agrarian change in Zimbabwe is not easy. But data from the ground is essential if a better idea of what has happened where and to whom is to be gained, and in turn influence policy thinking.

This is why we initiated our research in Zimbabwe and have encouraged others to do so elsewhere. We were lucky that we were not alone, as we were able to work with Sam Moyo and colleagues at the African Institute for Agrarian Studies, Prosper Matondi and colleagues at the Ruzivo Trust and others at the University of Zimbabwe. All have produced important studies, with research results that can be compared and contrasted with ours. There have also been numerous other studies, including many by Zimbabwean PhD and Masters students, some of whom were supported by the Livelihoods after Land Reform small grants fund[260].

The accumulating evidence is impressive, and provides a nuanced and differentiated account of the land reform process and its impacts. What it consistently does though is counter the standard media narratives about land reform as a universal disaster, challenging the prevalent 'myths' about Zimbabwe's land reform. Data and evidence is thus important, and as it accumulates it provides greater authority [chapter 59].

However not everyone is convinced. Even thoughtful commentators such as Martin Plaut, formerly of the BBC and a visitor to our research sites in 2012,

---

[260] http://www.lalr.org.za/zimbabwe/zimbabwe-working-papers-1

questioned our results as not 'really authoritative' [chapter 55]. There are a number of complaints he and others have raised over time about our work, some legitimate, others not. The reviews of our book have continued to come in and they offer a diverse array of perspectives[261].

One frequent complaint has been that our research has been biased because of the affiliations of the authors, and our connections to government agencies, such as Agritex[262]. In chapter 56 I tackle this particular issue, arguing that all research is necessarily positioned, but objectivity and rigour can be assured by a solid adherence to transparent research approaches, as well as a reflexive stance acknowledging how biases impinge. This has been our research philosophy, and one that I defend vigorously. That our team represented political views from across the spectrum helped, and the fact that some of our team were beneficiaries of land reform also assisted us getting a deeper, embedded perspective. Some of the commentators who have complained about the quality of our work from this standpoint clearly have not done rural research in Zimbabwe, and certainly not in the 2000s. Political sensitivities were running high, and fostering good relationships in the research sites was essential. Working with government staff on the ground did not colour our views or compromise our findings, but allowed us to engage in a debate about our results with a wide range of people, including those working in the field.

Another familiar critique of our work is that it is based on a case study approach, and is not representative of the situation nationally. This is correct. But I do not regard it is a fatal flaw [chapter 57]. Indeed, the approach we took: a single province, 16 representative farm sites across an agro-ecological transect, and a sample of 400, stratified according to various ranking approaches, provided a unique insight that allowed depth within the sites but also breadth across them. Where more work could be done is to give the sort of historical depth to the cases that Terry Ranger in his review calls for.

We have always been careful not to extrapolate beyond our cases, but instead make use of the wider studies that have been carried out elsewhere – covering

---

[261] http://www.zimbabweland.net/Reviews.html

[262] Scoones, I. (2013) *Documentaries on land reform in Zimbabwe*, blog, http://zimbabweland.wordpress.com/

nearly all corners of the country now [chapter 59] – to compare and contrast. The *Journal of Peasant Studies* special issue edited by Lionel Cliffe and colleagues that pulled many of these together provides an important overview, and generally supports our early findings, with important nuances and qualifications[263].

Basic data is important, but has also been found wanting. With a radically changed situation, old data sources are obsolete as are the data collection methods. A solid statistical base for assessing conditions in rural areas is essential for any sort of planning and development. As chapter 58 discusses, referring to Morten Jerven's excellent book, *Poor Numbers*, African data is often wildly inaccurate and misleading, and no basis for making decisions, creating rankings or assessing options. I look at three areas: agricultural production, migration and land ownership to illustrate the point for Zimbabwe.

A major priority for the future must be to reinvest in data collection capacities, both in terms of surveys, such as those carried out by ZIMSTAT, the statistical services agency, but also detailed case study work to get the complementary detail. In conditions of an almost complete lack of research information of any sort, and a media and academic commentary not rooted in empirical findings but more in ideological assumptions and political posturing, our work has contributed to a basic empirical foundation. We and others are continuing the work, and a wider body of data is being built up that will form the basis for more informed policymaking, as well as a longer-run reflection on this particular period in Zimbabwe's history.

---

[263] Cliffe, L., Alexander, J., Cousins, B. and Gaidzanwa, R. (eds.) (2011). Special Issue on Fast Track Land Reform in Zimbabwe. *Journal of Peasant Studies*, 38(5)

CHAPTER 55

WHEN IS RESEARCH 'REALLY AUTHORITATIVE'?

Reviews of our book[264] keep piling up; this time prompted by the publication of *Zimbabwe Takes Back its Land*[265], a more popular summary of the main studies of Zimbabwe's land reform.

The latest is by Martin Plaut in *African Arguments*[266]. He broadly agrees with our findings, but says he is still awaiting a 'really authoritative' account. His main complaint about both books, it seems, is that authors on both are not only researchers but also resettlement farmers, and beneficiaries of the land reform. This he says has resulted in biases in our accounts. Authorship, bias and evidence are themes I discuss further in chapter 56.

In Martin Plaut's piece he argues "if the backgrounds and politics of the authors intrude into the study it lessens its objectivity". Yes, I agree. But we equally cannot ignore our backgrounds and politics, and that's why I make the case for reflexivity as essential for enhancing rigour. Just because some authors of our book, just as the new one, come from diverse backgrounds, with different experiences and contrasting political positions, this doesn't mean that the data we collect and the evidence we present is necessarily 'biased'. In fact, I would argue, quite the opposite.

In the case of our book, the core team has worked together for nearly 25 years, and knows the study area intimately. That some of the team were beneficiaries of the land reform programme allowed us particular insights. But others of course were not farmers and not from the area, and, crucially, all of us have a passion for detailed fieldwork, systematic data collection and careful analysis.

---

[264] http://www.zimbabweland.net/Reviews.html

[265] Hanlon, J., Manjengwa, J. and Smart, T. (2012) *Zimbabwe Takes Back Its Land*. West Hartford, CT: Kumarian

[266] Plaut, M. (2013) 'Zimbabwe Takes Back Its Land – A review by Martin Plaut', *African Arguments*, 21 March

This is why we presented so much detail in the book (against the objections of our editors!), so it could be scrutinized, evaluated and critiqued.

In his commentary, Martin highlights BZ Mavedzenge in particular, the field team leader, whose farm he visited (which was incidentally purposely not in our study area) in 2011 as part of a BBC team. When it came out, I sent the review to BZ by email – direct to the farm, where if you go to a small hill above the house, behind the new chicken runs, and beyond the well you can get good service and download emails these days. He wrote straight back. He asks, "Does authoritative mean an aerial view from outsiders? Surely, as Chambers says, farmer first is the way forward…". He goes on, appreciating the rest of the piece, "Martin I think agrees there was much to see to be proud of about accumulation from below".

So how should BZ, as an author, be represented? As farmer, researcher, land reform beneficiary, former government civil servant, born and bred in Masvingo province, or what? He is of course all of these[267]; and each identity helps shape his insights and perspectives. In particular as a researcher, trained at agricultural college and then working at Matopos research station, before taking over the lead of the Department of Research and Specialist Services' Farming Systems Research Unit in Masvingo, BZ has unparalleled insights into the dynamics of farming systems in the area. This is why I have so enjoyed – and benefitted from – working with him all these years.

What about Martin Plaut? How should we read his review? As someone who was born and bred in apartheid South Africa, educated at universities with largely white students, or as someone who was centrally involved in the anti-apartheid struggle and the 1976 Soweto uprising, or as formerly Head of the Africa section of the BBC World Service, and a brilliant reporter on the Horn and Southern Africa, or, now retired, and a Fellow of the Institute of Commonwealth Studies? Again, he is all of these; and these experiences and positions allow him to carry out really authoritative, top-notch investigative journalism and writing (just check out his book[268] on South Africa to get a flavour).

---

[267] http://www.mixcloud.com/ids/land-interview-with-blasio-mavedzenge/

[268] Plaut, M., and Holden, P. (2012) *Who Rules South Africa?*, Johannesburg and Cape Town: Jonathan Ball Publishers

All authorship is so conditioned, but this should not imply bias. And we should avoid jumping to conclusions just because of the author's status or experience. Any evaluation must come through more rigorous assessment of data and analysis. This is the reason I have objected before to statements from the Commercial Farmers' Union, for example (see chapter 28[269]) – not because they are from the CFU, but because they are wrong! I have previously commented[270] both on Martin's otherwise excellent BBC radio pieces he did in 2011 on Zimbabwe, and also when certain information was presented on the costs of land reform, and replicated in articles on the BBC and elsewhere as fact.

BBC balance is an article of faith but sometimes does not serve the search for truth well. A journalistic piece that presents all sides as equivalent sometimes ends up being unbalanced. If equal airtime is offered to detailed, rigorous research undertaken over years and commentaries based on figures that seem to have been plucked from the air to suit the argument, this is not exactly balance in my view.

This is not to argue that both our book and *Zimbabwe Takes Back its Land* don't have silences, gaps and contestable arguments. Of course. That's why we publish, encourage debate and urge others to do more research. What we don't expect is our work – or indeed anyone else's – to be dismissed on the basis of who they are, rather than what they say.

It's not as if we don't have plenty of empirical evidence to go on these days. This accumulation of insights is getting seriously 'authoritative' and pointing, broadly but with important nuances, in the same direction. It's irritating sometimes that our book is the only one that gets mentioned (and now of course the new one), just because we hit the limelight (not least I suspect because the lead authors of both books are based in the UK, and are white and professors).

But actually there are piles of other research [chapter 60], researched and written by Zimbabweans, not least the impressive district studies led by Sam

---

[269] Scoones, I. (2011) *Fact check*, blog, http://zimbabweland.wordpress.com/

[270] Scoones, I. (2011) *BBC Crossing Continents: production declines?*, blog, http://zimbabweland.wordpress.com/

Moyo and team at the African Institute of Agrarian Studies, the book[271] by Prosper Matondi, based on the work by the Ruzivo trust team, plus numerous PhD and Masters studies, including those sponsored through the Livelihoods after Land Reform small grants programme[272].

Across these studies, we can triangulate, compare, synthesise and generate, yes, really authoritative insights. So, why the reluctance to accept the findings? Why the questioning of authors' credibility? Why the lack of counter-data coming forward? I think some of the answers do indeed lie in the positionality and politics of the commentators. It is difficult accepting a new situation, and rejecting positions long held. It is unsettling, discomfiting and challenging. But that is what good research – and indeed good journalism – sometimes has to do if we are to seek ways forward.

Just as Thomas Khun[273] argued now over 50 years ago, settled paradigms are difficult to shift for all sorts of political, social and institutional reasons, but when they do, then 'normal science' can proceed, and the new paradigm can be unpacked, contested, unravelled, adapted and elaborated. For most serious scholars in Zimbabwe, it is this normal science that is unfolding now, as we do follow up surveys, new rounds of case studies, and examine our older data in the light of new findings. Just as all good 'normal science', the new data both confirms, but also nuances and sometimes contrasts with, the early findings. I hope that Martin and others find our new contributions 'authoritative' enough!

---

[271] Scoones, I. (2013) *Two new books on Zimbabwe's land reform*, blog, http://zimbabweland.wordpress.com/

[272] http://www.lalr.org.za/zimbabwe/zimbabwe-working-papers-1

[273] http://en.wikipedia.org/wiki/Thomas_Kuhn

CHAPTER 56

WHO ARE THE AUTHORS? THE CHALLENGES OF POSITIONALITY, PARTIALITY AND REFLEXIVITY

All writing is inevitably positioned and partial. We all write from our experience, our history, our politics. But this does not mean that we can never engage critically with empirical realities. In our acceptance of a social constructivist take on knowledge, we should not resort to a desperate relativism where anything goes. There are plenty of philosophical traditions – critical realism[274] being the most prominent – that help us think about how to balance commitment to empirical investigation with critical reflection on positionality, and so the inevitable partiality of any exploration of complex realities. This requires transparency, accountability and reflexivity in research and writing.

This is of course particularly important when engaging with a subject as contested as land reform in Zimbabwe. In our book[275], we attempted to do this up-front in the Preface and Acknowledgements. As well as our declarations of institutional affiliation and funding from the UK government (ESRC and DFID), we had this (page ix):

> "*The Livelihoods after Land Reform project research team in Zimbabwe was led by Dr Nelson Marongwe, an urban and rural planner, of the Centre for Applied Social Sciences Trust in Harare. He has been supported by Professor Ian Scoones, originally an agricultural ecologist, based at IDS, and Dr Chrispen Sukume, an agricultural economist from the University of Zimbabwe. The Masvingo province field team was led by B.Z. Mavedezenge, formerly the regional team leader of the Farming Systems Research Unit (FSRU) of the Department for Research and Specialist Services in the Ministry of*

---

[274] Archer, M. S. and Bhaskar, R. (eds) (1998) *Critical Realism: Essential Readings. Vol. 6*, Oxford: Routledge

[275] Scoones, I., Marongwe, N., Mavedzenge, B., Mahenehene, J., Murimbarimba, F., and Sukume, C. (2010) *Zimbabwe's Land Reform: Myths and Realities*, Oxford: James Currey

Agriculture, but now of the Agritex (agricultural extension) department in Masvingo. He is also an A1 resettlement farmer in the province. He worked with Felix Murmibarimba, formerly also of FSRU and then Agritex, but now a full-time A2 sugar cane farmer in Hippo Valley, and Jacob Mahenehene, who farms in the communal areas near Chikombedzi, as well as having a new resettlement plot in an informal site in Mwenezi district."

Roger Southall[276] in his review of the book in *Africa Spectrum* picked up on this: "It is interesting, in this regard, to note that three of the authors, Blaise (sic) Mavedzenge, Jacob Mahenehene and Felix Murimbarimba, are themselves beneficiaries of the land reform". He continues: "There is certainly nothing wrong with this, and the research probably would have been impossible to conduct without their ability to negotiate the political and administrative landscape. But it does raise the question of whether their backgrounds shaped, blunted or constrained the political judgements of the research team as a whole". In a similar vein, Blair Rutherford[277] in his excellent review in the *Journal of Contemporary African Studies* [chapter 17], argues that "the authors' positioning of the book as a detached promotion of the empirical realities contradicts their textured analyses of contested histories and masks their own politics".

These are interesting commentaries reflecting directly on the challenges of positionality, partiality and reflexivity in authorship. On the following page to the quote above, we state:

"The research team came from very different backgrounds, with different experiences, outlooks and political persuasions. It made for an interesting, but productive, dynamic. We were always there to challenge each other's assumptions and biases, but what held the group together was the commitment to explore the empirical realities on the ground, and root our analysis and policy recommendations in such solid evidence."

---

[276] Southall, R. (2011) Too soon to tell? Land reform in Zimbabwe, *Africa Spectrum*, 46 (3): 83-97

[277] Rutherford, B. (2012) Shifting the debate on land reform, poverty and inequality in Zimbabwe, an engagement with Zimbabwe's Land Reform: Myths and Realities, *Journal of Contemporary African Studies*, 30 (1): 147-157

Revealingly, neither Southall nor Rutherford particularly picked up on this passage. Yet this was an attempt – perhaps inadequate – to be honest about the challenges of being positioned, but also to describe how we managed a reflexive process as an authorial group. Multiple authorship is challenging at the best of times, but it is especially so when interpretations are politically charged and contested. This is why we presented the book in a highly empirical way, while still engaging critically with the interpretations. The myths-realities contrast became the device to present these, with the aim of raising the debate about what happened during land reform. In this, as both Rutherford and Southall remark, we succeeded.

Southall argues that having land reform beneficiaries on the team may have coloured our judgement. I would beg to differ. Our methods and process of analysis would not have allowed for this, and as explained above we always engaged in a collective debate about findings. It has been implied that we had a bias towards ZANU-PF politics in our team, but this is not the case either. Around the 2008 elections, I recall that of those who could vote, we had one strong MDC-T supporter, one ZANU-PF supporter, one Makoni supporter, and two who were equivocal, and said they probably would not vote at all. As for myself, I would not count myself as a supporter of any political formation – indeed, as these chapters show, I am critical of them all!

Given backgrounds, politics and interests, it is therefore not surprising that the group did not agree with everything! It is also why, particularly at that time, it was not easy to write about the wider political context, and some of the political implications of our findings. This is a valid criticism of the book, made by both reviewers. This is now easier, given the passage of time and the change in political dynamic post 2009, and it is reflected, I hope, in more recent writings, including those included in this book.

A reflexive approach, combined with a critical stance, surely allows some valid insights from empirical study that cannot be so easily dismissed as simply emerging from personal, political or professional biases.

CHAPTER 57

MASVINGO EXCEPTIONALISM? THE CHALLENGE OF CASE STUDIES

One of the main complaints about our book is that it's mostly about Masvingo, and that it does not tell the whole story of land reform in Zimbabwe over the past decade or so. On all counts we are guilty. As we are clear in the book we are not making wider claims. This is a case study – of 16 sites in one province over 10 years. As Professor Terry Ranger remarks in his review of our book[278]: "Patterns emerge but the book pays admirable attention to variation and variety". Such a province-wide case study is still important, we maintain, as a basis for more in-depth comparison where contrasts and convergences can be teased out.

The Commercial Farmers' Union[279] of Zimbabwe and their supporters often make the point that Masvingo is 'exceptional', and that somehow are results should not be taken too seriously. They argue that this was not a 'real farming' area, and that something different happened there. Well, if this was not an important part of the commercial farming sector, why on earth did they not give up the land for resettlement many years before? Of course other areas in the Highveld are different, as we clearly state in the book. But, as we equally argue, there are some important broader patterns. And indeed, wider work that has emerged since has challenged in similar ways the five myths we lay out in the book.

A number of points are made about Masvingo 'exceptionalism'. First, of course, Masvingo is in the drier part of the country, where certain cropping and livestock rearing patterns prevail. This agroecological difference is of course important, but let's also remember that geographically the largest portion of the country is dry, with poor infrastructure and reliant on rainfed production, even in the former commercial sector. Second, the proximity to Harare is seen as a key factor in affecting the degree to which land was grabbed by elites through processes of violence and patronage. This again is true, and many of the high-profile cases

---

[278] Ranger, T. (2011) Zimbabwean diamonds, *Africa: The Journal of the International African Institute*, 81(4): 649-661

[279] 'CFU welcomes debate on land reforms', *The Zimbabwean*, 12 January 2011

where whole farms were taken by those well connected to the political-military elite are in these areas. But the pattern of 'cronyism' remains much under dispute [chapter 26]. Third, as Terry Ranger argues in his review, the longer-term histories of particular places are important both in the processes and outcomes of land reform. This is absolutely correct. As we point out in the book it is these micro-political contexts, influenced by histories – of the liberation war, chieftaincy and political party allegiances – that have had really important influences on what happened, where. He admonishes us for not referring more to a set of important historical district studies (by for example Alexander, Kriger, Maxwell, Moore, Ranger, Schmidt), but all of these fall outside Masvingo (indeed, all are from Manicaland). In Masvingo there is a perhaps surprising absence of such studies, beyond the important study of Great Zimbabwe by Joost Fontein, although we have some fantastically rich pre-colonial accounts from Gerald Mazarire and others.

These three factors will have a big influence on land reform processes and outcomes. But to what degree do these specificities (all variable indeed *within* Masvingo as we point out) affect the broad challenge of the five 'myths'? We now have a growing body of work available to assess this, including the AIAS six district study led by Sam Moyo[280], the three district study by Ruzivo Trust led by Prosper Matondi[281], and the growing array of more focused, farm-based studies by research students and others, supported for example as part of the 'Livelihoods after Land Reform' small grants call[282], and some collected together in the important synthesis volume of the *Journal of Peasant Studies* by Lionel Cliffe and colleagues[283]. These studies cover an increasing number of locations across Zimbabwe, with perhaps Matabeleland North and Midlands provinces being the least covered to date.

---

[280] Chambati, W., Dangwa, C., Moyo, S., Mujeyi, K., Murisa, T., Nyoni, N. and Siziba, D. (2009) *Fast Track Land Reform Baseline Survey in Zimbabwe: Trends and Tendencies, 2005/06*, Harare: African Institute for Agrarian Studies

[281] Matondi, P. (2012) *Zimbabwe's Fast Track Land Reform*, London: Zed Books

[282] http://www.lalr.org.za/zimbabwe/zimbabwe-working-papers-1

[283] Cliffe, L., Alexander, J., Cousins, B. and Gaidzanwa, R. (eds.) (2011). Special Issue on Fast Track Land Reform in Zimbabwe. *Journal of Peasant Studies*, 38(5)

While the results from this now large body of work show wide variation, there are also some important common patterns. Overall, our analysis of the five myths is supported by other studies: all are rejected. A more detailed and systematic cross-study assessment would certainly be valuable, but the deployment of the 'Masvingo is exceptional' narrative in order in some way to reject the validity and applicability of our findings is clearly inappropriate. And so is the argument that 'we need much more data from other places in order to take the wider significance of the Masvingo study seriously'. We have this data, and the body of work is growing: to date no one has dealt a killer blow to our study!

But what these other studies have done is nuance, extend and challenge some of the implications of our analysis. This is important. This is good research and how understanding progresses. Avoid the point-scoring, the summary rejections, and the attempts to side-line, but engage. This is certainly my attitude. The contrasts between studies certainly highlight all three of the factors highlighted above – agroecology, location and history – in interesting ways.

Clearly agroecology has a huge influence on what is possible in agronomic terms, but also the returns to investment, and so the incentives to invest in infrastructure, including greenhouses, irrigation and so on. This in turn influences the style of farming – higher potential areas offer opportunities for more intensive farming, where farm labour is important, and is more linked to the (still struggling) A2 sector. Paradoxically, until investment gets going (and this requires market confidence and stability as well as credit and financial services), it is the lower potential low-input areas based on smallholder family farm labour that are the more successful. Of course the tobacco story offers a different angle on this, and there are important lessons to be learned for the A2 farms more generally from this experience [chapter 2].

Proximity to urban centres, and particularly Harare, is again important. The attraction of big chefs is one dimension to this. It is certainly the case that the Mashonaland [chapter 36] provinces had substantially more A2 plots allocated during fast-track land reform. These were particularly prone to capture by elites as we have discussed elsewhere [chapter 26]. But we also have to differentiate between this sort of patronage – through manipulation of bureaucratic allocation procedures, for example – to the large scale 'grabs' of whole farms.

The high profile cases of these are almost exclusively in the high potential Mashonaland provinces, and although small in number they are large areas and the 'grabbers' are very high profile people. These are now euphemistically called 'large-scale A2' farms, and have been accepted as part of the new agrarian structure. The big question is whether these players gain the upper hand politically and assert a new dualism in farming, just with new owners. This would be a regressive move, undermining the aims of the agrarian reform. As a result an effective land audit and a close social, political and economic analysis of these new farms (and their new owners) will be essential. Here there certainly are important contrasts between provinces, and this must be an essential part of the wider political analysis.

Finally, longer-term histories of people and places are, as Terry Ranger, argues essential. This may not have a big impact on overall production patterns, for example, but the underlying authority structures, the role of different local elites, chiefs and others, as well as the political dynamic will all be influenced by such histories. This will have had an impact for sure – as it did across our sites in Masvingo – on land invasion and acquisition processes, as well as patterns of violence [chapter 22]. But it will also influence future governance arrangements, and the possibilities (or not) of 'rebuilding public authority from below' [chapter 20].

As Ranger correctly argues there will not be a 'Masvingo solution', and our book "is not the end but very much the beginning of a discussion". This discussion is now well under way, and supported by a range of scholarship mostly from Zimbabweans studying what happened where to build the bigger story of Zimbabwe's land reform.

CHAPTER 58

DODGY DATA AND MISSING MEASURES: WHY GOOD NUMBERS MATTER

In 2013 an excellent short book, *"Poor Numbers: How we are misled by African development statistics, and what to do about it"* [284] by Morten Jerven from Simon Fraser University in Canada was published (see this *African Arguments* [285] piece for a summary). It makes the case that African statistics are often worse than useless, and decisions, rankings and other assessments made based on such poor numbers are usually grossly misleading. Jerven comments (page xi):

> *"…the numbers are poor. This is not just a matter of technical accuracy. The arbitrariness of the quantification process produces observations with very large errors and levels of uncertainty. This numbers game has taken on a dangerously misleading air of accuracy, and the resulting numbers are used to make critical decisions that allocate scarce resources. International development actors are making judgments based on erroneous statistics. Governments are not able to make informed decisions because existing data are too weak or the data they need do not exist."*

He argues that this appalling state of affairs came about through a long neglect of statistical services in Africa, made worse by the withdrawal of state support during the structural adjustment period. He focuses in on the iconic statistic, the gross domestic product (GDP), and a few countries, including Nigeria, Malawi, Zambia and Tanzania. GDP figures are made up of various elements, and in many countries in Africa, agricultural income is crucial. Yet, as Jerven shows for Malawi, there are all sorts of reasons not to believe the figures, as political incentives in particular result in distortions (in the case of Malawi massively upwards to 'prove'

---

[284] Jerven, M. (2013) *Poor Numbers: How We Are Misled by African Development Statistics And What To Do About It*. Ithaca: Cornell University Press

[285] Jerven, M. (2012) 'Poor Numbers: How We Are Misled By African Development Statistics And What To Do About It', *African Arguments*, 20 November

the 'success' of the politically driven fertiliser subsidy policy). Also, in much of Africa, the informal economy is massive, and very poorly understood. There are ways of assessing informal economic activity, such as through assessing expenditures, but understandings remain often very limited. The result is that in countries where the informal economy is significant (most of Africa), there are large under-estimates in national income.

The consequences of all this are severe, the book argues. Planning and budget allocations are carried out on the basis of flimsy evidence, distortions arise as statistics are influenced by political interests, successes much hailed may be far from such, and in the endless pursuit of targets (driven for example by the Millennium Development Goal process), indicators may be meaningless, or the data simply made up or guessed. The highly popular country rankings on everything from GDP to good governance – including the latest offering coming from the Institute of Development Studies at Sussex (where I work), the Hunger and Nutrition Commitment Index[286] (HANCI) – thus create their own political economy. Informed by dodgy data and the even more dubious process of 'expert judgement', many rankings may be worthless. Dudley Seers (quoted by Jerven, p. 36), who went on to become the founding director of IDS, had this to say 60 years ago:

> "In the hands of authorities, such international comparisons may yield correlations which throw light on the circumstances of economic progress, and they tell us something about relative inefficiencies and standards of living, but they are very widely abused. Do they not on the whole mislead more than they instruct, causing a net reduction in human knowledge?"

A key complaint from Seers was the lack of attention to the 'subsistence economy'. This he referred to as the "well-known morass which those estimating national income of underdeveloped areas either skirt, rush across or die in" (again quoted by Jerven, p. 37).

Yet such measures and rankings inform opinion, resource disbursement and provide competitive league tables to which governments respond, often exacerbating the poor numbers problem, as yet more dodgy data is conjured up, combined and ranked in ways that make little sense.

---

[286] http://www.ids.ac.uk/project/hunger-and-nutrition-commitment-index-hanci

Zimbabwe is not covered by the book, but the core argument still holds. The Central Statistics Office, now ZIMSTAT[287], has been the main source of government data since the colonial era. Compared to many countries, it has impressive capacity and a very strong track record. One thing that could be said of the colonial and Rhodesian authorities is that they were very keen on data. From the Rhodesian Yearbooks to the regular national income and expenditure surveys, data was collected, collated and compiled rigorously and consistently.

Statistics are after all about measurement and control – they are the very essence of the state, as the term suggests. In his brilliant history of statistics, *The Taming of Chance*[288], Ian Hacking relates how states were developed alongside statistical services, including cadastral surveys, taxation systems and population counts. In Jim Scott's terms the ordered, controlling and regulated way of 'seeing like a state'[289], is very much wrapped up in counting, surveying and so being able to control, through a form of Foucauldian governmentality at the core of modern statehood.

While there are clearly negative aspects to this form of state capacity, there are also positive attributes. A committed developmental state cannot allocate funds, direct energies and plan for the future without a good statistical base. Negotiations with donors, steering of investments and prioritisation of expenditures are impossible. Equally, without solid data, political biases, bureaucratic whims and donor influence can overtake planning and budgeting to the detriment of developmental objectives.

Jerven concludes on the state of African statistics: "…the data are based on educated guesses, competing observations, and debateable assumptions, leaving both trends and levels open to question and the final estimates malleable" (p. 108). He continues: "Decisions about what to measure, who to count, and by whose authority the final number is selected do matter" (p.121). This is why he recommends the revitalisation of African statistical services and, perhaps just as importantly, the improvement of capacity to interrogate and interpret data, including from qualitative insights.

---

[287] http://www.zimstat.co.zw/

[288] Hacking, I. (1990) *The Taming of Chance*, Cambridge: Cambridge University Press.

[289] http://www.nytimes.com/books/98/04/19/reviews/980419.19graylt.html

Based on our work in Zimbabwe, let me offer three examples that complement Jerven's cases, and contribute to the same bigger point that good numbers matter.

Agricultural output data[290]: Zimbabwe's agricultural data comes from a variety of sources, including annual crop surveys, market surveys and assessments of throughput at marketing depots. In the past, when the sector was dominated by a few large farms, it was relatively easy to get a picture of production each year. Output from the communal areas was assessed through state marketing channels through marketing boards for most of the agricultural commodities, especially maize (but also cotton, tobacco and beef). While statistics on cotton and tobacco remain reasonably good, as their marketing is channelled through few players, the production and marketing of maize and beef, by contrast, has changed dramatically since land reform.

Today there are diverse marketing channels, including much locally-focused marketing and little reliance on the old marketing board routes. And with many more farms across the country (around 150,000 new units in the A1 schemes alone), field-level monitoring by extension agents is nigh on impossible. For important crops such as the small grains (millets, sorghum), groundnuts, many oilseeds and beans, as well as smallstock, we know virtually nothing about total production and marketing.

The bottom line is that we don't know how much food is produced and where, nor do we know how much is stored and marketed. Despite the attempts of Fewsnet[291], ZimVAC and others, the estimates are increasingly guesswork, especially as sampling frames and data collection protocols have not changed sufficiently to respond to the dramatically reconfigured agrarian structure[292].

Each year we get conflicting estimates of how dire the harvest is going to be, and the consequences this will have for food imports, and food aid. With such uncertainties, this becomes a critical area of political contestation: between

---

[290] Scoones, I. (2012) *Fact check*, blog, http://zimbabweland.wordpress.com/

[291] http://www.fews.net/pages/country.aspx?gb=zw

[292] Scoones, I. (2013). *'Food crisis in Zimbabwe: 2.2 million at risk. But where do the figures come from, and what do they mean?'*, blog, zimbabweland.wordpress.com

government and the donors, and even between international agencies. Claiming a food 'crisis' may be the only way of securing international funds, as sustaining an 'emergency' has been essential to continued international engagement through 'humanitarian' aid. Such a response may well be justified; but it may be not. The problem is often we don't know.

Migration data [chapter 40]: Similar uncertainties centre on population data and migration-related demography. While we know that migration, particularly to South Africa, has increased, we have absolutely no idea how many people have moved permanently there (or indeed to other destination countries, although the data for the UK, for example, is better). Large numbers are bandied around, which serve particular politically purposes; in South Africa (linked to xenophobic, anti-immigrant rhetoric) and in Zimbabwe and internationally (supporting the narrative that people are 'fleeing').

But the figures of course don't take into account the long-term pattern of circular migration whereby people move temporarily, or indeed increasingly seasonally. If we were to believe the figures, there would be far fewer people in Zimbabwe than there seem to be. For example, the preliminary results for the 2012 census[293] show that the population has increased by 1% over a decade and stands at nearly 13m. Even within the country we don't know where people are living. There is an assumption that the urban areas are growing, as people flood to the cities. But is this the case? Debbie Potts[294] doubts this data for sub-Saharan Africa generally, but until we get better locational census data that accounts for regular movement, we will not know.

Land ownership data [chapter 26]: This is perhaps the most contested, and in the absence of a proper land audit, we cannot know. But when 'surveys' purport to present data that show that "40% of the land was seized by Mugabe and his cronies", and these figures get reported in the international media as fact, we are in trouble. Examples of this short-cut journalism and recycling of 'facts' include cases from the BBC (on the Hard Talk[295] show with Patrick Chinamasa) and the

---

[293] http://www.zimstat.co.zw/dmdocuments/CensusPreliminary2012.pdf

[294] Potts, D. (2012) *Whatever Happened to Africa's Rapid Urbanisation?*, London: Africa Research Institute, Counterpoints

[295] http://www.youtube.com/watch?v=3DRDWRBmxmo

UK Guardian (in a link put in by the paper in an otherwise good piece by Simukai Tinhu[296]). The earlier land audits by Utete and Boka have shown categorically the problem of elite capture in the A2 sites, and our detailed province-specific work in Masvingo supports this. But the scale is nothing like that claimed.

This poverty of data leads to a poverty of understanding, and so a distortion of debate. We should not be ignoring the abuse of the land reform programme by some politically-military connected elites, and the ownership of multiple farms is clearly contrary to any regulation, but our focus should equally not be only on this issue, and the wider picture, based on realistic data, needs to be central. This is why, in terms of the Global Political Agreement and in line with the now agreed constitutional commitments, a proper land ownership and use survey (an audit) is critical.

If you don't know how much food is being produced, how many people are in the country or have left and who owns what land, then how can you begin to make plans for the future? As contributors to other headline statistics, including GDP, such figures may result in major distortions.

For example, in Zimbabwe, GDP figures have been used to show the dramatic decline, and then impressive recovery in the formal economy (see the shower of graphs in the 2013 budget statement[297]), yet, as I have argued before, even in the depths of the crisis in the late 2000s, economic activity was far higher than measured. The 'real economy' – informal, often based on barter exchanges, sometimes illegal, much of linked to cross-border trade – was thriving, despite the collapse in the core, formal economy. It had to: this is how people survived. If you believed the figures on the formal economy, where the numbers were collected, people would have been suffering far more than they did.

As the formal economy has recovered, this has been registered in the statistics, but the informal economy still exists, and indeed the 2000s saw a massive restructuring of economic activity, not only in the agricultural sector, but across

---

[296] Tinhu, S. (2013) 'Why Zimbabwean voters are deserting Morgan Tsvangirai', *The Guardian*, 23 April

[297] http://www.zimtreasury.gov.zw/index.php?
option=com_content&view=article&id=79:the-minister-of-finance-hon-t-biti-presented-his-2013-national-budget-statement-&catid=40:scrolling

the economy towards more small-scale, informally-based enterprises. This is not a bad thing, as it provides the basis for more inclusive, employment generating, broad based growth. But if it is not understood, measured and recorded, it does not feature in planning and crucially budget allocation discussions.

While it may seem that a focus on statistical services is a rather dry and dull subject, it is in fact essential. ZIMSTAT has a small 'did you know?' box on their website's front page[298]. It says: "The likely success of development policies in achieving their aims will be improved by the use of statistics". They are right. Revitalising statistical services, and improving their capacity to carry out national-level, macro-census type work, as well as smaller, more focused surveys, complemented with qualitative insights, is vital.

If development is to be successful, a thorough-going and honest debate on the quality of data and how to improve it is essential. Jerven's superb book discusses an important topic with clarity and honesty; and for donors thinking of investing in government capacities in Zimbabwe again, it is well worth a read.

---

[298] http://www.zimstat.co.zw/

CHAPTER 59

A GROWING EVIDENCE BASE: YET MORE INCONVENIENT TRUTHS

In one of his Sokwanele "land debate"[299] contributions, Dale Doré used his slot to critique our work in Masvingo. Since the publication of our book, *Zimbabwe's Land Reform: Myths and Realities*[300], in November 2010 we have had plenty of reviews[301], and a number of critiques. Most common is the refrain, that Masvingo is different to other areas (of course it is, see chapter 57). Others have focused on the credentials and backgrounds [chapter 56] of the research team, while others have questioned our sampling and methodology. Still others have called us names familiar to the discourse from the liberation struggle (sell-outs, collaborators, sympathisers, liberals, apologists and so on). Others have been plain bonkers or simply abusive, and I won't share these, in case there is a family readership of this book.

All this shows the heated nature of the debate, and frustrations felt. Doré's piece focuses on methodology, while offering no new data to counter our arguments. He questions our approach to the study of complexity in particular which aimed at discovering emergent patterns from diverse data, arguing instead for a model-driven reductionism. In this regard he has problems with our chapters on labour and markets, suggesting that they are neither novel nor revealing. Well, others disagree, and so do I. This data offers, I would argue, fundamentally new insights into labour regimes and market processes, which have not been discussed before, and certainly both chapters analyse the processes and outcomes in great detail. The frustrations Doré feels may be due to disciplinary preferences (he's an economist), but exploring patterns and processes on the ground in great detail, I

---

[299] Dore, D. (2012) 'Myths, reality and the inconvenient truth about Zimbabwe's land resettlement programme', *Sokwanele*, 13 November

[300] Scoones, I., Marongwe, N., Mavedzenge, B., Mahenehene, J., Murimbarimba, F., and Sukume, C. (2010) *Zimbabwe's Land Reform: Myths and Realities*. Oxford: James Currey

[301] http://www.zimbabweland.net/Reviews.html

believe has important merits, and reductionist approaches may do violence to the complexity observed.

Also, as part of his methodological assault, he disputes our use of baselines against which change is measured. But if you read the book you can see we were careful on this – using data on nearby communal areas, the past work of Bill Kinsey and colleagues on old resettlements[302], and the limited available data on the production and economics of commercial farms. And in relation to the baseline costs on investments, I am afraid he missed the detail in the footnotes which contains all the assumptions: the analysis cannot thus so easily be dismissed as 'sheer nonsense'.

Doré goes on to accuse us of simply creating 'straw men' myths to ease the flow of our narrative. This is an argument I have heard before. Surely, people have argued, no-one ever believed these myths! Well, just take a look at any media commentary, donor document and many academic pieces and you will see these myths (and many more) are alive and well. A particularly pure form appeared in the press penned by UZ Professor Tony Hawkins[303] if you need convincing further. Later, in the piece Doré also accuses us of lack of triangulation, an approach to probing the robustness of data. Triangulation may be of methods (and we used every method, qualitative and quantitative, we found appropriate) or of cases (and again the site comparisons, within and between clusters, was central in the book), although we do admit that we did find it difficult to gain perspectives from former farm owners and workers, despite many attempts. Finally, Doré accuses us of making 'egregious' 'false claims' about the process of land reform. Again, I beg to differ. Our book offered the stories of what happened on 16 farms – all were different (as is clear from studies from elsewhere). The simplistic picture Doré paints, backed up not by empirical information but by broad proclamations, is not enough to understand the diversity of settings, processes and outcomes of Zimbabwe's land reform.

---

302 Kinsey, B. (1999) Land reform, growth and equity: emerging evidence from Zimbabwe's resettlement programme, *Journal of Southern African Studies*, 25 (2): 173-196

303 Hawkins, T. (2012) 'Counting the cost of Zimbabwean land reform', *Politics Web*, 1 November

Two years on (and why did it take this long for this review to emerge?), we actually have many more cases to compare with, improving possibilities of triangulation. These include our Masvingo studies, the African Institute of Agrarian Studies district level research[304], the Ruzivo Trust studies (now a book[305]), the Livelihoods after Land Reform small grant studies[306] and a growing number of PhD studies, some which were reported on in the *Journal of Peasant Studies* special issue[307]. It is an impressive array, with pretty good geographical coverage, although clearly still some gaps.

While there are important variations across sites, there is an emerging, common story that Doré and others still find difficult to accept. These are indeed inconvenient truths. The accumulating and converging evidence points to the following:

A1 farms are doing relatively well (although could do better), with a solid 'middle farmer' group within them who are reinvesting profits from agriculture in their farms. By contrast, A2 farms have struggled, although things have improved since the end of hyperinflation and in the multicurrency environment since 2009. They have been greatly assisted by contract farming arrangements that have provided much needed capital and inputs.

Private and community investment in the resettlement areas is significant, especially in the A1 sites. But more needs to be done, with clear needs for public investment in infrastructure.

Capture of farms by high level, politically-connected elites has taken place, and this varies between different parts of the country, especially in relation to proximity to Harare. However even in these areas, the dominant story remains small and medium scale A1 and A2 farmers. A1 farmers, particularly on land that

---

[304] Chambati, W., Dangwa, C., Moyo, S., Mujeyi, K., Murisa, T., Nyoni, N. and Siziba, D. (2009) *Fast Track Land Reform Baseline Survey in Zimbabwe: Trends and Tendencies, 2005/06*, Harare: African Institute for Agrarian Studies

[305] Matondi, P. (2012). *Zimbabwe's Fast Track Land Reform*. London: Zed Press

[306] http://www.lalr.org.za/zimbabwe/zimbabwe-working-papers-1

[307] Cliffe, L., Alexander, J., Cousins, B. and Gaidzanwa, R. (eds.) (2011). Special Issue on Fast Track Land Reform in Zimbabwe. *Journal of Peasant Studies*, 38(5)

was invaded and occupied, are largely from nearby communal areas and small towns, while A2 farmers are predominantly former or serving civil servants, teachers and business people, with urban connections.

The potential for production across the resettlements is far from being realised due to inefficiencies in input markets, a lack of credit and rural finance and the high costs of transition in infrastructure, and up and downstream industries. However, production has not collapsed, and is booming in some commodities and areas. Markets may be informal, but they generate employment and spin-off benefits from economic linkages in an area.

There are nuances and variations – yes complexity – but the picture is increasingly clear, as are the policy challenges. The now infamous five myths we set out to examine in Masvingo are rejected countrywide, although with important qualifications – as indeed we offered in the 288 pages of small type in our book for Masvingo.

ENDPIECE

The final chapter that follows offers an overview of the key policy conclusions from our work. These were originally published in our book in 2010, but remain relevant today. Our research findings suggest a very different narrative to that often pushed by the media and wider commentariat. These have important implications. For sure they need nuancing, contextualising and amending for different settings, but they suggest a way forward for Zimbabwe's agriculture and rural areas that capitalises on the land reform's successes while recognising the failures.

Unfortunately the political parties, donors, and many policy advisors inside and outside Zimbabwe, persist with the myths we tried to demolish in 2010. This has been why the continued debate and discussion on the Zimbabweland blog has been necessary. Hopefully this book will contribute to a wider sharing and deepening of this discussion.

As Zimbabwe moves forward, this sort of empirically-based evidence is essential. The debate however does not stop here, and the blog will be carrying new updates and reflections, including results from our on-going work in Masvingo.

CHAPTER 60

POLICIES FOR LAND, AGRICULTURE AND RURAL DEVELOPMENT

In the build-up to the 2013 elections, all the major political parties failed to grasp the implications and opportunities of the new agrarian structure following land reform. Whether positioned around a populist, nationalist narrative or one focused on private investment and individual entrepreneurship, the policies do not focus on the importance of a new group of 'emergent' or 'middle' farmers, as part of a socially and economically differentiated rural population [chapter 18]. The new agrarian structure, with a tri-modal pattern (involving large, medium and small scale farms), also has important implications for all areas of policy, whether infrastructure, services, finance and so on.

In our 2010 book, we started from the realities of farmers in A1 and A2 farms acquired through the post 2000 land reform programme. We argued that these new farmers are not like communal farmers, nor larger scale commercial farmers. They are different, with different aptitudes, skills, needs and potentials. We equally argued that we don't have to start from scratch. There is much to build on in terms of initial investments, and the skills and knowledge of the new settlers are significant. These are new people with new production systems engaging in new markets – all with new opportunities and challenges.

What then should the top priorities be now to meet these new demands – and particularly to support those 'new' middle farmers who are already 'accumulating from below'? Here I identify four (drawn from our final chapter):

1. Infrastructure investment, research and extension support and rural finance

Getting agriculture moving requires investment, and this means private individuals, businesses and the state working together. Yet a vibrant agricultural sector always is reliant on solid state support – to provide basic infrastructure, extension support, and public research. This has been a long-term lesson, both in Zimbabwe, and elsewhere. Following land reform in 2000, there has been vanishingly little support, from government, donors or others. Where subsidies have been offered they have often been misused. With new people on the land, a major investment is required to reconfigure the basic infrastructure for new uses. The old patterns, relevant to large-scale farms, are no longer appropriate. Investing in roads, schools, health clinics, dams, irrigation schemes, dip tanks and so on is essential. While individual entrepreneurs are making a difference through private investment, these basic public investments are a vital complement. In addition, research and extension is vital. But the new farmers are often highly educated and well-connected. This opens up new opportunities: the old style intensive extension system probably doesn't make sense. For example, support for marketing or input supply via mobile phone updates, or agricultural extension or business planning advice offered via the Internet offer real opportunities. One of the big constraints on agriculture currently is finance [chapter 14]. Approaches to loan arrangements with new forms of collateral are required, with state guarantees to private bank loans. Accessible, cheap finance could open up multiple opportunities.

2. Securing the land

Security of land tenure is an essential prerequisite for successful production and investment in agriculture. Tenure security arises through a variety of means [chapter 27]. Existing legislation allows for a wide range of potential tenure types, including freehold title, regulated leases, permits and communal tenure under 'traditional' systems. All have their pros and cons. Policymakers must ask how tenure security can be achieved within available resources and capacity; how safeguards can be put in place to prevent land grabbing or land concentration; and what assurances must be made to ensure that private credit markets function effectively. Lessons from across the world suggest there is no one-size-fits-all solution centred on freehold tenure. Instead, a flexible system of land administration is required – one that allows for expansion and contraction of farm sizes, as well as entry and exit from farming. While the excesses of elite patronage and land grabbing must be addressed through a land audit, a successful approach, overseen by an independent, decentralised authority, must not be reliant on technocratic diktat.

3. Fostering local economic development

Land reform has reconfigured Zimbabwe's rural areas dramatically. No longer are there vast swathes of commercial land separated from the densely-packed communal areas, the inheritance of the colonial Land Apportionment Act. Today, small-scale farms are nearby medium and large-scale farms, sharing labour, technologies, market chains, skills and expertise. This has created 'multiplier effects' in land reform areas – economic linkages from new farms to the wider economy [chapter 13]. The land reform has given rise to the growth of new businesses to provide services and consumption goods. Such local economic development potentials are far from fully realised, and to date there has been little support to this wider, new rural economy. To make the most of the new mosaic of land uses and economic activities, an area-based, local economic development approach is required. This would facilitate investment across activities, adding value to farm production. An area-based approach needs to draw in the private sector, farmer groups and government agencies, but with strong leadership from a revived local government, with rethought mandates and rebuilt capacities.

4. Giving farmers a voice

Reflecting a wide range of interests, the new resettlement farmers are highly diverse in class, gender and generational terms. This diversity has many advantages, adding new skills and experiences, but it is also a weakness. Formal organisation in the new resettlements is limited. There are of course emergent organisations [chapter 36] focused on particular activities – a garden, an irrigation scheme, a marketing effort, for example – but these are unlikely to become the basis of political representation and influence. Because politics has been so divisive in recent years, many shy away from seeing political parties as the basis for lobbying for change, and there are few other routes to expressing views. Building a new set of representative farmers' organisations, linked to an influential apex body, will be a long-term task, and will be highly dependent on the unfolding political alliances in rural areas. In contrast to the past when smallholders could easily be marginalised and were courted only at elections for their votes, the new farmers – and particularly the burgeoning group of 'middle farmers' – now control one of the most important economic sectors in the country. Today, this new politics of the countryside [chapter 19] cannot be ignored.

A new debate on land and agriculture in Zimbabwe

Many of these four themes do of course chime with recommendations that are now appearing in policy documents. However, the real implications of the land reform and capturing the potentials of a new agrarian structure must be front and centre, rather than assuming that the job ahead is only to offset the downsides of the fast-track programme or recapture an assumed ideal past.

A new debate on land is required, and this needs to be reflected in policy debates. The challenge for the future is a new one however. As the then head of agricultural extension Masvingo province put it back in 2006: "We don't know our new clients: this is a totally new scenario".

If given the right support, the new farmers can drive a vibrant agricultural revolution in Zimbabwe. Of course, this has happened before: with white commercial farmers in the 1950s and with communal area farmers in the 1980s. Both past agricultural revolutions required support and commitment from outside, something that has been starkly absent since 2000. Zimbabwe's green revolution of the 1980s has been much hailed, but this only involved perhaps 20% of farmers, mostly in high potential communal areas and was quickly extinguished following structural adjustment. The nascent green revolution in the new resettlement areas potentially has far wider reach, both geographically and socio-economically, and must not meet the same fate.

A smallholder-based agricultural revolution could indeed be the basis of wider growth and development in Zimbabwe [chapter 13]. Now is the time for some strategic policy thinking, not blinkered by ideology or false images of the past. Such thinking requires a deeper understanding, based on the facts on the ground, of what is going on, and what might be possible if the right investment and support was offered.